TITUS

TITUS

Conqueror of Jerusalem

Nicholas Jackson

GREENHILL BOOKS

Titus: Conqueror of Jerusalem

First published in 2026 by
Greenhill Books,
c/o Pen & Sword Books Ltd,
George House, Units 12 & 13
Beevor Street, Off Pontefract Road,
Barnsley, S. Yorkshire S71 1HN

www.greenhillbooks.com
contact@greenhillbooks.com

ISBN: 978–1–80500–216–1

The Publisher's authorised representative in the EU for product safety is Authorised Rep Compliance Ltd., Ground Floor, 71 Lower Baggot Street, Dublin D02 P593, Ireland. www.arccompliance.com

CIP data records for this title are available from the British Library

Maps by Peter Wilkinson

Printed and bound in the UK by CPI Group (UK) Ltd, Croydon, CR0 4YY.

Typeset in 11.5/14.4 pt Arno Pro Regular and Arno Pro Display

TO MAÏNA

CONTENTS

ILLUSTRATIONS AND MAPS

Plates

Titus, *ca.* 79, in a bust found on the island of Pantelleria (*Ed Euthman, CC BY-SA 2.0*)

Vespasian, Vatican Museum, Rome (*Author's Collection*); Julia, only daughter of Titus, in the collection of the Getty Villa, California (*CC0 1.0 Universal*); relief of Britannicus and Nero, found in the ancient city of Aphrodisias in Turkey (*Turkish Archaeological News*); bust of the Emperor Domitian (*Toledo Museum of Art*)

Map of the Roman province of Judea and the surrounding region (*Peter Wilkinson*)

The palace at Caesarea Maritima (*Ian Scott, CC BY-SA 2.0*); the palace of Herod Agrippa II, Caesarea Philippi (*Mboesch, CC BY-SA 4.0*)

Jotapata, seen from the north-west (*Google Earth PhotoSphere*); the site of the ancient town of Gamla (*Michael Baram*)

Map of Jerusalem (*Author*)

Replica Roman battering ram, in the National Military Museum, Bucharest (*Cristian Peter Marinescu-Ivan, CC BY-SA-2.0*); loading a replica scorpion artillery weapon (*Hans Splinter, CC BY-ND 2.0*); the Western Wall in Jerusalem (*Dennis Jarvis, CC BY-SA 2.0*)

The Siege and Destruction of Jerusalem by the Romans Under the Command of Titus, by David Roberts (*private collection*); *Destruction of the Temple in Jerusalem* by Francesco Hayez (*Gallerie dell'Accademia, Venice – CC BY-SA-4.0 International*); *The Triumph of Titus: The Flavians,* Lawrence Alma-Tadema (*Walters Art Museum*)

Herculaneum ancient beach and vaulted boat houses (Emanuele Antonio Minerva, Ministry of Culture)

Double-headed snake armlet found in the House of the Golden Bracelet, Pompeii (*Sailko, CC BY-SA 4.0*); Plaster casts and remains of the four victims found in the House of the Golden Bracelet, Pompeii (*Peter Macdiarmid, Getty News Images, License 2102410004*)

Roman legionary *testudo* formation, cast of Trajan's Column, National Museum of Romanian History (*Joe Marbel, CC BY-SA 2.0*); Praetorian Guards, marble relief, Louvre-Lens, France (*Author's Collection*)

Three views of the underside of the Arch of Titus, Roman Forum, Rome. (*all Author's Collection*)

Colosseum, Flavian Amphitheatre, Rome ; Temple of Peace, or Forum of Peace, Rome. (*both Author's Collection*)

Laocoön and His Sons, Vatican Museum, Rome (*Author's Collection*)

'Villa di Tito', Rieti Province, Italy (*McMaster University, CC BY-ND 2.5 CA*)

Titus, Vatican Museum, Rome (*Author's Collection*)

Illustrations in Text and Family Tree

All images of coins are reproduced courtesy of the Classical Numismatic Group, LLC.

Rabbi Fishman Maimon's postcard (*Yeshiva University, Special Collections. Presented by the Leah Adler Memorial Fund*)

Maps

PREFACE

Titus stands out as the first biological son of a Roman emperor to succeed his father to the throne. He was a charismatic leader whose audacious exploits as a young *Caesar* thrust him repeatedly into peril during the Jewish War. He epitomised the Flavian dynasty,[1] his life unfolding amidst Nero's despotism, the turbulence of civil war, the suppression of the Jewish rebellion and the grandeur of triumph. From the chaos of the 'Year of Four Emperors' to the smouldering ruins of Jerusalem, Titus navigated an ever-changing empire.

Titus' behaviour was a product both of his time and of his privileged upbringing, leading him to be despised initially as Vespasian's heir, despite his successful capture of Jerusalem following the Judean rebellion. He was remarkable as a ruler. Despite wielding absolute power, he succeeded in rebranding his image to one of benevolence and appears to have ruled with compassion and fiscal prudence. His leadership was tested by a series of calamities: the cataclysmic eruption of Vesuvius, a devastating fire in Rome and a rampant disease epidemic. While history ranks him among the 'good emperors', his short reign raises a thorny question: were his positive attributes genuine and deep-rooted or was his true nature masked by the brevity of his time on the *sella aurea*, the golden chair?

This biography delves into the complexities of Titus' reign, unravelling the man behind the legends, exploring the layers of his character and examining the enduring impression of his brief yet impactful rule. Six ancient works make it possible to piece together Titus' life and times; five of these are primary and contemporary sources to the extent that the authors lived during the Flavian period.

The Roman knight and historian Gaius Suetonius Tranquillus published his collective biographies of *The Twelve Caesars*, from Julius Caesar to

Domitian, around thirty-eight years after the death of Titus.[2] He was probably around ten years old when Titus came to power, studying in Rome at the time, and was later a friend of Pliny the Younger (introduced below). Filled with anecdotal details, Suetonius' account of Titus is unfortunately very brief.

Cornelius Tacitus, historian and senator, who lived through the Flavian period, compiled his *Histories* about twenty-five years after the death of Titus. He was born around AD 58 and supported by Vespasian in the award of senatorial status, the *latus clavus*, probably in 76. Titus clearly favoured Tacitus and awarded him a quaestorship in 81 as his attaché. His books were written in a terse style and, due to lost volumes, unfortunately end in 70, shortly after Vespasian came to power.[3]

Flavius Josephus was a Roman-Jewish historian who was a Jewish general during the uprisings. He was captured by Vespasian and Titus, and to survive offered his loyalty to the Roman cause and earned their respect as a trusted advisor. He accompanied Titus closely during the siege of Jerusalem and witnessed many events first-hand. After the rebellion, while in Rome under Flavian patronage, he wrote a detailed account of the war entitled *The Jewish War*. His work provides a unique level of detail for Roman military campaigns under Vespasian and Titus, albeit biased towards both the Roman perspective and prevailing Flavian propaganda.

Both Pliny the Elder and his nephew Pliny the Younger were prominent figures in Roman society in the Flavian period. While their works and letters do not focus specifically on Titus, they provide valuable information about the social, political and cultural context of his reign, including the renowned description of the eruption of Vesuvius in two letters written by Pliny the Younger. The correspondence describing the eruption, approximately twenty-five years after the event, was sent in response to a request from Pliny's friend, the aforementioned historian Tacitus.

The later Roman historian Dio Cassius, writing over 130 years after Titus' death, produced two works that covered Titus but they have only survived as a summarised narrative condensed by John Xiphilinus, a Byzantine monk from the eleventh century. Nevertheless, the abridgements provide useful details regarding major events.

Although we have these sources, there are erroneous details, gaps and areas of ambiguity that force the writer of Roman history to use speculative language such as 'could', 'probably', 'likely' or 'possibly'. My approach, therefore has been to state facts without discussion when the narrative of our sources is clear, when there is corroboration between them or when validated by other means of evidence such as archaeology, numismatics and epigraphy. When the evidence is less compelling, I have attempted to summarise the details. Where there is little or no evidence, I have proposed plausible hypotheses or stated simply that we cannot know.

As for modern sources, there are numerous works referenced throughout the book and I am particularly indebted to the scholarly work of Professor Brian Jones, who published his biographies *The Emperor Titus* and *The Emperor Domitian* in 1984 and 1993, respectively. Professor John Nicols's *Vespasian and the Partes Flavianae* has been an invaluable source for the chronology of the Jewish War (which incidentally uses the Julian calendar). I am also grateful to the late Professor Barbara Levick, whose *Vespasian* provides a masterful narrative of his life with reference to Titus.

Recognising the magnitude of the Jewish War in response to the uprisings in Judea, alongside the unusually detailed contemporary documentation, it becomes essential for any author writing about Titus to deeply delve into the conflict. The initial Jewish uprising, igniting a powder keg of hatred against the Roman occupiers and neighbouring Greek populations, was just the first of three major periods of rebellion. The second wave of uprisings occurred in the diaspora regions of Libya, Egypt and Cyprus, as well as Judea, necessitating Trajan's intervention in 116–17. The third, of 132–5, was spurred by Hadrian's plan to rebuild Jerusalem as a Roman colony bearing his name. Each of these revolts drove Jewish refugees into the diaspora, creating a legacy of displacement and transformation under Roman rule.

Following convention, Roman costs are generally cited in this book in *sestertii*, abbreviated as HS. Roman coinage was denominated as follows: 1 *aureus* (gold) = 25 *denarii* (silver) = 100 *sestertii* (brass) = 200 *dupondii* (brass) = 400 *asses* (bronze). To put the values into perspective: one loaf of bread was around two *asses*; one litre of average wine, five *asses*; a donkey several thousand *sestertii*; an unskilled slave around 2,000 *sestertii*; a highly educated or skilled slave over 20,000 *sestertii* and a well-appointed town house in Rome around two million *sestertii*. A Roman legionary could earn 900 *sestertii* a year in this period.[4] At the state level, the largest annual cost was maintaining Rome's professional army, which consumed nearly 80 per cent of the imperial budget (lower-range estimate around 643 million *sestertii* a year).[5]

*

I would like to express my gratitude to those whose expertise, insights, and generosity have enriched this book. Professor Pedar Foss (DePauw University) and Professor Steven Tuck (Miami University) provided invaluable guidance on the dating of the Vesuvius eruption and details on Pompeii's survivors, respectively. Professor Mordechai Aviam (Kinneret Institute for Galilean Archaeology) and Dr Danny Syon (Israel Antiquities Authority) offered assistance regarding Jotapata and Gamla, respectively. Professor Stephen Kay (British School in Rome) provided his first-hand expertise on the archaeological evidence for the Flavian residence in the Apennines. I am thankful to Stephen Dando-Collins for his help in deciphering the complex array of Roman forces deployed during the Jewish War. I am also grateful to Dr Simon Elliot for his expert review of the entire manuscript and his thoughtful, diligent feedback, as well as to Professor Philip Matyszak for taking the time to critique the early chapters. Special thanks to Edward Handyside for his professional editing and wise adjustments to the manuscript. My sincere thanks also goes to David Swain for his tireless review of the raw manuscript and his many keen observations, and to Donald Sommerville, whose remarkable editorial precision and dedication once again refined both the narrative and its accuracy. Finally, I am especially grateful to Michael Leventhal of Greenhill Books, whose trust, advice, and support have been invaluable throughout this journey. While I have greatly benefited from the wisdom and generosity of these individuals, any errors or misinterpretations remain entirely my own.

Nicholas Jackson

CHRONOLOGY

All dates are AD.

3 Birth of Sabinus II, Titus' uncle (*ca.*)

6 Judea becomes equestrian sub-province of Syria

9 Birth of Vespasian (17 November)

14 Death of Augustus (19 August), accession of Tiberius (17 September)

28 Vespasian's vigintivirate (*ca.*), birth of Queen Berenice (*ca.*)

33 Sabinus II praetorship (*ca.*)

35 Vespasian's quaestorship (*ca.*)

37 Death of Tiberius (16 March) and accession of Caligula (18 March)
   Death of Antonia Minor, ally of Vespasian (1 May)

38 Vespasian's aedileship (*ca.*)

39 Birth of Titus (30 December)

40 Vespasian's praetorship (*ca.*)

41 Assassination of Caligula and accession of Claudius (24–25 January)

42 Vespasian commander of Legio II *Augusta* in Germania

43 Claudius' invasion of Britannia under Plautius with Vespasian and
   Sabinus II as legion commanders (spring–summer)

44 Sabinus II consulship
   Claudius' triumph in Rome over Britannia; names son Britannicus
   Vespasian awarded *ornamenta triumphalia* (*ca.*)
   Death of King Herod Agrippa I
   Roman procurators govern Judea

47   Vespasian returns to Rome from Britannia (late in the year)
     Vespasian and Sabinus II possibly adlected into the patrician class (*ca.*)
     Titus and Britannicus start schooling together (*ca.*)

48   Messalina executed

49   Claudius marries his niece, Agrippina the Younger

50   Claudius adopts Nero (25 February), Agrippina given title Augusta

51   Birth of Domitian (24 October)
     Vespasian's first consulship (towards end of year as *consul suffectus*)
     Nero dons his *toga virilis* (*ca.*)

53   Birth of Domitilla II, Titus' sister (*ca.*)

     Nero and Octavia marriage

54   Claudius death and Nero's accession (13 October)
     Corbulo appointment to restore Armenia status quo
     Titus fifteenth birthday (30 December)

55   Titus dons his *toga virilis* (*ca.*)
     Nero poisons Britannicus (11 February)

56   Sabinus II first term as prefect of Rome (*ca.*)

59   Nero orders execution of his mother, Agrippina the Younger

60   Titus' vigintivirate (*ca.*)

61   Sabinus II second prefect of Rome
     Titus' military tribunate, Germania Superior (*ca.*)

62   Titus' military tribunate, Britannia (*ca.*)

63   Vespasian proconsul governorship of Africa (*ca.*)
     Titus returns to Rome from Britannia (*ca.*)
     Titus and Arrecina Tertulla marry

64   Titus' quaestorship (*ca.*)
     Birth of Titus's daughter Julia
     Death of Arrecina Tertulla

65   Titus and Marcia Furnilla marry
     Pisonian Conspiracy
     Titus and Marcia Furnilla divorce

66 Judean rebellion breaks out in Caesarea (spring)
    Nero tours Greece, accompanied by Vespasian and Titus (summer)
    Cestius departs Antioch to suppress rebellion (autumn)
    Cestius retreat, Battle of Beth Horon and loss of Judea
    Nero summons Corbulo to Greece and forces his suicide (*ca.* October)
    Nero appoints Vespasian general for the Jewish War (December)
    Titus appointed commander of XV *Apollinaris* (December).

67 Vespasian arrives in Syria to muster army (February)
    Titus arrives in Alexandria
    Vespasian and Titus unite at Ptolemais (spring)
    Start of siege of Jotapata (May)
    Massacre at Mount Gerizim (25 June)
    Capture of Japha (20 June).
    Titus leads breaching of Jotapata (1 July)
    Vespasian captures Josephus (early July)
    Massacre at Joppa (July/August)
    Vespasian and Titus guests of Agrippa II and Berenice at Caesarea
      Philippi (August)
    Capitulation of Tiberias (8 September)
    Titus captures Tarichea (September)
    Battle on Sea of Galilee (September)
    Massacre at Tiberias stadium (September)
    Mucianus arrives in Syria as new governor (October)
    Fall of Gamla (23 October)
    Titus captures Gischala (end of October)
    Galilee recaptured, Titus and Vespasian return to Caesarea
    Nero returns to Rome from Greece (December)

68 Capitulation of Gadara to Vespasian (4 March)
    Vespasian learns of Vindex uprising against Nero (April)
    Placidus subdues Perea region (spring)
    Vespasian campaigns in Judea and Idumea (spring)
    Titus' diplomatic missions to Syria
    Nero's suicide and accession of Galba (9 June)
    Vespasian in Caesarea receives news of Nero's death and halts
      campaign (end of June)
    Domitilla II and Q. Petillius Cerialis marry (*ca.*)

69   Year of the Four Emperors
     Germanian legions hail Vitellius emperor (2 January)
     Galba assassination and Otho accession (15 January)
     Titus aborts trip to Rome to return to the East (January)
     Sabinus II third term as Prefect of Rome (*ca.*)
     Birth of Domitilla III, Titus' niece (*ca.*)
     Limited military action in Judea and Idumea (March)
     First Battle of Bedriacum, Otho defeated (14 April)
     Otho suicide (16 April)
     Vitellius accession (19 April)
     Vespasian's Mount Carmel meeting in Syria (June)
     Death of Domitilla II (*ca.*)
     Egyptian, Judean, Syrian legions hail Vespasian as emperor (1, 3, 15 July,
         respectively)
     Mucianus leaves Syria with Vespasian's expeditionary force (mid-Aug.)
     Pro-Vespasian forces under Primus advance into Northern Italy
         (September)
     Mucianus reaches Moesia (mid-October)
     Adriatic naval fleet declares for Vespasian (17 October)
     Primus victorious at second Battle of Bedriacum (24–25 October)
     Capitoline Battle, Temple of Jupiter destroyed and Sabinus II killed
         (19 December)
     Primus enters Rome, street battles, Vitellius killed (20 December)
     Senate hails Vespasian emperor, Mucianus reaches Rome
         (21 December)

70   Vespasian II and Titus I consulships in absence in Alexandria
         (1 January)
     Lex de imperio Vespasiani (January)
     Titus leaves Caesarea to unite his army outside Jerusalem (early April)
     Titus repositions his forces against Jerusalem's defences (mid-April)
     Roman attack of the Third Wall (*ca.* 22 April)
     Romans breach Third Wall and occupy New Town (*ca.* 7 May)
     Romans breach Second Wall (*ca.* 11 May)
     Start of siege works against Fort Antonia (*ca.* 12 May)
     Construction of circumvallation around Jerusalem (*ca.* May–June)
     Fall of Fort Antonia (5 July)
     Titus orders razing of Antonia (17 July)

Start of Temple assault (*ca.* 20 July)
Capture of Temple and destruction of the Holy of Holies (10 August)
Fall of Jerusalem (7 September)
Vespasian in Rome (end September)
Titus in Caesarea, celebrates Domitian's eighteenth birthday
   (24 October)
Titus in Berytus, celebrates Vespasian's sixtieth birthday
   (17 November)
Traianus in Cappadocia and Paetus in Syria (*ca.* December)
Titus Imperator I

71   Vespasian III and Nerva consulships (1 January)
Titus in Zeugma (early January)
Titus in Antioch (end January)
Titus in Alexandria (March–April)
Domitian suffectus consulship (*ca.* spring)
Domitian and Domitia Longina marry (*ca.*)
Titus in Rome and joint triumph with Vespasian (*ca.* June)
Titus awarded *tribunicia potestas* for the first time and proconsular
   power (1 July)
Vespasian appoints Titus Praetorian Guard Prefect (*ca.* summer)
Titus Imperator II

72   Vespasian IV and Titus II consulships (1 January)
Mucianus III consulship (29 May)
Lesser Armenia annexed
Kingdom of Commagene annexed
Titus Imperator IV

73   Domitian II and Valerius Catullus Messallinus consulships (1 January)
Titus and Vespasian censorship (April)
Birth of Domitian's daughter
Romans capture Masada
Traianus starts governorship of Syria
Titus Imperator V

74   Vespasian V and Titus III consulships (1 January)
Titus and Vespasian end their censorship (October)
Birth of Domitian's son, Titus Flavius
Titus Imperator VIII

75 Vespasian VI and Titus IV consulships (1 January)
    Berenice and Agrippa arrive in Rome
    Temple of Peace inauguration
    End of Capitoline Temple reconstruction (*ca.*)
    Josephus publishes his *Jewish Wars* (*ca.* 75–79)

76 Vespasian VII and Titus V consulships (1 January)
    Titus Imperator XII

77 Vespasian VIII and Titus VI consulships (1 January)
    Agricola governor of Britannia

78 Titus Imperator XIV
    D. Junius Novius Priscus and L. Ceionius Commodus consulships
        (1 January)

79 Vespasian IX and Titus VII consulships (1 January)
    Titus dismisses Berenice from Rome
    Caecina–Marcellus conspiracy
    Vespasian's death (23 June) and Titus' accession (*ca.* 24 June)
    Vesuvius eruption (24–25 Aug.), Titus' first visit to disaster area
    Julia and Titus Flavius Sabinus IV marry (*ca.*)

80 Titus VIII and Domitian VII consulships (1 January)
    Deification of Vespasian
    Titus' Baths inauguration
    Colosseum inauguration
    Restoration of the Julio-Claudian coinage
    Berenice brief visit to Rome and second departure
    Titus' second visit to Vesuvius' disaster zone (spring)
    Great fire in Rome
    Major epidemic in Rome
    Titus Imperator XV

81 Flavius Silva Nonius Bassus and Asinius Pollio Verrucosus consulships
        (1 January)
    False Nero episode (*ca.*)
    Titus Imperator XVII
    Titus' death (13 September) and Domitian accession (14 September)
    Titus' deification (after 1 October)

THE CURSUS HONORUM

An overview of the senatorial career ladder, the *cursus honorum*, in the Flavian imperial period. The table does not address some of the nuanced paths that could be taken under special circumstances.

Post Title and Duties	*Posts available*	*Term served*
Vigintivir. A junior official involved in an array of administrative roles. Not part of the official *cursus honorum*, this was a stepping stone before entry into the senate.	20	1 year
Military tribune. Important preparatory phase serving as an officer in a legion before entering the senate. Before or after the Vigintivirate.	many	1–2 years
Quaestor. The first step of a senatorial career, the position included formal entry into the senate proper and usually financial duties.	20	1 year
Aedile. Optional and not a strict requirement for higher office, duties included managing public events and buildings.	4	1 year
Praetor. Senior judicial and administrative responsibilities. On completion of his term the holder qualified for governorship of a minor province or command of a legion.	*ca.* 10	1 year
Consul. The highest executive office in the senate, the *ordinarius* consul took post at the start of the new year and could hand over to a *suffectus* consul later in the year.	2	months
Proconsul. Posts could include: governorship of a senatorial or imperial province, legion commander, general of a military campaign, curator of major infrastructure, Prefect of Rome, additional consulships or important religious roles.	many	varied

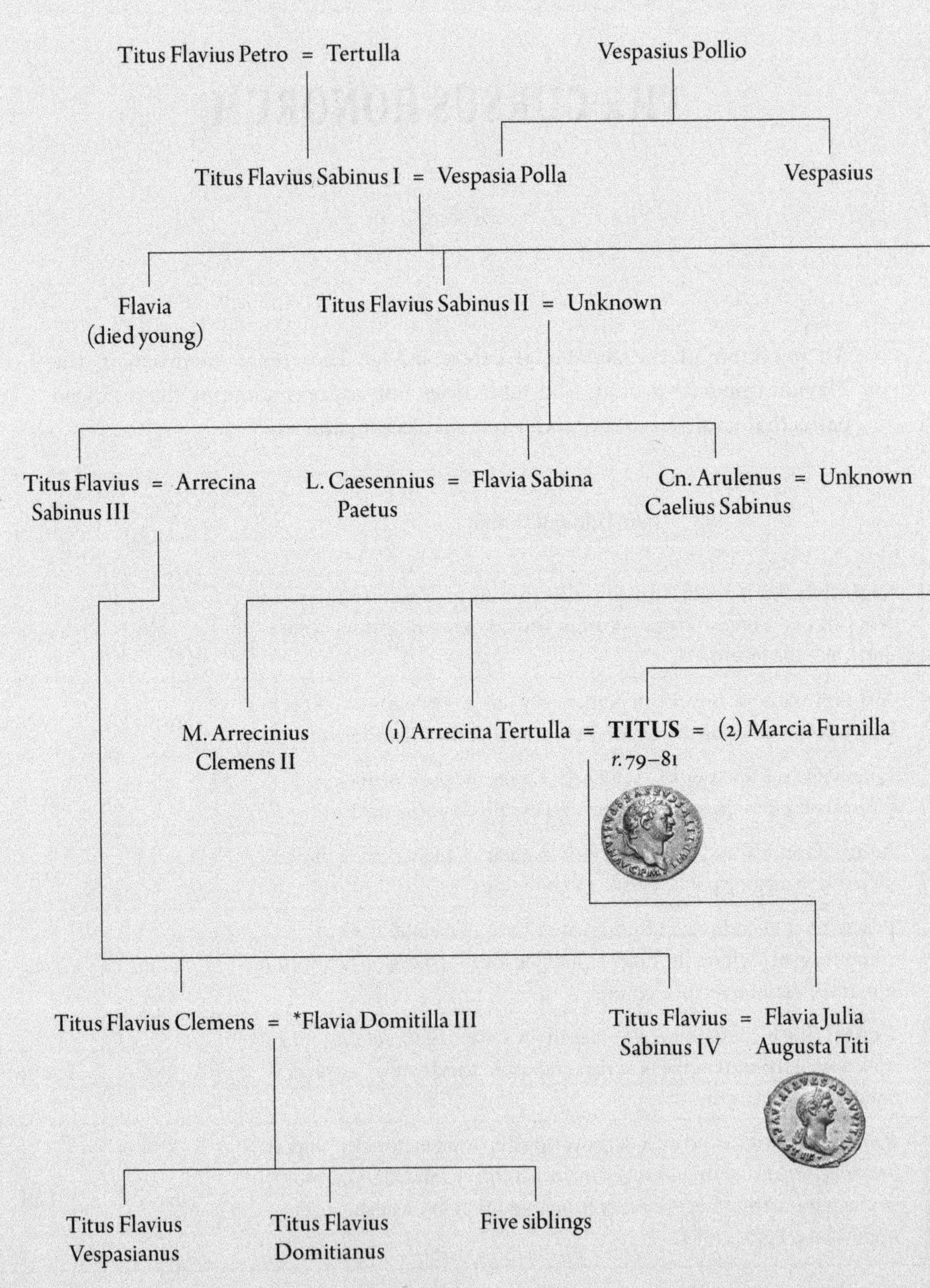

Titus Flavius Petro = Tertulla
Vespasius Pollio
Titus Flavius Sabinus I = Vespasia Polla
Vespasius
Flavia
(died young)
Titus Flavius Sabinus II = Unknown
Titus Flavius = Arrecina
Sabinus III
L. Caesennius = Flavia Sabina
Paetus
Cn. Arulenus = Unknown
Caelius Sabinus
M. Arrecinius
Clemens II
(1) Arrecina Tertulla = TITUS = (2) Marcia Furnilla
r. 79–81
Titus Flavius Clemens = *Flavia Domitilla III
Titus Flavius = Flavia Julia
Sabinus IV   Augusta Titi
Titus Flavius
Vespasianus
Titus Flavius
Domitianus
Five siblings

FLAVIAN FAMILY TREE

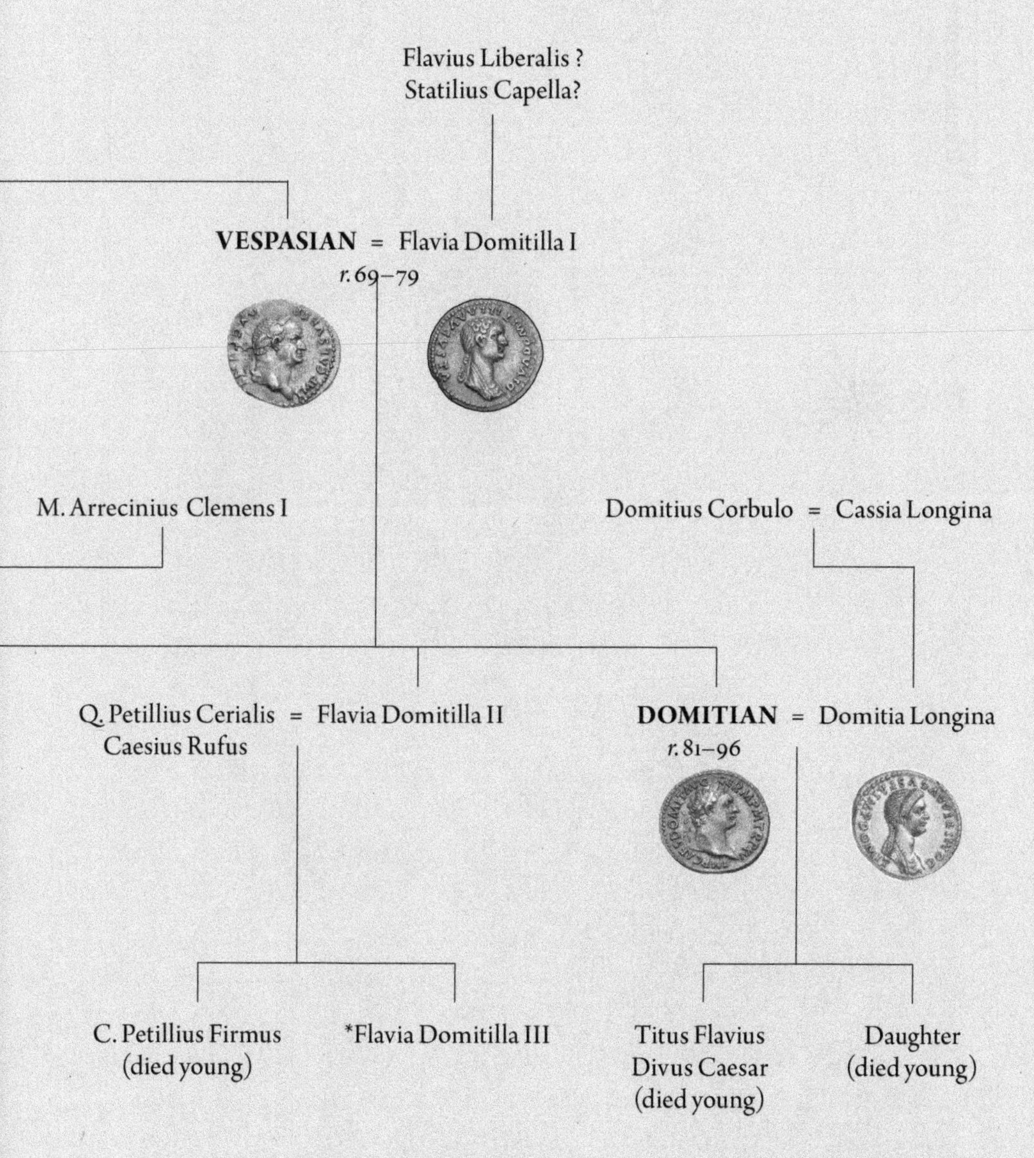

Flavia Domitilla III shown twice to fit tree structure.

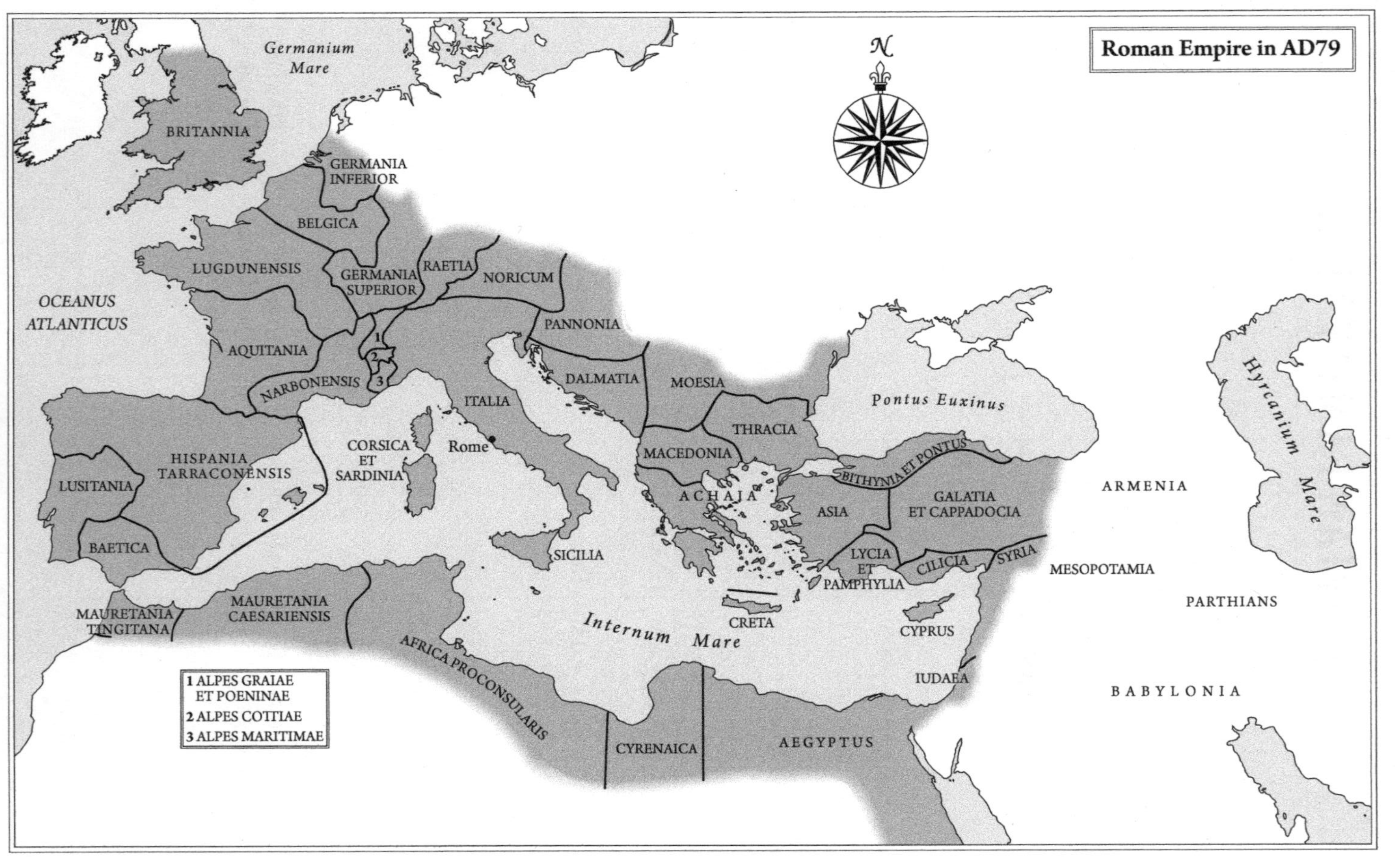

Roman Empire in AD79
Germanium Mare
BRITANNIA
GERMANIA INFERIOR
BELGICA
LUGDUNENSIS
GERMANIA SUPERIOR
RAETIA
NORICUM
OCEANUS ATLANTICUS
AQUITANIA
PANNONIA
1
2
3
NARBONENSIS
DALMATIA
MOESIA
Pontus Euxinus
ITALIA
THRACIA
MACEDONIA
BITHYNIA ET PONTUS
ARMENIA
Hyrcanium Mare
CORSICA ET SARDINIA
Rome
HISPANIA TARRACONENSIS
ACHAJA
ASIA
GALATIA ET CAPPADOCIA
LUSITANIA
BAETICA
SICILIA
LYCIA ET PAMPHYLIA
CILICIA
SYRIA
MESOPOTAMIA
MAURETANIA TINGITANA
MAURETANIA CAESARIENSIS
Internum Mare
CRETA
CYPRUS
PARTHIANS
AFRICA PROCONSULARIS
IUDAEA
BABYLONIA
1 ALPES GRAIAE ET POENINAE
2 ALPES COTTIAE
3 ALPES MARITIMAE
CYRENAICA
AEGYPTUS

FIRST DISASTER: VESUVIUS ERUPTS

In August AD 79, the idyllic landscape of Campania was torn apart in a cata-clysm unlike anything the Romans had ever witnessed. Over the course of just twenty-four hours, Mount Vesuvius unleashed a staggering estimated four cubic kilometres of molten rock, ash and pumice, blotting out the sky and suffocating the land.[1] Thousands perished, their lives swallowed by the ashen clouds, and many more were displaced.[2] The volcanic fallout dispersed over thousands of kilometres across the Mediterranean.[3] The once wealthy and prosperous agricultural region, blessed with fertile soils, home to some of Italy's most luxurious villas and served by several ports trading across the Roman Empire and beyond, was entombed beneath the volcanic debris. It was perhaps the greatest natural disaster in European history and the first well-documented eruption.[4] Emperor Titus, barely two months into his reign, had to face this catastrophe, the first of three disasters to afflict his rule.[5]

Morning, 24 August: Several days of tremors and earthquakes and the dis-appearance of water springs forewarned of the event that commenced with an initial explosion while the population went about their daily business. This opening volcanic activity created a fifteen-kilometre-high eruption column that spread east in the wind.[6] Pompeians and other inhabitants in the vicinity of Vesuvius would have been startled and concerned. They were accustomed to tremors in the region but not an actual eruption.[7] Indeed, only a few scholarly Romans would have had any notion of a volcanic eruption and those living in Pompeii and the vicinity considered Vesuvius a mountain.[8]

Unknown to them, an enormous bolus of pressurised magma underneath the volcano had built up, fed by a deep chamber several kilometres below.[9] Eventually, as the molten rock forced its way closer to the surface and mixed with ground water, the pressure dropped and dissolved gases bubbled out in a manner similar to the opening of a bottle of sparking water. This first outburst was the prelude to an immense eruption of mixed gases, solids and liquids. Residents under this portentous easterly cloud saw a small accumulation of pumice and ash scatter across their summer Campanian countryside. Rectina, a friend of Pliny the Elder, was so concerned by this initial eruption that she sent a mounted courier to her friend with a message pleading to be rescued.[10] Her villa may have been right under the shadow of Vesuvius.

1 p.m., 24 August: A colossal explosion proclaimed the main eruption. Tearing apart Vesuvius's peak, a gigantic churning upsurge of magma, poisonous fumes, pumice, ash and rock, mixing violently with atmospheric gases, soared into the sky. A deafening sonic boom radiated out and shockwaves ripped into the atmosphere. Within just ten minutes, the column reached over twenty kilometres in height.[11]

Some thirty kilometres west in Misenum, Gaius Plinius Caecilius Secundus, better known as Pliny the Younger, was staying at the family villa with his mother, Plinia Marcella, and his uncle, her brother, Pliny the Elder. Pliny the Elder was *praefectus classis*, admiral of the Classis Misenensis naval fleet, moored at the large Roman port in Misenum.[12] Plinia Marcella pointed out a cloud of 'unusual size and appearance' over the distant Vesuvius. The younger Pliny observed the evolving column and thought it resembled a pine tree branching out.[13] He was describing the prevailing atmospheric winds that were driving the cloud south-east towards Pompeii and beyond. In his honour, as the first to document in detail the stages of a volcanic eruption, this is termed the *Plinian* phase or type of volcanic eruption.

Shortly after the start of the Plinian phase, white pumice began to fall on Pompeii and surrounding areas under the main axes of the spreading column. It would accumulate at around fifteen centimetres per hour and therefore quickly covered everything. For many observers, panic set in. We know from the number of corpses found in Pompeii that the majority managed at least to exit the town.[14] Chances of survival would have been reasonable for those who grabbed just a few of their most precious possessions and immediately moved in the right direction, away from under the fallout zone and far from the volcano. The first hours were critical because roads would have quickly disappeared and familiar landmarks rapidly become masked. As the level of light faded, victims would also have become disorientated as the horizon blurred between the fallout-laden skies and the blanketed landscape. Breathing would have become laboured due to sulphur dioxide, carbon dioxide and airborne volcanic particulates.[15] The majority in the danger zones would have been on foot, with only a fraction able to use a horse or boat. Depending on the baggage they carried and whether they had young children, disabled individuals or elderly persons with them, people who fled immediately could have covered around twelve kilometres within three hours if they headed directly away from the fallout axes.[16] Otherwise, taking too long to depart, moving too slowly or fleeing in the wrong direction, would have meant wading through ever growing drifts of pumice and ash, increasing the probability of becoming lost and stranded.

2 p.m., 24 August: In Pompeii, around fifteen centimetres of pumice and ash now covered the entire town and surrounding countryside, eerily white-washing the landscape. At a temperature of 120–140°C, the pumice would have burned any bare skin and scorched hair, requiring anyone outside to cover themselves as much as possible for protection.[17] People remaining in the town or exposed in the countryside or coastline would have been deeply alarmed for their safety. Nothing is known about the reaction of local authorities or any troops in the area, except for Pliny the Elder's fleet at Misenum. The Romans had fire brigades in major community centres but no first-line emergency services. In short, nothing at a population level could have been done and we shall see that Pliny's ships do not appear to have succeeded in any rescues. To the west of Pompeii, perched on a cliff-top overlooking the bay, the fashionable seaside town of Herculaneum – named after the Greek god Hercules – with its prominent townhouses and surrounding palatial villas, was only getting a light dusting from the fallout given its position upwind. However, its close proximity to the vent and the vast eruption column, now towering around thirty kilometres into the sky, also triggered a mass exodus of the estimated 5,000 inhabitants.[18] Meanwhile in Misenum, the eruption column seen from that distance was significant enough to warrant Pliny the Elder, who had a keen interest in natural history, to order a light ship from his fleet to be prepared in order to go and observe the event more closely. He offered to take his nephew with him but the younger Pliny declined in preference of his studies. At their distance, they were clearly unaware of the magnitude of the unfolding disaster.

3 p.m., 24 August: Just about to leave his villa, Pliny the Elder received the message sent earlier in the morning from Rectina. Her plea to be picked up convinced Pliny to change his plans from an observational expedition into

a rescue mission. The admiral promptly ordered large quadrireme vessels to be launched. With two rows of oars on each side, they were capable of around six knots; meaning a trip of around three hours to reach the coastline near the suburban Oplontis area.[19]

In Pompeii and elsewhere under the main fallout zone, the white pumice, ash and rock fell relentlessly across the landscape. For those who sought shelter in public or private buildings, the weight of the volcanic deposits began to cause the collapse of the weaker or more poorly constructed refuges. One can imagine people desperately trying to keep exits clear, comforting children, gathering possessions and seeking the best location for shelter. Outdoors, other than its singeing heat, the falling generally smaller pieces of pumice were not life-threatening given their small size and lightweight porous nature.[20] More hazardous were larger chunks of pumice, limestone and other volcanic rock falling from the proliferating column that would reach at its peak around thirty-three kilometres in height.[21] Daylight continued to fade, worsening the perilous situation.

Sunset, 24 August: The Plinian phase continued to evolve and *grey* pumice now began to fall.[22] This was a signal unknown to anyone at the time that materials within the exploding column were being derived from deeper levels within the magma chamber.[23] By around this time, half a metre or more of pumice mixed with ash and rock had accumulated, causing many roofs and walls to collapse across Pompeii. The failing infrastructure claimed many casualties and trapped others with no hope of being rescued.[24] Those who had fled at the start and were able to move quickly might have reached safe distances by now. However, those in slower-moving groups would have struggled to reach safe positions, particularly if they had delayed their departure.

Pliny the Elder's flotilla of quadriremes had reached the other side of the Bay of Naples where they were hit by an increasingly lethal fallout. Pliny the Younger later recounted details to the historian Cornelius Tacitus that he probably acquired from interviewing naval officers:

> Now ash was falling on the ships, hotter and heavier the nearer they approached; then pumice, and even stones, blackened, burnt, and broken by fire.[25]

They were too late. The fallout had created a floating carpet of pumice and ash on the surface of the sea, making it impossible for Pliny's boats to reach any port. They also encountered unexpected shallows, presumably due to massive seismic shifts in the level of the seabed.[26] A helmsman pleaded with his admiral to turn back and, after some hesitation, Pliny decided to head ten kilometres south-east to Stabiae, where he hoped to find another friend, Pomponianus. He had abandoned any hope of finding Rectina.

7 p.m. 24 August: Pliny the Elder made land at Stabiae and was probably able to moor his vessels in the large port if it remained open – or, otherwise, he could have beached them. The resort town was extremely wealthy, with some of the finest villas in the Roman Empire, exquisitely adorned and designed and reaching new levels of architectural perfection.[27] One example, the Villa San Marco, covered 11,000 square metres, roughly 1½ times the size of a soccer pitch. Indeed the whole coastline around the Bay of Naples was a prime real estate playground for rich Romans escaping the summer heat of Rome, lounging in opulent villas, gorging on oysters and consuming fine wines at parties. The town of Stabiae stood on a fifty-metre-high headland that afforded speculator views over the Bay of Naples. Like Pompeii, it was directly under the central axes of the fallout, but its location seventeen kilometres from the vent meant a slower accumulation of deposits. Pomponianus had already transferred his important belongings to a boat, ready to leave when favourable winds permitted. He was terrified and Pliny tried to reassure him. Feigning calm, Pliny asked to bathe at his friend's villa and they had dinner together afterwards.

In Pompeii, more than half a metre of pumice and ash had now fallen on the town. This placed unsustainable strain on most roofs, colonnades and other structures, resulting in the further collapse of buildings. The fallout continued ceaselessly and would eventually reach as high as 2.8 metres at the Vesuvius Gate of Pompeii; only the second and third storeys of buildings protruded above this. In the suburban area of Oplontis, 1.8 metres would ultimately build up. Around 10 per cent of the fallout comprised fist-sized rocks, which would have been lethal projectiles falling at terminal velocity.[28] To the north-west in Herculaneum, still upwind of the fallout, those waiting or unable to flee would have observed the luminescent glow of super-heated materials at the base of the column. In Misenum, Pliny the Younger experienced ever more violent earthquakes.[29]

7:00–8:00 p.m., 24 August: No one still trapped in Herculaneum would have seen the next horror coming in the pale darkness: a pyroclastic surge – a turbulent mass of ash, rock fragments and super-heated gases hugging the ground and moving fast – descended the western, southern and south-eastern flanks of Vesuvius.[30] Billowing down at around 100–180 km/hr, it took just minutes to hit the idyllic seaside town.[31] The surge ripped off roof tiles and knocked down colonnades but walls generally survived. It was the extreme heat, not the force, that was deadly. The searing temperature carbonised wood and boiled the sea surface as the surge continued across the bay. A pyroclastic flow, a denser mix than the surge, immediately followed. Over 300 people had taken refuge in twelve boat chambers lining the beach. The first surge was over 550 °C and killed everyone instantaneously. Their hands and feet violently contracted in the heat and their soft tissues vaporised in seconds.[32] In some cases, the pressure of the steaming brains of victims exploded their skulls.[33] On the beach, several mothers with young children and people with disabilities had gathered as some of the last to evacuate, in vain hope of escape by sea. The surge also killed them instantly, some of their skulls also exploding and their bones being utterly consumed.[34] The beach was opened to the public for the first time in 2024; the morbidly curious can observe the clusters of skeletal remains. For around two kilometres north-west and two kilometres south-east along the coast, many more doubtless perished.[35] A victim lying on a wooden bed in the Collegium Augustalium in Herculaneum was engulfed in the surge, his body fat ignited, soft tissues vaporised and his brain vitrified into glass[36] – a gruesome but instant death. This first surge marked the overlapping start of the second, *Peléan*, phase of the eruption. The fallout continued for several more hours but the column at a height of around thirty-three kilometres had begun a series of deadly collapses.[37]

1 a.m., 25 August: A second massive pyroclastic event, larger than the first, discharged from Vesuvius and spread in all directions from the vent.[38] Moving extremely fast, up to a staggering 300 kilometres per hour, this surge was capable of immense physical destruction. It smashed down walls and roofs that had survived the first surge in Herculaneum. Reaching around seven kilometres south-east, the flow engulfed Boscoreale and Oplontis, killing sixty-four people.[39]

2 a.m., 25 August: Another pyroclastic flow and surge, of over 300 °C and with enormous kinetic energy, billowed out in all directions.[40] In the darkness, the super-heated black clouds would have appeared to be riddled with flames and lightning. Striking Herculaneum, Boscoreale and Oplontis, its force tore apart buildings protruding from the deposits of the prior events.[41] In some parts of Herculaneum, the event left behind a layer of ash several metres thick. It reached further than the first and would have killed anyone in its path. However, it did not reach as far as Pompeii.

During the night, fallout continued to amass at Stabiae. Frail and exhausted, Pliny the Elder had managed to sleep but Pomponianus and others on vigil decided to wake him. They were afraid he would be trapped in his room as the volcanic deposits piled up in the courtyard. Moreover, frequent earthquakes threatened to bring down Pomponianus' villa. They agonised over whether to stay outdoors in case of collapse or remain indoors to avoid the fearsome fallout. In the end, they found the resolve to remain outside and tied cushions on their heads as a means of protection.[42]

6.30 a.m., 25 August: A pyroclastic current blasted out west, south and south-east from the vent and had enough energy this time to reach much further. It got as far as the northern walls of Pompeii, over ten kilometres away, but was exhausted at that distance and fizzled out.[43] A flow followed directly after and totally buried the rest of Herculaneum except the upper part of the theatre. A layer nearly ten metres thick in certain areas was dumped by this fourth flow, sufficient along with subsequent pyroclastic currents to extend the coastline at Herculaneum by around 400 metres.[44]

A small reprieve followed that allowed many Pompeians still alive to emerge from their hideouts and crawl across the fallout that blanketed their town.[45] In Misenum around this time, Pliny the Younger, his mother and his uncle's visiting friend from Spain had endured a night of violent earthquakes and observed a 'dim and faint' dawn. Their home was at risk of collapsing and, fearing for their lives, they finally decided to join the masses fleeing west out of Misenum. Their wagons, probably carrying some of their most valuable and precious possessions, could not be kept under control even on level ground, due to the earthquakes.[46]

7:30 a.m., 25 August: The collapse of the Plinian column, its vast contents dropping like an avalanche of rock and ash, generated a huge current that swept over Pompeii.[47] The event lacked sufficient force to cause major structural damage but was still able to claim the lives of most remaining Pompeians who either scrabbled for survival in its concentrated path or were trapped and engulfed by its noxious contents.[48] Just prior to the arrival of this deadly pyroclastic flow, a woman over fifty years of age and a man between thirty-five and forty had taken refuge in the dining room of a house known as Casa del Fabbro, in what would normally have been a bustling area a few blocks from the main theatre.[49] The couple were huddled on a *triclinium*, the type of reclining couch that the Romans used when eating meals. The man was disabled due to Pott's Disease, a complication of tuberculosis spreading to the spine causing severe arthritis in the intervertebral joints.

His condition had evidently prevented him from fleeing, and the woman, probably his devoted mother, had stayed with him to the very end.

Alone and likely terrified, a child around eight years of age, presumably separated from its parents or perhaps a child slave, had found transient sanctuary in the central bath complex of Pompeii.[50] The baths were the largest in Pompeii and construction had not been fully completed at the time of the eruption. However, the sturdy walls and arches of the complex had offered protection until the deadly event engulfed the facility and the poor child choked to death.[51]

On the north-western edge of Pompeii, the impressive House of the Golden Bracelet boasted three levels of finely appointed living areas.[52] It was constructed on a slope with its upper storey at street level on one side. The residents enjoyed the luxury of an atrium-style arrangement, including three dining rooms, a private bath suite and numerous reception rooms. Several areas had fine views of the Bay of Naples and likely benefited from cooling sea breezes during the hot summer months. No expense had been spared: all the main rooms were decorated with fashionable intricate frescos ranging from fantastical architectural scenes to garden landscapes filled with birds and flowers. Other frescos pleasing to the eye were fine depictions of Dionysus, the god of wine, becharmed by the beautiful young Ariadne of Naxos, and of Alexander the Great's marriage to Roxana during his Asian conquests. On the ground floor, a formal garden with box hedges, flower beds and a semi-circular pond were overlooked by vaulted rooms: one a summer dining room complete with its own *nymphaeum* (grotto fountain). Water flowed down from the apse between the marble dining couches and into the garden pool where it sprinkled again from the elegant water features.

Once the height of fine living, the garden by this time was buried, its elegance lost beneath the pumice and ash. Cowered in an alcove near a staircase, two adults – a male and female – and two young male children had decided to stay rather than flee. Recently shown to be unrelated genetically, one can only guess why the four were hiding together.[53] The woman was clearly very wealthy, with an ornate solid-gold double-headed snake armlet weighing 610 grams and worth 8,200 HS in metal value.[54] Possibly the wife or widow of the property owner, she wore other gold and gemstone jewellery and had clutched forty *aurei* and 172 *denarii* – equivalent to more than five years' wages for a Roman soldier.[55] As they perished in the pyroclastic event, the woman held one of the young children on her belly in their last moment alive, the other child lay nearby and the man hunched up his limbs.

In the opposite south-eastern corner of the town, a large *palaestra* or gymnasium with an expansive open-air courtyard surrounded by a portico and high walls had served as a prestigious facility for the training of Pompeian youths.[56] Many had gathered here desperate for refuge under the elegant Augustan-era arcades. A few victims already lay dead, buried in the fallout and probably killed by collapsing structures. That didn't deter sixty people from gathering in the *palaestra*, perhaps sensing some safety in numbers. Suddenly engulfed in the pyroclastic flow, they would have struggled to breathe, pressing their faces into the ground, each covering their nose and mouth with their hands while gasping for air, eventually overcome as ash clogged their lungs.[57]

Seven blocks to the west in one of the wealthiest homes in Pompeii, Casa del Criptoportico, nine individuals had managed to survive the fallout phase.[58] Magnificently appointed, the house had two rare attributes: its own private bath suite and cryptoporticoes. The former was exceptional and the latter a much sought after feature of covered passages and corridors, providing a cool space for leisure and rest during the ferociously hot Campanian summers. Cleverly designed windows allowed light into the cryptoporticoes but not the outside heat.[59] The passageways surrounded a garden and presumably the owners, family members and their most loyal slaves had remained, the sturdy arched roofs of the cryptoporticoes probably providing a sense of protection. Amongst them, they had jewellery, coins and a key in their possession. Exhausted from a sleepless and fearful night, the arrival of the killer pyroclastic flow drove them into the garden, where they succumbed to the ash.

7.30–8:30 a.m., 25 August: Unbeknown to the Romans, the final, phreatomagmatic, phase had begun. The disrupted Earth's crust had allowed the water table to interact with the magma chamber resulting in thermal contraction, a new short-lived eruption column and the beginning of the inward collapse of Vesuvius.[60] With little or no sign of dawn emerging through the ash-laden atmosphere, the subsequent total collapse of the column generated a colossal pyroclastic current that dwarfed all proceeding events. The event discharged its vast swirling black clouds in all directions from the vent and had sufficient energy and mass to encase the entire Bay of Naples.[61] The massive hot pyroclastic flow billowed over Pompeii, already buried in over two metres of pumice, rock and ash and with only the tallest buildings still visible above the desolate ghost town. The event utterly inundated the town; its energy knocked down or damaged structures in its path. A few remaining survivors who had miraculously managed to scramble above the fallout, inside and outside, or found spaces protected from the deposits, were enveloped in the dense gaseous mix of fine particles that exploded into open areas or seeped into cavities.[62] Unlike at Herculaneum, it might not have been exposure to intense heat that killed them, but rather the presence of the ash clouds swirling around for an estimated seventeen minutes, that suffocated all the remaining wretched victims.[63]

Away to the south-east, Pliny the Elder with a few companions had decided to move down to the shoreline, which, despite the dawn, was in total darkness caused by the dense volcanic clouds. Using torches and lamps to help illuminate their route, they were dismayed to find a raging sea with no possible hope of a nautical escape. A sheet was laid out for the elderly statesman to lie down on and he repeatedly called for water to drink. The stranded group witnessed the vast black turbulent clouds of the pyroclastic current plunging its way towards them:

> Then fire and the smell of sulphur – the harbinger of flames – turned
> the others to flight and roused him.

Pliny's weak constitution meant that he suffered acutely from the particle-laden atmosphere mixed with poisonous volcanic gases. Able to make a last stand with the help of two slaves to lift him up, he finally collapsed, asphyxiated. His body was recovered the next day.[64] The scale of this pyroclastic event, able to reach Stabiae around twenty-one kilometres from the vent, left an eighty-centimetre-thick deposit.[65]

Thirty kilometres to the west in Misenum, Pliny the Younger and his mother were also caught by this event. As they laboured to escape amongst the fleeing crowds, he was able to see the coastline from their position and witnessed the sea dramatically receding, stranding countless fish and other 'sea creatures'. Pliny was observing the formation of a tsunami in the Bay of Naples created by seismic activity. From his position, he also saw the volcanic flow as a 'fearful' black cloud illuminated by lightning and 'great tongues of fire'. At this point, their Spanish visitor pleaded with them to think more for their own safety and, clearly terrified for his own wellbeing, dashed off alone. Pliny described the actual descent and dissemination of the pyroclastic flow:

> … the cloud sank down to earth and covered the sea; it had already
> blotted out Capri and hidden the promontory of Misenum from sight.

Pliny's mother begged her son to flee, knowing that her frailty hindered his flight. Ashes still falling all around them, Pliny described the pyroclastic current reaching them a staggering thirty kilometres from Vesuvius' vent:

> I looked round: a dense black cloud was coming up behind us,
> spreading over the earth like a flood. 'Let us leave the road while
> we can still see,' I said, 'or we shall be knocked down and trampled
> underfoot in the dark by the crowd behind.' We had scarcely sat down
> to rest when darkness fell, not the dark of the moonless or cloudy
> night, but as if the lamp had been put out in a closed room. You could
> hear the shrieks of women, the wailing of infants and the shouting of
> men; some were calling their parents, others their children or their
> wives, trying to recognise them by their voices.

Still shrouded in darkness, they nevertheless survived and were able to see the distant volcanic flames through the gloom. Under heavy fallout they struggled on and stopped periodically to shake off heavy showers of ashes.[66]

Remaining morning, 25 August: The finally exhausted magma chamber destabilised the entire structure of Vesuvius, causing the roof of the inner volcanic chamber and the remaining external mountain top to collapse into the void, creating a new caldera and a pyroclastic flow that reached six kilometres from the vent. Despite the caldera creation, the phreatomagmatic phase was still able to generate more events, churning enormous amounts of ash and rock over considerable distances.[67] Finally, the darkness 'dispersed into smoke or cloud' in Misenum as glimmers of daylight returned.[68] An utterly barren landscape emerged in the pale light, covered in ash like snow. Pliny and his mother returned to their home, which was buried under drifts of ash. Still unaware of Pliny the Elder's fate, they had to endure continued aftershocks, probably forcing them to camp outdoors.[69] The Younger Pliny, aged seventeen, inherited his uncle's full estate and went on to have an illustrious senatorial career, serving under the Emperor Trajan and dying in service as the Governor of Bithynia-Pontus.[70]

So ended the cataclysmic eruption of Vesuvius that wiped out a large proportion of Roman Campania with an eruptive force equivalent to around twenty-four megatonnes of TNT, 1,600 times or more the yield of the Hiroshima atomic bomb.[71] One of the wealthiest regions of Italy, teeming with prosperous towns, coveted by wealthy Romans for its exquisite villas and sought after by farmers for its prime farmland, along with countless industries, was utterly destroyed. The natural disaster remains deeply enigmatic to modern visitors of Pompeii and Herculaneum and is still studied by historians, volcanologists and geologists.

Titus' Response to the Disaster and its Survivors

Early news would likely have arrived in Rome late on 25 August as the eruption ended. The full nature of the disaster, humanitarian and financial, was only appreciated as further news flooded in over the proceeding days. Some survivors with relations, friends or resources in Rome could have arrived from around the 28th, able to describe events first-hand.[72] One can easily imagine Titus' reaction as one of sheer disbelief and shock at the unfolding news. The catastrophic eruption was a staggering blow to Titus, as the Campania region was highly populated, one of the most agriculturally productive parts of Italy and home to many elite Roman citizens, including senators. The immediate reports of entire towns – Pompeii, Herculaneum, and Stabiae – being buried under volcanic ash, along with widespread destruction and loss of life, would have emphasised the enormous scale of the disaster. Titus, a man known for his compassion, would have been deeply moved by the human cost. Like many fellow superstitious Roman citizens, Titus would have recognised the symbolic significance of such a disaster occurring so early in his reign. As a new emperor, tasked with demonstrating his legitimacy and capability, he knew the catastrophe was a test of his leadership.

Titus acted decisively. He probably arrived for his first visit before the end of August.[73] Surveying the desolate, ghostly landscape, he almost certainly experienced the after-tremors that typically follow such volcanic eruptions. He would also have witnessed the mass displacement of destitute survivors. Astutely, Titus appointed a special commission led by two ex-consuls, chosen by lot to 'supervise the restoration of the region and bestowed on the inhabitants … gifts of money'. It would have been immediately clear that enormous sums would be required to deal with the catastrophe. As a result, he tapped into his own imperial funds to support the recovery efforts. Additionally, in the disaster zones he also diverted the estates of those who had died without heirs to a fund dedicated for rebuilding.[74] It would have also been apparent to Titus and his advisors that large sources of tax revenue were lost. Campania was well-known for its extensive vineyards that accounted for a significant proportion of the peninsula's profitable wine production.

It was totally impossible to locate and dig out roads, ports or other public facilities lost under the millions of tonnes of volcanic debris and it was unworkable to build on the surface of the wasted areas because the ground was highly unstable and required months, if not years, to solidify gradually due to rainfall, and even longer for topsoils to develop for farming.[75] Moreover, the fields of ash were a direct health hazard to humans and animals in terms of respiratory disease. Therefore, Titus' central disaster-policy decision, later inherited by his brother Domitian, was to restore and build up the towns that had survived in the region to cope with refugees setting up new lives. It appears that Titus and his consular commission did not direct survivors to any given refugee areas.[76]

Displaced individuals and communities sharply raised the population numbers in the regional towns that took them in. As a result, Cumae's amphitheatre was expanded and new public baths, aqueducts and roads built.[77] Titus is credited with restoring edifices in Neapolis.[78] Eventually a new theatre and Odeon were completed for the displaced communities settling there.[79] Water was a quintessential need and the Aqua Augusta (Serino) Aqueduct required significant repairs together with the replacement of lead pipe conduits that fed from it. The aqueduct was still able to bring water to places like Neapolis but construction started immediately after the eruption to bring online an overhauled water system that ultimately required fifteen years to complete.[80] Only a few kilometres to the west, the crucially important port of Puteoli also received imperial support for the influx of survivors, such as a large new amphitheatre, baths, roads and harbour works. The port was allowed to expand its boundary under a renewal of its colonial status.[81]

On the human side, we know very little about the survivors but can glean some stories. Caius Sulpicius Faustus and Caius Sulipicius Onirus, for example, who both had financial dealings in Pompeii, managed to make it out and resettled in Cumae. Indeed, several identifiable families made it to Cumae, such as the Aelii, Caecilii and the Licinii. Resettled families also prospered by making good marriages.[82] M. Caninius Botrio, from Herculaneum, fled with his family and built a new life in Neapolis. Another, unnamed, native of Pompeii survived and moved to Neapolis; this man later served as an army officer, dying in far-off Dacia.[83] To recognise these new resettled communities, a statue was set-up in Neapolis and the dedication records the foremost and resplendent district of the Herculaneans; one can conclude that they were settled into a new suburb of the city – and a good one, not a slum.[84] Families managed to flourish and in Puteoli, among the next generation of survivors, M. Gavius Puteolanus was named after the new town in which his parents had first found shelter and then presumably established a home.[85] Some lost businesses were able to thrive again. Pompeii had once produced large quantities of garum, a fermented fish sauce that was the ketchup of the Roman world. Survivors of this trade relocated to Puteoli and opened up garum production not seen before in the port.[86] These are all examples of individuals with ample resources or munificent acquaintances and certainly many people displaced by the eruption were less fortunate and they probably created slums in various towns or took their chances further afield, perhaps on the streets of Rome. It is quite probable that Roman looters ventured into the wasted areas digging tunnels in search of precious valuables. However, Pompeii, Herculaneum, Stabiae and other places were eventually forgotten until their rediscovery especially from the eighteenth century.[87]

As Titus surveyed the desolate, grey, ashen wastelands left in the wake of the catastrophe, his thoughts undoubtedly wrestled with the daunting task that lay ahead. Having ascended to the Principate just nine weeks prior, he was confronted with the immense challenge of addressing this natural disaster. In such a trying time at the dawn of his reign, Titus perhaps found guidance in the example set by his father, Vespasian, renowned for his pragmatic and prudent leadership style. Drawing inspiration from his father's legacy, Titus would have felt a deep sense of responsibility towards his citizens and prioritised their wellbeing through swift effective disaster management. Overall, Titus' response to the Vesuvius disaster demonstrated his commitment to effective governance and his probable desire to emulate the leadership qualities of his father and uphold the honour of his Flavian family.

CHAPTER 1

HUMBLE BEGINNINGS

The Flavii

Navigating the corridors of power in first-century imperial Rome required wealth, resilience and robust connections in terms of patronage, allies and friends. The first five emperors from Augustus to Nero hailed from the illustrious Julio-Claudian family, emphasising the privileged lineage that was a prerequisite for imperial ascent. However, the AD 69 civil war, known as the Year of the Four Emperors, witnessed a transformation in the dynamics of power.[1] The traditional requirement of noble birth was gradually overshadowed by the influence of Rome's legions, a shift laid bare during the tumult of civil strife. Military might, always an underlying force behind an emperor's accession, emerged more prominently during this period. As we delve into Titus' journey to the Principate, we find further departure from aristocratic origins. His father, Vespasian, came from an equestrian family and his early senatorial career was uneventful.[2]

Titus' paternal great-grandfather, Titus Flavius Petro, came from Reate (Rieti) in the Latium region of Italy. Founded in the Apennines by the ancient Sabine people, it was approximately seventy-five kilometres north-west of Rome along the age-old Via Salaria. In 48 BC, Petro, serving as a centurion on Pompey's side, fought in the famous Battle of Pharsalus in central Greece against the victorious Julius Caesar.[3] Surviving the battle, he received a pardon, an honourable discharge, and transitioned to a career as a tax collector. His wife Tertulla, Titus' great-grandmother, had an estate in a coastal colony called Cosa, in south-west Tuscany. Their son, Titus Flavius Sabinus I, Titus' paternal grandfather, started his career as a customs supervisor in Asia and attained some fame as an honest tax gatherer – 'cities honoured him with statues'.[4] With an acumen for finances and sufficient capital accumulated, he returned from the East and settled in the Alps amongst the upwardly mobile Helvetii to start a banking business. Sabinus married Vespasia Polla, and their union was a prestigious match; her father, Vespasius Pollio, held the rank of Camp Prefect in a Roman legion and her brother, Vespasius, was a senator who attained a praetorship. Thus, Titus' paternal great-uncle became the first in the family to reach senatorial rank, elevating the family's status to low-level gentry. However, as will soon be apparent, Sabinus' wealth and possibly unique connections with Germanicus, brother of the future Emperor Claudius (41–54) and their mother Antonia Minor would serve as a launch pad for his future career.[5] Sabinus and Vespasia Polla had three children: Titus Flavius Sabinus II and Vespasian, the uncle and father of Titus respectively and Flavia, their firstborn, who died at a very young age.[6]

Titus' father, Vespasian, was born on 17 November AD 9, five years before the death of Augustus, in a rural settlement called Falacrinae, further north along the Via Salaria from Reate (Rieti), in the modern-day commune of

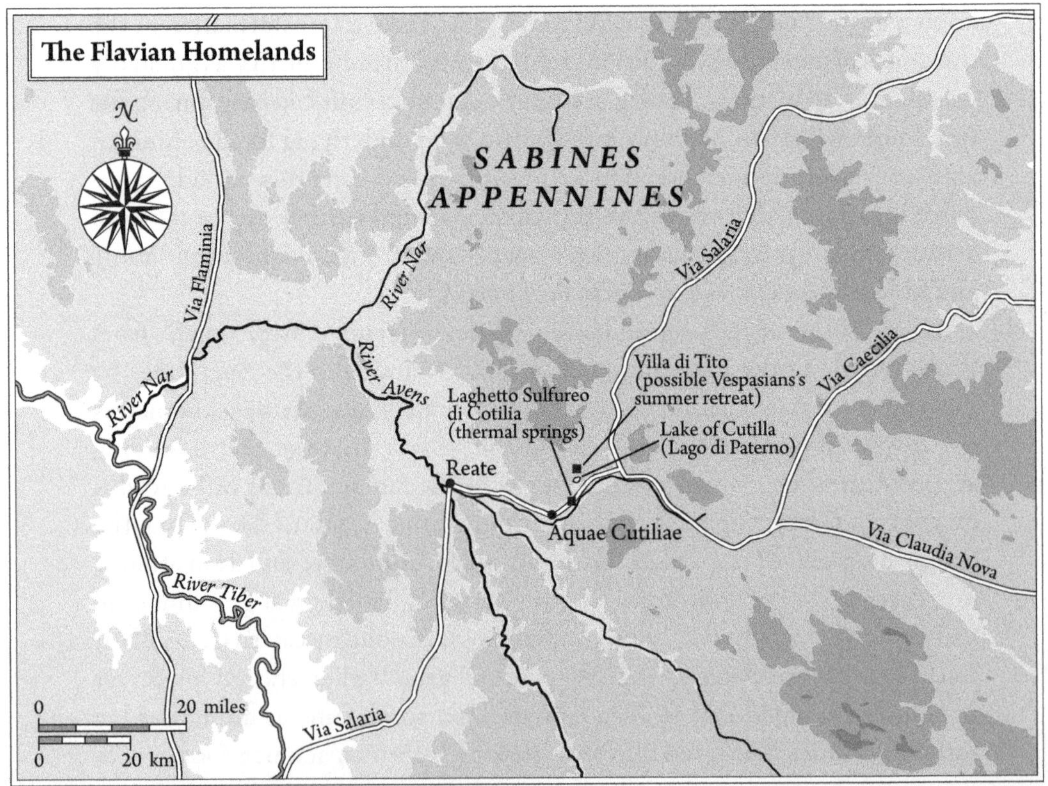

Cittareale.[7] As emperor, Vespasian would later build a summer villa in the region of his unassuming birthplace.[8] His brother, Sabinus II, was approximately six years his senior.[9] They were raised by their paternal grand-mother, Tertulla, on her property at Cosa. Deeply fond of those childhood years, Vespasian frequently revisited the home throughout his life and maintained the estate as he remembered it to cherish his memories.[10] He would always retain his accent from those regions and it later suited him politically never to shy from his rural roots in contrast to the ostentatious ancestry of the Julio-Claudians.[11]

In stark contrast to his father's equestrian lineage, it is speculated that Titus' mother, Flavia Domitilla I, might have been the illegitimate child of a slave and a Roman knight called Statilius Capella from Sabrata in Africa. Although Statilius is believed to have cared deeply for Domitilla, her birth status was a problem. Due to her lowborn background, Roman law prohibited Vespasian from marrying Domitilla. To overcome this legal obstacle, Vespasian may have sought the assistance of one of his freedmen, Flavius Liberalis. It is suggested that Flavius Liberalis falsely claimed paternity over Domitilla to secure a legal ruling declaring her free at birth and consequently eligible for Roman citizenship. The arrangement likely proved beneficial for Flavius Liberalis, who, with Vespasian's patronage, rose to prominence as a civil servant. In return, Vespasian may have gained advantages through his connection with Domitilla, as Roman marriages were typically strategic rather than driven by personal affection. It is plausible that Domitilla's ties through Statilius to Sabrata, a wealthy ancient trading city on the northern coast of Africa, played an important role in shaping her husband's evolving career, especially during a period when Vespasian was uncertain about entering politics and less concerned about her origin.[12]

Vespasian's Early Career

Titus' uncle Sabinus II paved the way for the Flavii in terms of a senatorial *cursus honorum*, meaning he had acquired enormous wealth and patronage to qualify and advance. By around 33 he had held a praetorship, in the later part of Tiberius' reign (14–37).[13] Vespasian was initially reluctant to follow in his brother's footsteps but eventually conceded after insistent comments from his mother.[14] Around the period of his brother's praetorship, Vespasian was posted for approximately three years to Thrace as a military tribune, probably with the Legio IV *Scythica*.[15] Next, around the age of twenty-six,

Vespasian's quaestorship saw him assigned by lot to the peaceful senatorial provinces of Crete and Cyrenaica as a financial magistrate.[16]

At this juncture of his *cursus honorum*, Vespasian was struggling to make a political mark. The aedileship in this period was a greatly diminished position, far from the original authority it held over the maintenance of Rome in the Republican period.[17] The Emperor Augustus had found it hard to fill the positions. Yet Vespasian failed in his first attempt for election and came in last place with his second.[18] In this new position the erratic Emperor Caligula (37–41) found reason to be furious with him for neglecting his duty as an aedile to keep the streets of Rome clean. He ordered some soldiers to cover Vespasian's toga with mud to humiliate him. The Roman historian Suetonius tells us that it was later considered a portent of his future reign:

> ... an omen interpreted to mean that one day the soil of Italy would be neglected and trampled on as the result of civil war, but that Vespasian would protect it and, so to speak, take it into his embrace.[19]

At this time, in the autumn of 39, Caligula's reign darkened further following allegations of a conspiracy in Germania Superior. The emperor travelled to the province accompanied by his two sisters, Agrippina and Livilla, and his ex-brother-in-law Marcus Aemilius Lepidus, who had been married to Caligula's third, now deceased, sister Drusilla. Caligula ordered the execution of the Roman governor Gaetulicus for his role in the affair.[20] Lepidus and Caligula's sisters were also accused of plotting against the emperor, as well as committing adultery. Lepidus was executed and Agrippina bore the remains of her lover back to Rome. The two sisters were later exiled by Caligula to the Pontine Islands.[21]

Despite this ominous purge and a background of high tension between Caligula and the Senate, Vespasian secured his praetorship appointment, perhaps in 40, meaning that his selection would have been approved by Caligula the year before. How did Vespasian achieve such a position after an uneventful start to his senatorial career? As a young man, as well as during and after his marriage to Domitilla, Vespasian had a relationship with Antonia Caenis, who was the freedwoman and private secretary of the stately Antonia Minor.[22] Vespasian was very close to Antonia Caenis and she was apparently 'his wife in all but name even when he became Emperor'.[23] It's hard to over-emphasise the enormous influence of Antonia Minor up until her death in 37; she was the daughter of the famous Mark

Antony, the niece of the Emperor Augustus, sister-in-law of the Emperor Tiberius, paternal grandmother of the current Emperor Caligula and the mother of the great general Germanicus and the future Emperor Claudius. Therefore, Antonia Caenis would have given Vespasian extraordinary insights into the machinations of the imperial court and almost certainly helped him secure extremely valuable patronage.

When Agrippina brought Lepidus' cremated remains back prior to her eventual exile there was a debate in the Senate after which the remains were denied a Roman burial. Vespasian, as praetor designate, relying on uncertain support from Caligula, supported the motion to prevent the burial. Thwarting Agrippina would come back to haunt Vespasian. After Caligula's hyped-up victory against the Canninefates in Germany in early 40, Vespasian proposed special celebratory games. As praetor, he was expected to pay part of the cost of the games from his own resources and this caused him significant financial stress. When Caligula was back in Rome, Vespasian was invited to dine one evening in the palace and he later thanked the emperor in front of the Senate.[24] Like others, Vespasian was not above grovelling before Caligula. After his praetorship, Vespasian probably remained in Rome and observed the tumult of Caligula's assassination on 24 January 41 and the subsequent accession of Claudius.[25]

Titus' Birth and Early Upbringing

Far from the image of a future emperor born amongst opulent surroundings, Titus was born on 30 December 39, in a 'small, dingy, slum bedroom' close to a construction called the Septizonium in Rome.[26] The location of the Septizonium remains unknown and its translation means 'seven zones', which could, but does not necessarily, mean that it was a seven-storey building.[27] The house of Titus' birth was preserved and open to the public during Hadrian's reign, when Suetonius wrote his *Twelve Caesars* around eight decades later.[28] It must have been a novelty to visit the squalid birthplace of one of Rome's great emperors. Given that Vespasian was a senator, typically an indication of considerable wealth, the family had clearly fallen on very hard times.

There were many ambitious Roman senators in the past who had risked enormous debts in pursuit of political advancement, as contributing towards lavish public games in Caligula's honour the year before to please the despotic emperor would have done. In any event, Titus' family in this period appear to have been living in a lowly apartment block in a less desirable part of Rome, probably with no running water and, at best, shared tanks in the building for sewage disposal.

The next documented part of Titus' life is the astonishing transformation from the slums of his birthplace to the imperial court, where he was educated alongside the Emperor Claudius' son, Britannicus, fourteen months his junior.[29] This meant that Titus was granted the finest, most privileged, education available in the Roman world. As we shall see later, the careers of his father, Vespasian, and his uncle, Sabinus II, benefited from the patronage of Emperor Claudius. As one extraordinary reward, the emperor's wife Messalina and the emperor's extremely influential freedman, Narcissus, probably agreed to have the two boys co-educated. Perhaps Titus already stood out amongst prospective young candidates for the privilege.

It is assumed that their schooling together commenced in 47, with Britannicus and Titus six and seven years old, respectively. Teaching would presumably have been conducted in the emperor's primary residence in the Domus Tiberiana on the Palatine Hill. Titus was most likely escorted every day to the palace by his *pedagogue*, typically a slave, who was trusted to supervise the young child. Once installed in their teaching area in the palace, a series of renowned tutors taught them both the same curriculum. One tutor was called Sosibius but his background is not recorded though he was probably a freedman.[30]

The two boys were first taught reading and writing (in Latin and Greek), and arithmetic. A wax tablet for writing and an abacus for calculations were principal tools for learning and they probably began to use precious papyrus scrolls and ink given their fortunate level of education. A typical day had around five to six hours of teaching, with physical exercise and bathing concluding the day. At around twelve years of age, under a *grammaticus* tutor, their syllabus advanced into the disciplines of language and literature; content ranging from poetry to history, amongst others. As their education advanced, they would have benefited from access to some of Rome's finest public and private libraries. Daily life at the imperial palace would also have exposed them to some of the routines of Claudius' court: security details, visiting dignitaries and the many senators passing in and out every day – invaluable lessons for the young Titus in the arts of politics and diplomacy.[31]

Beyond the age of twelve, in the year 51 for Titus, studies would turn to rhetoric and oratory. The former was a much sought-after skill for any aspiring senator, designed to develop the 'science of speaking well'.[32] One aim for the application of rhetoric to oratory discourse was the ability to persuade others what ought to be done. The *rhetor* tutor would have laboured with Titus and Britannicus to teach them the disciplines of structuring an argument, the arrangement of the narrative to articulate the argument, the style of speaking appropriate for a given audience and the importance of delivery.[33] One can easily imagine a process of selecting a topical subject, the application of rhetorical tools and many hours of subsequent declamation, perhaps on rare occasions in front of the Emperor Claudius himself. Titus would also have studied law rigorously, a process designed to instil a deep understanding of Roman ruling and prepare him for a career in public service.

For physical exercise, they received privileged instruction from the Praetorian Guard Prefects themselves: Geta, Crispinus and later Burrus.[34] Youth entertainment clubs were also venues for training, where children and adolescents of comparable age participated in athletics, hunting, riding and military exercises.[35] The end result of Titus' education, fit for a future emperor, was the formation of a cultivated young man well versed in literature, the arts and various other subjects, bilingual in Latin and Greek, able to deliver effective speeches, as well as being skilled and dexterous in physical pursuits:

> Though not tall, he [Titus] was both graceful and dignified, both muscular and handsome, except for a certain paunchiness. He had a phenomenal memory, and displayed a natural aptitude alike for almost all the arts of war and peace; handled arms and rode a horse with great skill; could compose speeches and verses in Greek or Latin with equal ease; and actually extemporised them on occasion. He was something of a musician, and had mastered the harp. It often amused him to compete with his secretaries at shorthand dictation, or so I have heard; and he claimed that he could imitate any handwriting in existence and might have been the most celebrated forger of all time.

Suetonius[36]

In a true tale of rags to riches, Vespasian and his family had risen from impoverished conditions at the time of Titus' birth to a position in which his son was tutored alongside Emperor Claudius' son. Patronage and favour from Claudius had facilitated Titus' remarkable education within the imperial court and Titus had become a loyal friend of Britannicus, the heir apparent. With rustic and unassuming ancestries, Titus' father and uncle had managed to launch their senatorial careers and survived the turbulent reign of Caligula.

CHAPTER 2

THE RISE OF THE FLAVII

Vespasian's forebears had never reached the prestigious senatorial position of consul, which marked the pinnacle of a senator's career. In the realm of Roman politics, he was perceived as a *novus homo*, a new man, despite the extinction of many of Rome's noble families as a consequence of purging during the civil wars at the close of the republican era.[1] Nonetheless, his father, Sabinus I, had accumulated considerable wealth through banking and possibly forged vital connections with Germanicus, Emperor Claudius' brother. This affiliation provided access to a network of distinguished families associated with the Claudii. Vespasian also enjoyed favour from Claudius' influential freedman, Narcissus. Moreover, his enduring close relationship with Antonia Caenis, the highly trusted freedwoman and aide to Claudius' mother, Antonia, further solidified his connections within the influential inner circles of the imperial court.[2]

The accession of Claudius in January 41 was therefore a watershed moment for the Flavian brothers. They could now capitalise on their network of connections. In 42 Narcissus helped secure Vespasian the command of Legio II *Augusta* based in Germania, one of four legions subsequently selected for Claudius' conquest of Britannia. Indeed, the rapid appointment of Vespasian soon after Claudius' accession is a clear indication that he was well known to the Emperor and his close allies, and had the necessary acumen to take on the command for an invasion.[3] Vespasian's brother, Sabinus II, was also appointed to command a legion in the campaign. They were clearly powerful siblings.

Devicta Britannia

In 55 BC, the great Roman general, Julius Caesar, had landed in Britannia with two legions for a reconnaissance. Caesar's venture into the exotic and mystical British Isles caused a sensation back in Rome in awe of their general's audacity. He returned the following year with a formidable army of five legions; after landing near Ramsgate, East Kent, his force punched north-west to the River Thames. The otherwise shrewd general appears to have undertaken this campaign rashly and was soon needed back in Gaul due to the risk of uprisings so he returned empty-handed, without booty or royal captives. Caligula contemplated an invasion in AD 39 but never left the shores of the Dutch coast, although he probably made preparations that Claudius later utilised.[4]

Why then did the newly installed Emperor Claudius invade Britannia? The cost of garrisoning and improving the infrastructure of the region outweighed returns from taxation. Moreover, the Oceanus, the English Channel, was already an excellent natural border for the western Roman Empire. Instead, Claudius needed to follow the long-standing formula for Roman political success to fortify his Principate: namely, the demonstration of military prowess through conquest and the extension of the Roman peace, *Pax Romana*. This was critical for the new emperor because, unusually, he had no military experience whatsoever.[5] This significant deficit was all the more acute given his father and brother's almost legendary military endeavours. Claudius required more than a fracas with a conveniently disruptive Germanic tribe. He needed to expand the empire and be remembered through the ages. The mythical isles on the fringe of the western Empire were an ideal candidate and south-eastern Britain was already partially subdued, making the initial conquest a low-hanging fruit for the emperor.[6]

Aulus Plautius Silvanus (hereafter Plautius) was appointed general of the invasion force. A steadfast Claudian loyalist, he is thought to have governed Pannonia and may have quashed a revolt against Claudius in 42. Vespasian's II *Augusta* is thought to have joined IX *Hispana*, XIV *Gemina* and Legio XX.[7] Along with Vespasian and Sabinus II, the proven military leader Cnaeus Hosidius Geta was also appointed a *legatus legionis*. Plautius assembled a total force of around 40,000 men, including auxiliaries, on the coast. An enormous armada of around 1,000 vessels, drawn from across the Roman Empire, was readied to ferry across the invasion force.[8]

In the spring or summer of 43, milder weather brought sufficiently calm seas for Plautius to muster his troops for the Oceanus crossing. However, his legions were not immune to the superstitious nature of the Roman people, afraid to venture beyond the limits of the known Roman world. It required the remarkable intervention of Narcissus, evidently posted to represent Claudius during his initial absence, to convince the rank and file to board the fleet.[9] It is not known with certainty, but the fleet likely beached at Richborough in Kent.[10] Unopposed, the first activity for Plautius' army was the construction of defensive works to shield the precious naval vessels.

The Roman column advanced west, probably via Durovernum (Canterbury), to the River Medway, where the Catuvellauni had massed under the leadership of two brothers: Togodumnus and Caratacus.[11] The location where Plautius attempted to cross the Medway has been much debated and new thinking suggests he may have selected a front west of Maidstone along the river at East Farleigh, Barming and Teston, where the river was historically fordable and where there was no impeding marshland.[12] The Medway was nevertheless a significant barrier that the Britons erroneously assumed their enemy could not easily cross. The Romans, however, had the equivalent of modern-day special forces: the Batavian auxiliary cavalry. These elite troopers were recruited from what is now the Dutch Rhine delta region and were highly skilled in river crossings. In full armour and with weapons, they were able to swim across rivers while guiding their mounts and using them to carry their shields and helmets. In a disciplined manner, they could cross wide turbulent rivers such as the Rhine and Danube while maintaining ordered ranks.[13] Thus, Plautius ordered his special forces to cross the Medway, presumably at a wide and faster-flowing section of the river where the Britons thought the Romans would not attempt to cross and therefore out of sight from their defensive lines. The special operatives reached the opposite bank, remounted and attacked. They focussed on the unprotected British chariot division to incapacitate the tethered horses. This was a major setback for Togodumnus and Caratacus because the lightweight, fast-moving chariots were a critical part of their army, able to disrupt enemy formations and move with agility across a battlefield.

Capitalising on this opening advantage, Vespasian led his legion across the Medway at a shallower fordable area. This was a bold and dangerous move. The Britons would have heavily defended any areas suitable for wading. Selecting an area where the water's depth was around 1.25m or less, a Roman legionary would have been able to wade when the speed of the river's flow was low.[14] In loose formations, the cohorts advanced on the opposite bank. After considerable effort and probably significant casualties, Vespasian withdrew the II *Augusta*, unable to establish a bridgehead. Unusual for field warfare in this period, which was typically settled in a single day, Plautius called a halt to action to continue on the morrow. Led this time by Geta, the force presumably attacked the same position as Vespasian. The legion commander was almost captured, suggesting a fierce engagement, but the disciplined and larger Roman forces eventually routed the Britons. Plautius was then able to move his whole force across the Medway and pursue the retreating army.[15]

The Britons withdrew north along routes known only to them. At this time, the Thames was much wider and shallower than today, and its flood plains created wide inaccessible marshes. This was a challenging barrier for the Romans to navigate. Once again, Plautius gave the order for the specialised Batavian cavalry to swim across when necessary to spearhead the Roman attack and other troops in the meantime managed to find a crossing point further upstream. Despite difficulties with swampy areas and some losses, the Batavii were able to rout the Britons.[16] Togodumnus does not appear to have survived, leaving Caratacus to rally what remained of his forces, although many dispersed and returned to their homesteads and farms in the wake of defeat.[17]

Plautius had what he needed now to send word to Claudius to join the conclusion of this first campaign. This was almost certainly prearranged and Claudius arrived subsequently with all the pomp befitting a Roman emperor, supposedly riding on an elephant and accompanied by his Praetorian Guard and a retinue of senators in their glimmering white and purple-trimmed togas. It would have been a sight to behold; the Britons would never have seen an elephant before. Claudius marched against the important town of Camulodunum (Colchester), which fell without incident, and he subsequently received the capitulation of several tribal kings. Caratacus slipped away and went on to resist the Romans for several years. Claudius stayed for only sixteen days, suggesting that he began his return journey very soon after arriving at Camulodunum. He had the victory he desired and was awarded the title of Britannicus and a triumph by the Senate. His son was also given the title Britannicus and became known by that name.[18]

Vespasian remained, and in 44 led a campaign that first consolidated gains in West Kent and Sussex before advancing south-west through Hampshire,

Dorset and Devon. While in Hampshire, he crossed over to the Isle of Wight and captured the island.[19] His forces systematically defeated any Britons who resisted:

> ...he fought thirty battles, subjugated two warlike tribes, and captured more than twenty towns, besides the entire Isle of Vectis [Wight].

Suetonius[20]

Vespasian did not sweep through these territories easily; he campaigned for four long years, only returning to Rome towards the end of 47.[21] Titus was four years old when his father left but, on his return he was greeted by a fast-growing boy who had started his education with Britannicus in Rome. With his mother, they had been placed under the care of Titus' grandfather, Sabinus I, in Aventicum while Vespasian was away on campaign.[22] The battle-hardened *legatus* was awarded the *ornamenta triumphalia* to acknowledge his distinguished role in the conquest of what is now southern England and notably appointed to two priesthoods.[23] In the meantime, his brother Sabinus II had been awarded a consulship in 44 as a reward for his services. The Flavii were on the rise.

Imperial Court Treachery

Vespasian's return to Rome after his military conquests in Britannia coincided with power shifts within the imperial court, starting with the downfall of Claudius' wife Messalina in 48, executed following a mysterious plot involving her lover.[24] Still a poor judge of women who attracted him, Claudius promptly married his beautiful but treacherous niece, Agrippina, lifted from exile.[25] She was dangerously ambitious and would allow nothing to get in her way. The marriage itself required a change in the law to allow an uncle to marry a niece and it is very likely that Agrippina influenced the demise of Messalina.[26]

Claudius' new wife utterly dominated him. In 50, he awarded her the prestigious honour of *Augusta*, essentially anointing her as Empress.[27] Agrippina also wasted no time in promoting her own son Nero over Claudius' biological son, Britannicus.[28] Titus, by now a very close friend of Britannicus, would have followed many of these unfolding events. Agrippina not only secured Nero's adoption by Claudius, but also disposed of the man betrothed to Claudius' daughter, Octavia, to allow her engagement to Nero.[29] They would later marry in 53.[30] A year after his adoption, Nero was prematurely allowed to claim his *toga virilis*, the toga of manhood, before the normal age of fourteen and this heralded his introduction into formal public life.[31] From 51, coins were struck showing Nero as *Caesar* on the reverse, Claudius on the obverse.[32] The portrait on these coins depicts Nero as the archetypally idealised Julio-Claudian prince, the same virtuous profile Augustus used for his grandsons and heirs, Caius and Lucius. There could be no doubt to anyone that Agrippina had successfully thrust Nero into the position of an heir to the purple. In a sinister move, Agrippina had Sosibius, the tutor of Britannicus and Titus, executed on grounds of treason against Nero. She separated her son's education, placing him under the tutelage of celebrated philosopher and senator, Seneca.

Unprotected by his father, Britannicus could do little at his age and Agrippina worked actively to marginalise him. He was effectively imprisoned within the palace and barred from access to his father.[33] It is hard to understand why Claudius allowed this harsh treatment to happen to his own son.[34] The loss of his mother as a protector was a major factor. Moreover, manipulated by his wife, the Emperor of Rome seems to have become his empress's puppet. It is also possible that, in Claudius' mind, Nero and Britannicus were both potential heirs just as Augustus had positioned Caius and Lucius.

Claudius, with Agrippina (Junior), *aureus*, struck 50–51, Lugdunum mint.
Sear I, no. 1885.

Vespasian now had to lie low. Agrippina had not forgotten his slight against her back in 39 when he spoke against her returning the ashes of her lover to Rome. These were threatening times for the Flavii: Narcissus was no longer able to support them and Claudius' patronage had become lethargic. Nevertheless, Vespasian received his suffect consulship at the end of 51.[35] This was the least prestigious of the multiple annual consulships but it would make him an ex-consul of Rome. In the same year, Titus' brother Domitian was born; Titus was twelve years old. His sister, Domitilla II, was probably born later, in early 53.[36]

Eventually Agrippina's scheming went too far and Claudius became angry with her devious activities:

> He would not endure her behaviour, but was preparing to put an end to her power, to cause his son to assume the *toga virilis*, and to declare him heir to the throne. Agrippina, learning of this, became alarmed and made haste to forestall anything of the sort by poisoning Claudius.
>
> *Dio Cassius*

Whether Agrippina actually poisoned Claudius or he expired from natural causes, we will never know. The timing suggests foul play. He died at sixty-three years of age on 13 October 54.[37] Narcissus was forced to commit suicide very shortly thereafter. Nero, three months from his seventeenth birthday, was hailed as emperor by the palace Praetorian Guards on the same day as Claudius' death and was whisked away to the Praetorian Camp for further acclamations. He was then escorted to the Senate where his accession was ratified.[38]

Amongst other factors, age had played an important role in allowing Nero to eclipse Britannicus. The gap of three years was significant because it provided the opportunity for various appointments, or planned positions, that came with power. Agrippina and her allies had gone to great lengths to make Britannicus appear immature compared to his adoptive brother.[39] Britannicus, almost certainly consulting Titus and other friends, would have feared for his life. He was the most prominent rival for the Principate and his fourteenth birthday, when he could claim manhood, was only four months away.[40] A warning came before the end of 54, when Julius Densus, an otherwise unknown equestrian, was charged with treason on the grounds of favouring Britannicus, but the case was later overturned.[41] In the following year, Agrippina's grip on Nero began to wane. Used to getting her own way, she resorted to condemning and threatening her son.[42] Consumed with rage, she ranted apparently that she would take Britannicus to the Praetorian Guards as the true biological heir of Claudius.[43]

Unsurprisingly, it is thought that Nero arranged for the poisoning of Britannicus to eliminate his rival. Britannicus was effectively trapped at this time and had no living senior male relatives to protect him. On 11 February 55, just three days before Britannicus' fourteenth birthday, Nero struck. At a family dinner, a food taster for Britannicus – exemplifying that the fear of poisoning was a common concern – cleared a warm drink for consumption.

Since it was too hot for Britannicus, it was cooled with spiked water. The fast-acting poison caused Britannicus to convulse and Nero coolly dismissed it as his usual epilepsy, an affliction not hitherto mentioned in contemporary sources. Even Agrippina, present at the dinner, was apparently shocked by the gruesome, cold-blooded murder. Titus was supposedly next to his friend and had tasted the same concoction. He was seriously ill for a long time but survived. Nero arranged for the rapid burial of Britannicus without honours or ceremony.[44]

Fifteen years old at the time of Britannicus' death, Titus was not a threat to Nero or Agrippina. His father was an ex-consul awaiting his moment to advance his career further and his uncle was away in Moesia as governor. More importantly, the Flavii were not a noble family and in Nero's eyes could never possibly aspire to reign. Besides, they had all been loyal to the Julio-Claudian dynasty from which Nero descended.

Sestertius, struck 50–54, Balkan mint. Obverse, Britannicus; reverse Mars. Exceptionally rare and sold in 2010 for $65,000. *Sear I*, 1908.

The Demise of Agrippina and the Start of Titus' Career

Initially controlled by his mother, Nero became increasingly intolerant of Agrippina's conspiring and interference. Her insistent 'over-watchful, over-critical eye' drove him to cut her power and privileges, take away her guard and eventually expel her from the palace. Agrippina, always the fighter, threatened her son and was even violent towards him, pushing him to a point of no return.[45] In 59, after a bizarre failed attempt to drown her in a collapsible boat, he ordered his henchmen to slay her at a villa to which she had retreated after the incident.[46]

With Agrippina gone, Vespasian prospered again after years in which the empress had stifled his career in favour of others.[47] This recovery did not happen overnight and he had to wait until around 63 to secure a proconsular position as governor of Africa. There was a queue of many more-eligible ex-consuls ahead of Vespasian, better able to capture Nero's and his henchmen's attention. Members of Titus' wider family appear to have had more success in finding the emperor's favour. Titus' cousin's husband, Caesennius Paetus, was consul in 61. Caesius Rufus, Titus' brother-in-law, was given command of a legion in 60. His uncle secured a second stint as the Prefect of Rome starting in 61, an important role maintaining public order in Rome through the urban cohorts and nightwatchmen.[48] In the meantime, probably in 60, Titus was twenty years old and secured a position amongst the imperial *vigintivirate* – literally 'the twenty men'.[49] This office was a prerequisite for a future senatorial career and awarded by the emperor himself. Not a role in the Senate proper, the post in Rome lasted one year in one of four colleges, depending on social standing: the *tresviri monetales,* mint magistrates; the *decemviri stlitibus iudicandis,* assigned to the civil courts; the *quatuorviri viarum curandarum,* maintenance of Rome's streets; and the *tresviri capitales,* supporting the criminal courts.[50] The most distinguished college was the *tresviri monetales,* reserved in particular for patricians and individuals earmarked as promising future commanders.[51] Since Emperor Claudius may have made Vespasian a patrician for his services,[52] it is possible Titus was therefore given such a position.[53] Titus would have greatly benefited from the experience, learning and helping to manage Rome's crucially important mints.

In the following year, Titus was ready for his military tribunate. Following in his father's footsteps, he was posted to Germania Superior as a *tribunus laticlavius* to become second-in-command of a legion. The position was part of a political career, designed for the incumbent to observe and learn the strategic and operational activities of a Roman legion.[54] Here, Titus showed an aptitude for military matters and was praised for his work in Germania. Further following his father's postings, he went on to the new province of Britannia, becoming a *tribunus laticlavius* with one of the garrison legions.[55]

Although formally second-in- command, these young aspiring senators were new to military life; the real authority beneath the legionary commander rested with the seasoned camp prefect, the *primus pilus* – senior centurion – and the fifty-nine other centurions. The *tribunus laticlavius* also nominally outranked the *tribuni angusticlavii,* five tribunes of equestrian class who usually had some experience. A *tribunus laticlavius* like Titus was therefore typically regarded as a very 'green' officer and it was down to the individual how much he wanted to glean from the one to three years of service.[56] There were no known major uprisings in Germania during Titus' commission, and by the time he reached Britannia in 62, Boudica's revolt had been crushed. Londinium (London) had been destroyed by the rebels and it is quite probable that Titus witnessed part of the reconstruction and its new designation as the capital.[57] Titus may have been exposed to a variety of experiences as a *tribunus laticlavius*: dispensing orders on behalf of the *legatus legionis*; issuing punishments; leading manoeuvres; negotiating with envoys; commanding a division during engagements and learning the many aspects of how a legion functioned on the march or when encamped.[58]

Marriage, Quaestorship and the Pisonian Conspiracy

Back in Rome in 63 after completing his military tribunate, Titus showed that he was perhaps rather conceited. In opting to pursue a stint in the law, he saw a means to enhance his popularity, probably by taking on high-profile legal cases.[59] Perhaps he found inspiration in the esteemed figure of the Republic, Cicero, who had achieved great renown as an advocate and orator. During this period, Vespasian was occupied with his governorship of Africa, though this did not hinder him from arranging a suitable marriage for his son, now appropriately in his early twenties. For an ambitious individual like Titus, a Roman marriage had little to do with affection and represented a significant opportunity to expand connections by forming an alliance with another influential family. The marriage dowry also played a crucial role in facilitating such unions and may have been extremely important to the Flavii given Vespasian's continued dire financial situation after his proconsulship in Africa.[60]

Titus' bride was Arrecina Tertulla, daughter of Marcus Arrecinus Clemens who had been one of the Praetorian Guard commanders during Caligula's reign. This position was the most senior role open to equestrians and arguably one of the most powerful appointments in Rome. Thus, although the family was equestrian in status, Clemens was likely a powerful and wealthy man. The match demonstrated that Vespasian had political clout and the marriage probably went ahead in 63.[61]

Thereafter, Titus entered the Senate to take up one of the twenty annual quaestorship positions open for 64.[62] Senatorial elections selected the candidates but the successful ones like Titus would have had support from Nero when they declared as candidates the year before. Nero knew Titus very well and it is quite possible that Titus' skills in the arts captivated the young emperor, who adored such pursuits. A quaestor could be posted in Rome, Italy or a senatorial province and his role was to manage financial matters such as taxation and debts. Four of the quaestors were attached to the consuls and two to the emperor.[63] Posts as attachés of the emperor were normally reserved for patricians and almost certainly hand-picked by the emperor himself. We do not know the precise nature of Titus' quaestorship, but on completion it would have been normal to endure a gap period until his twenty-eighth year when he could seek a praetorship.[64] During his quaestorship it is likely that Arrecina and Titus had a daughter, Julia Titi, but Arrecina passed away, possibly during childbirth or of complications following delivery.[65]

It was important for the ambitious Titus to remarry quickly and he wedded Marcia Furnilla who was a 'very well connected' woman.[66] Her paternal grandfather had been proconsul of Africa, a sought-after senior position for a senator. As expected, there were connections between the families: Marcia Furnilla's uncle was probably a friend of Vespasian and previously proconsul of Asia, a relationship that would have helped secure the match.[67]

With Titus' quaestorship concluded, 65 was marked by a thwarted major plot against the emperor. Arguably the beginning of the end for Nero, the Pisonian Conspiracy signalled a sinister turn in his Principate with the open purging of his enemies, real and perceived. Moreover, it exposed the deeply ingrained hatred of Nero across wide sections of Roman society: patricians, equestrians and the Praetorian Guard. However, the conspiracy was not a tight group of individuals with rigorous designs under one ideology, but rather a 'loose confederation' of like-minded people desperate to remove what they saw as a tyrant.[68] In April, the wealthy statesman Gaius Calpurnius Piso was accused of leading a conspiracy against Nero that included several officers of the Praetorian Guard. The sheer numbers of those involved almost certainly doomed the secrecy. With the plot uncovered, Nero persecuted both the guilty and innocent, resulting in nineteen deaths and thirteen exiles.[69] The legendary Seneca, for several involved in the plot their *de facto* leader to replace Nero, and once the emperor's own tutor, perished in the cull. Even the children of those condemned were brutally 'banished from Rome and then starved to death or poisoned'.[70] The Pisonian Conspiracy sent shockwaves through Rome's elite and beyond.

The Flavii were acutely aware of the dangerous repercussions of being associated with anyone even loosely connected to any conspiracies, real or not, so they acted swiftly after the Pisonian conspiracy. Titus' wife, Marcia Furnilla, had relatives who had fallen from grace and had connections to the Pisonian rebels.[71] As a result, Titus promptly divorced his wife, probably in 65. Vespasian also severed connections with two friends, who were executed and exiled in this period, to save himself from incrimination.[72]

Such practices, long applied since the Republican period, exemplified the fickle nature of marriage alliances and friendships in the wake of political fall-outs.

As the year 65 closed, Titus had turned twenty-seven years of age. He was already a widow and a divorcé, and his daughter Julia Titi, presumably from his first marriage, was one year old. During his childhood, both his father and uncle had led legions and distinguished themselves in the conquest of Britannia, pleasing the Emperor Claudius in doing so. Benefiting from subsequent imperial rewards and patronage that included his father's consulship, the family may have been elevated to patrician status and Titus granted a unique education alongside Claudius' own son. During his adolescence, the menacing rise of Agrippina as empress had checked Vespasian's career and, following the death of Claudius, Titus witnessed first-hand the poisoning of Britannicus at the hands of the new emperor, Nero.[73] The deeply unsettling death of his close friend would not be forgotten; later, as emperor, Titus would install a gold statue of Britannicus in the palace and an ivory equestrian statue of him would be paraded into the Colosseum during events.[74] As a young man entering his senatorial career, Titus observed Nero's increasingly totalitarian behaviour that resulted in the death of Agrippina and many more among Rome's aristocracy. After a series of conspiracies, Titus' family had survived the wrath of Nero by actively distancing themselves from anyone who could even remotely be connected with the subversions. Moreover, Titus's own career had advanced with Nero's support, securing his quaestorship after his military training as a *tribunus laticlavius*. He was ready for the next challenging and often hazardous step up the senatorial career ladder: *per angusta ad augusta,* 'through difficulties to honour'.

Nero, *aureus,* struck 64–65, Rome mint. Reverse, Jupiter holding a thunderbolt in his right hand and a vertical sceptre in the left. The coin type commemorates Nero's deliverance from the Pisonian conspiracy. *Sear I, no. 1930.*

CHAPTER 3

THE PATH TO POWER AND WAR

With his elite enemies in Rome eliminated or at least terrorised temporarily into acquiescence, Nero travelled to Greece in the summer of 66 to wallow in the fine arts and cultural delights of the region that he adored.[1] Drawn by his fascination for such aesthetic pleasures, Nero's prolonged visit was a grand tour of several famous centres: Athens, Delphi, Corinth and Olympia. The architectural wonders of that era combined monumental structures with columns, exquisite stonework and awe-inspiring designs. While Rome boasted impressive edifices, Nero would undoubtedly have been captivated by the Parthenon, a supreme example of Greek architecture dedicated to the goddess Athena, and its commanding situation on the Acropolis in Athens. He visited the Temple of Apollo in Delphi, an exquisite construction featuring Doric elements and spectacular views over the valley below from its vaulted position on the slopes of Mount Parnassus.[2] Topping his list of marvels, Nero almost certainly visited the revered Temple of Zeus in the sanctuary of Olympia. One of the Seven Wonders of the ancient world, the temple was an extraordinary architectural achievement exemplifying the finest craftsmanship of the age. It housed a colossal statue of Zeus made by the Greek sculptor Phidias in the fifth century BC. Towering over twelve metres high, the breath-taking statue used ivory and gold panels on a wooden framework to fashion Zeus, seated on a giant throne adorned with precious metals and stones.[3]

In addition to these architectural triumphs, Nero would have also seen many wonderful bronze and stone statues, seemingly perfect depictions of nature in proportion and expression. On the itinerary of his tour of public and private buildings, he encountered an array of outstanding potteries, mosaics and paintings portraying religious and mythological scenes in intricate detail. Many such works of art were purchased or taken back to

Rome on the emperor's orders.[4] Nero's fascination with athletics led him to attend various sporting events, including the renowned Olympic Games. His indecorous participation in a chariot racing event at the Olympics shocked his contemporaries and the competition resulted in a perilous accident that nearly cost him his life. Nevertheless, amidst controversy, Nero was dubiously proclaimed the victor and received a crown.[5]

During this period, Vespasian had either travelled to Greece with Nero or joined him later in 66.[6] His inclusion in the imperial retinue was a clear sign that he was favoured by the emperor; selected as a *comes*, a companion.[7] Vespasian was a trusted senator with a solid military reputation. Nero needed such a man in his travelling court because crucial imperial business still needed to continue. Vespasian was also shrewd and recognised the political advantages of being close to the emperor, able to influence his decisions and seize on opportunities as they arose.

Moreover, it is thought that Nero's Hellenic tour was initially devised as part of a wider eastern excursion; both Nero and Vespasian may well have had designs on conquest.[8]

Titus was also part of the retinue.[9] Educated alongside Britannicus with insights into the imperial court of Claudius and an acquaintance of Nero since childhood, he had all the necessary skills and experience to navigate the scheming politics amongst the entourage of the emperor. In short, father and son commanded a strong presence in the touring imperial court. Despite such a bearing, Vespasian apparently tested Nero's patience by avoiding some of the emperor's singing recitals and supposedly finally incurred his wrath by falling asleep at one of his concerts.[10] As a punishment Vespasian was dismissed from the court and scuttled away to a nearby village, presumably to let the dust settle.

Jewish Revolt

In the spring of 66, as Nero prepared for his infamous trip to Greece, the Jewish rebellion ignited in Caesarea Maritima, located on the coast of modern-day Israel.[11] Augustus had gifted the settlement to King Herod the Great, who constructed a new metropolis at the site and named it after his imperial benefactor.[12] The magnificent city port, complete with a protective breakwater, docks and sailors' quarters, became an important trading centre in the region.[13] At that time, the uprising did not alarm Nero. Unbeknown to the emperor, violence would spread swiftly into widespread disorder, destruction and the loss of the entire province.[14] Not since the Illyrian

Revolts (AD 6–9) sixty years earlier had *Pax Romana*, the Roman peace, been tested under imperial rule.[15]

Some 129 years before the Jewish Revolt, the legendary Roman republican general Pompey the Great marched into the Kingdom of Judea during his eastern campaigns to intervene in a power struggle for the throne. His intervention led to the capture of Jerusalem, where he entered the Temple's Holy of Holies, desecrating a space that only the High Priests were permitted to enter under Jewish Law. Despite this sacrilege, Pompey did not loot the Temple's priceless contents and the next day ordered the officials to cleanse their Temple.[16] He then appointed a puppet High Priest and continued his Eastern campaigns. Judea became a client state until AD 6, when misrule led Augustus to convert the kingdom into a subprovince of Roman Syria. Initially, Roman equestrian prefects governed the region. After 44, following the death of King Herod Agrippa I, Judea came under direct Roman control and was administered by procurators. Auxiliary soldiers policed the region and were local recruits.[17]

What factors led to this major Jewish rebellion? Firstly, Roman disrespect for Jewish religious monotheism stirred tensions among the population, such as Caligula's sacrilegious order to erect his statues in Jerusalem's Temple sanctuary.[18] The Jewish people strongly resented the Roman disregard for their beliefs and practices. Secondly, years of corrupt and inept Roman procurators in Judea, coupled with their oppressive policies, led to widespread discontent. Gaius Julius Severus Albinus had plundered and stolen properties from Judeans[19] and the romanised local ruling elite were seen as crooked and colluding with the Romans, which fuelled attacks against the wealthy classes.[20] Thirdly, a heavy array of levies on landed properties and poll taxes, as well as tolls and duties, made worse by massive Roman exploitation, exacerbated socio-economic grievances and disparities amongst the Jewish population.[21] Lastly, there were growing national sentiments amongst separatists advocating resistance against Rome. The death of King Herod Agrippa I two decades earlier, the last Jewish King of Judea, dashed expectations of greater autonomy that came with his passing, fuelling separatist ideology.

All this festering discontent materialised into bloodshed in the Roman administrative capital, Caesarea, between Jewish and Greek communities fighting over ownership of the city. Nero had decreed that the Greeks were rightful owners, creating a tinderbox of wrath, ready to ignite. The spark finally came when some Greeks desecrated a Jewish synagogue by sacrificing birds at its entrance. Roman military intervention was required to break up the fighting.[22] At his disposal, the procurator Florus commanded auxiliary infantry and cavalry posted throughout his region, particularly in the large urban centres. These soldiers were local recruits and would have been 'indistinguishable from their peers when out of their uniform'.[23]

News from Caesarea spread quickly to Jerusalem, raising alarm. The wholly incompetent Florus, to make matters worse, seized seventeen talents of gold from the Temple treasury in Jerusalem on the pretext that it represented unpaid taxes for his emperor. This was a very large appropriation, around 445 kilograms of gold worth over 5.5 million HS. Conflict broke out, and Florus had to flee Jerusalem, leaving only a skeleton crew of soldiers to protect the leading priests and the city council, called the Sanhedrin.[24] Florus subsequently marched his troops back to Caesarea.

At this point, Caius Cestius Gallus (hereafter Cestius), governor of Syria, was separately called on to intervene by Florus and the Jewish authorities.[25] The governor sent one of his military tribunes to investigate together with Herod Agrippa II, the last descendant of Herod the Great, who ruled as a faithful client king of Rome. Agrippa II did not rule Judea like his father Agrippa I had; instead he reigned over territories outside the heartland called the Tetrarchy of Philip, bestowed on him by the Emperor Claudius. The two delegates failed to establish any order and the uprising took an irretrievable turn when the Roman fortress at Masada was attacked and the garrison slaughtered.[26] Eleazar ben Ananias, the son of the High Priest, ended the practice, honoured since the reign of Tiberius, by which sacrifices were made at the temple to the Roman people and the emperor, which was seen as laying the 'foundations for war with Rome'.[27] Further chaos descended on Jerusalem as competing factions vied for control over the city. Political leaders pleaded with Florus and Agrippa II to intervene but only the latter responded, sending 2,000 cavalry to support the city. However, the sinister Sicarii, extremists whose names derived from the Latin word *sica*, meaning dagger, known for their concealment of such weapons, infiltrated the trouble and escalated the uprising. Agrippa's cavalry, 'outnumbered and outmanoeuvred', failed to gain control and the High Priest Ananias' house and the King's palace were torched.

It was now mid-July 66, and the Antonia Fort was the scene of further conflict. The magnificent structure was a large military building commissioned by Herod the Great and named after Mark Antony. It was placed strategically north of the Temple to provide protection for the sacred centre.

The fortress housed Roman soldiers and served as the headquarters for the Roman garrison in the city. A short siege resulted in its abandonment and the surviving Roman forces and local loyalists fled to Herod's Palace before surrendering – only to be executed. Elsewhere, chaos descended into genocide. Greek factions in Caesarea massacred the Jewish population. Twenty thousand lives were reportedly taken. There can be little doubt that Florus approved the atrocity; any fleeing individuals were rounded up by the Romans.[28] The appalling massacre sent shock waves through Judea, triggering widespread acts of vengeance. The anarchy led to the death of the High Priest Ananias, who was discovered by rebels hiding beneath an aqueduct and killed for fraternising with the Romans.[29]

Utilising the efficient imperial post system, dispatches carried in coaches and boats would have required approximately forty-five days to reach Rome from Caesarea.[30] A comparable timeframe was likely needed for the messages to reach Nero in Greece. Consequently, by early September, it is conceivable that both Nero and Rome were aware of the widespread uprisings unfolding in the region. However, the situation on the ground demanded immediate action before any imperial direction could be received.[31]

The provocation and incompetence of Florus necessitated urgent intervention from Cestius, who commanded substantial military forces as governor of Syria. Understanding the gravity of the situation, Cestius acted. Mobilising Legio XII *Fulminata*, assembling detachments of around 2,000 men from each of the three other legions stationed in Syria, along with auxiliary troops, wings of cavalry and contingents from Agrippa II and other independent rulers, Cestius created a formidable force of approximately 35,000–45,000 soldiers.[32] The legionary detachments taken from IV *Scythica*, VI *Ferrata* and X *Fretensis* were probably necessary to make up numbers because XII *Fulminata* may still have been depleted since a challenging Armenian campaign. The legate Gallus, probably related to Cestius, led XII *Fulminata* and his second-in-command was probably a tribune called Placidus.[33] Governor Cestius' intention was to quell the unrest and restore Roman authority in the province. The stage was set for a critical episode in the Jewish Revolt, and the outcome of Cestius' campaign would shape the course of events in the months to come. Meanwhile Florus remained in Caesarea, with several cohorts of auxiliary troops.

In the autumn of 66, Cestius left Antioch and headed south into Judea to execute his plan. His army was divided and contingents dispatched to strategically important locations to regain control using brute force with no mercy. Josephus, a military leader in Galilee involved in the conflicts who eventually switched over to the Romans in 67, recorded the Jewish War first-hand. For this period, his summary was simple:

> [Cestius and the Romans] ravaged the land, killed a great number of inhabitants, looted their property, and burnt their villages.[34]

Judea was put to fire and the sword. The widespread and merciless onslaught targeted every facet of life and infrastructure, aiming systematically to crush any inclination towards dissent, both physically and psychologically. Eventually taking the conflict to Jerusalem, Cestius' army camped on Mount Scopus, north-east of the city.[35] Employing traditional Roman military tactics, relentless assaults and attempting to undermine the defences of Jerusalem yielded some success. Nevertheless, Cestius made the surprising decision to withdraw from the city, leaving the Jewish resistance perplexed. The Roman general's choice, probably suggested by his subordinate commanders, was likely driven by a combination of concerns, including the vulnerability of his supply line, the formidable nature of Jerusalem's fortifications, the approaching winter season and the potential arrival of outside reinforcements to aid the Jewish defenders.[36]

Roman forces on the march typically employed a highly organised and disciplined structure that provided the best defensive tactics to a long line of troops stretched over several kilometres, from the vanguard to the rearguard. However, constant harassment from nimble, lightly armed Jewish fighters took its toll on the Roman column, which refused to break formation. It would have taken Cestius one day to reach a camping place at Gibeon, north-west of Jerusalem, but during the twelve-kilometre march the pursuing Jewish soldiers forced the abandonment of large amounts of baggage.[37]

This was a disaster for Cestius' men because one of the mainstays for a marching legionary or auxiliary was his *sarcina*, or baggage pack. This contained clothing, personal items, rations, camp equipment and various tools. A proportion of the marching troops must have been fighting for their lives to have been forced to abandon their packs to use their shields and weapons to defend themselves and the column. Mules from the baggage train, carrying tents and other supplies, were also lost. The commander of the detachment from VI *Ferrata*, a tribune called Longinus, and a cavalry squadron commander were killed, an indication that the Jews may have been deliberately picking out men of rank conspicuous on horseback.[38]

Aerial view of the Beth Horon Pass, Israel.
The ancient road linking the coastal plains to Jerusalem had a pinch point at Beth
Horon where it passed over a section of steeply ridged rocky terrain. The Roman
general Cestius suffered significant losses here in 66 on his retreat to the coast.
Google Earth with author's annotations.

The isolated hilltop at Gibeon, about fifty metres higher than the surrounding landscape, provided a vantage point and defensible position for the Romans. However, it was vulnerable and liable to be cut off and lacked supplies, Cestius' hand was forced after two days of hesitation. His indecision allowed other Jewish rebels to swarm into the area. Realising that his position was deteriorating rapidly, Cestius gave the desperate order to slaughter all the pack animals and wagon teams, except those carrying artillery missiles and weapons, to allow a hastier retreat.[39]

Breaking camp, the Romans marched west directly for the coast, where open ground would give them a strong advantage. Along the route, the Roman column needed to proceed through the pass of Beth Horon, a descending mountainous defile with steep drops in places along the way. Anticipating this route, the Jewish forces, led by Simon Ben Giora, Eleazar ben Simon and other generals, had set an ambush around a neck of the ravine.[40] In such a setting, the Romans had to form into a narrow column – and the mêlée began when the Jewish fighters around the Romans hailed down missiles.[41] Typically the Roman cavalry would have swept in to protect the flanks, but the nature of the terrain rendered them useless. Hemmed in and unable to counter-attack, the Romans found their position was extremely vulnerable; soldiers desperately raised shields and edged slowly forward. Nightfall offered a reprieve and spared the Romans from further massacre.[42]

The cover of darkness allowed Cestius to regroup in the town of Lower Beth-Horon but the Jews encircled the position, expecting to attack again at dawn. Calling together his officers, Cestius devised a guileful plan to escape. Four hundred of the bravest men, essentially given a suicide mission, were selected to stand on rooftops and call out the security watchword to dupe the Jewish host into thinking that the full army remained barricaded in the town. In the meantime, Cestius led out the remainder of his army, and by dawn they were already over five kilometres away. Discovering the Roman escape, and slaying the valiant Romans who had remained, the Jews pursued Cestius as far as Antipatris, but there they had to stop as the coastal plains afforded the upper hand to the Romans.[43]

The Battle of Beth Horon was a great victory for the Jewish uprising and a humiliating defeat for Rome. The Romans lost over 5,000 infantry and nearly 500 cavalry, as well as abandoning many siege engines and their ammunition in Lower Beth-Horon that would later be used against them.[44] Cestius marched to Ptolemais, where he left two cohorts of XII *Fulminata* and a squadron of cavalry before he scurried back to Antioch with his remaining army, ashamed of his failed campaign.[45]

Rome had lost Judea. The Jews, now emboldened by their victory, took charge of their destiny and established a new government with Joseph ben Gurion and Ananus the High Priest (not to be confused with the High Priest Ananias) initially in charge.[46] Eleazar ben Simon rose to prominence, assuming the role of 'supreme commander', bolstered by his newly acquired wealth following the capture of Cestius' lost war chest during his retreat.[47] They also sent generals out to command different districts of Judea to strengthen defences, gather resources and restore order.[48] What had started as a violent conflict over the sacrifice of a bird on the steps of a synagogue in Caesarea, fuelled by decades of oppression and local infighting, had ended with imperial Rome losing control of a province. And a wealthy province to boot.

Flavian Appointments for the Jewish War

The Jewish uprising and loss of Judea posed a critical challenge for Nero, demanding a reliable and skilled general to quell the rebellion. Cestius' devastating defeat and failure to retain the province would have shocked Rome, further weakening Nero's position among the elite. Nero feigned a lack of concern by blaming poor Roman leadership in the region but he was actually extremely anxious to select a qualified general he could trust deeply.[49] His advisors, including Vespasian, would have recommended taking a quick decision because the rebellion could spread further in the

East and the Parthian Empire was a threat if they took advantage of Rome's vulnerability in the region.

Nero selected Vespasian for this crucial role due to several factors. First and foremost, loyalty and trust played a vital part in the appointment. Nero acknowledged Vespasian's unwavering dedication to imperial authority, demonstrated through his service under the previous emperor, Claudius. The recent Pisonian conspiracy involving senators, equestrians and military figures had heightened Nero's paranoia and he needed a man with the right family background that he could trust fully with such enormous military power. Furthermore, Vespasian's *triumphalia ornamenta* from Claudius for his achievements in Britannia showcased his loyalty to the Principate. Vespasian's brother, Sabinus II, had been appointed Praefectus Urbi, Prefect of Rome, for a second time by Nero and had been in the post since 61, a clear sign that Nero fundamentally trusted the Flavii. Secondly, Vespasian possessed proven military expertise and experience. He had led a legion effectively during the Britannia campaign and subdued resistance in the south-west after years of arduous campaigning. Known for his disciplined and methodical approach, Vespasian was a dependable commander on the battlefield. Thirdly, the emperor perceived Vespasian as a non-threatening figure.[50] Despite Vespasian's possible elevation to the patrician class by Claudius, his humble family background and modest origins rendered it inconceivable to Nero that he could ever aspire to the Principate, a position long dominated by the illustrious pedigree of the Julio-Claudian dynasty. Nero saw Vespasian as someone who would prioritise his military command over any ambitions for the imperial throne, making him a favourable choice. Furthermore, Vespasian's presence as a confidant of Nero in Greece made him readily available for the immediate assignment. Clearly, Vespasian was also forgiven for nodding off during Nero's recital. By appointing Vespasian, Nero sought ultimately to demonstrate his commitment to maintaining Roman control over the province and reinforcing his image as a strong and competent emperor.

During this period, Nero had summoned an esteemed general called Corbulo from the East to Greece. Corbulo's impressive achievements included securing a vital peace with the Parthians after years of campaigning and diplomacy. However, on his arrival in Corinth in October 66, Nero's fear, jealousy and paranoia led him to demand Corbulo's suicide. This brazen incident would have further fuelled growing resentment against Nero. Vespasian's appointment was made against the backdrop of removing a general Nero no longer trusted.[51] Placing Vespasian in a crucial command position allowed Nero to manage potential rivalries or discontent among other ambitious generals or factions. Vespasian's respected standing and network of supporters within the military establishment would play a significant role in maintaining stability during such turbulent times.

Hence, enormous power was placed in Vespasian's hands. He was designated *legatus Augusti pro praetore expeditio Iudaeae*. This meant he represented the Roman emperor (*legatus Augusti*), acting with the authority of a praetor (*pro praetore*), in command of the Judean task-force dealing with the Jewish uprising in Judea (*expeditio Iudaeae*). The position made him governor of Judea, albeit the province was lost to the rebellion. Cestius had since died, so Vespasian was also effectively the acting governor of Syria and general of all the forces in that province, pending a new appointment. Vespasian was the most powerful Roman in the eastern empire.[52]

Titus was in Achaea, where he had been with Nero, and was also called up to command.[53] Now aged twenty-seven, he was appointed commander of XV *Apollinaris* under his father.[54] It was highly unusual at the time for a son to serve as a legate under his father.[55] Vespasian would have recommended Titus for the post and Nero agreed. The emperor may have recognised Titus' swift divorce of his wife Marcia to distance himself from the Piso conspiracy against Nero. Josephus also provides another reason:

> [Nero] noted too the value of Vespasian's sons as a guarantee of his loyalty, and saw how their youthful vigour could be the muscle to match their father's brain.[56]

The appointment was clearly a promotion for Titus given that legionary legates were normally selected from the ex-praetor population of senators, a post Titus had not yet attained.[57] Thus, father and son headed east.

CHAPTER 4

THE JEWISH WAR: CAMPAIGN OF 67

Roman Command

With his *imperium* – the power to command – granted, Vespasian set out from Greece, crossed over the Hellespont (Dardanelles strait) and travelled overland to the Syrian capital of Antioch.[1] The journey would have taken around eight weeks and the newly appointed general arrived in February 67, where he called to arms Legio X *Fretensis* based in the province.[2] Eight legionary cohorts of the heavily depleted XII *Fulminata* moved to Laodicea (Latakia) in Syria and the disgraced legate, Gallus, was packed off back to Rome.[3] It is possible that two remaining cohorts of XII *Fulminata*, supported by a squadron of cavalry, waited for further orders in the ancient port of Ptolemais.[4]

Meanwhile, Titus had left Greece for Alexandria in Egypt, normally a risky journey during the winter months in antiquity. Presumably unseasonably fair weather must have permitted the open-sea crossing. Titus was a risk-taker when it came to his own welfare and after two weeks of precarious sailing, he arrived safely to take over the command of his appointed legion, XV *Apollinaris*, and he also mustered V *Macedonica* under the command of a tribune.[5] Both legions had been in Egypt preparing for Nero's anticipated Ethiopian expedition that was for now postponed.[6]

This was a prominent moment for the young Titus, his first charge of a Roman legion. Legio XV had a notable history in which it had seen much action. Founded originally by Julius Caesar around 49 BC to replace legions he had transferred to Pompey, Legio XV went on to serve in the war against Sextus Pompeius where it won its nickname *Apollinaris* and took the griffin as its new emblem. Octavian, who later became the Emperor Augustus, employed the legion in Illyricum for his campaigns there in 35–33 BC. Two years later the legion participated in the Battle of Actium against Antony and Cleopatra.[7]

Now it served Titus and with his legion on full ceremonial display, he would have entered the legion's fortress dressed in the striking military attire of a *legatus legionis*: a richly decorated bronze cuirass with scarlet *cincticulus* ribbons tied in bows above his waist as a symbol of his command; an ornate *gladius*; red cloak and leather *caligae* (shoes).[8] He would have mounted a tribunal to address a limited number of select officers and legionaries within earshot and described the uprising in Judea that required the legion to march and unite with his father's army to crush the rebellion and restore Rome's honour. Titus probably gave the same address to V *Macedonica*, also under his responsibility.

The Roman command structure for the war was typical for a large imperial expeditionary force of the period:

Titus Flavius Vespasianus   General, *legatus Augusti*, supreme commander of all the Roman forces sent against the Jews on behalf of the emperor. All strategic decisions and orders, and where possible all major tactical and operational decisions, required his approval.

Sextus Vettulenus Cerialis   Legate of V *Macedonica*, taking orders from Vespasian and with a direct commission from Nero to command the legion. He would take over the legion when it arrived in Ptolemais after being led there by Titus from Egypt. He was a client of Vespasian and shared similar Sabine origins.[9]

Marcus Ulpius Traianus   Legate of X *Fretensis*, also under Vespasian, a *novus homo* like Vespasian and well known by the general. Traianus might have accompanied Vespasian in Greece as a client.[10] Traianus and Titus had been brothers-in-law.[11] He was the father of the future emperor, Trajan.

Titus Vespasianus   Legate of XV *Apollinaris*, also under Vespasian, the least experienced of the legates.

Other notable officers:

Tribune (probably of XII *Fulminata*): Placidus[12]

Decurion: Aebutius (attached to Agrippa's allied forces)

Centurion: Antonius (commander of the garrison at Ascalon)[13]

Tribune of XV *Apollinaris*: Domitius Sabinus[14]

Tribune: Sextus Calvarius[15]

Tribune of V *Macedonica*: Paulinus[16]

Tribune of X *Fretensis*: Gallicanus[17]
Tribune: Nicanor (ex-commander of III *Gallica*)[18]
Lucius Annius (probably a tribune)[19]
Gaius Valerius Clemens (cavalry commander)
Decurion: Valerianus[20]

Consilarii Trusted members of the general's *consilium* (council of advisors). Usually, senior officers and others hand-picked for their military experience or specific expertise such as engineering and tactical know-how. There were probably representatives of the *tribuni militum* (military tribunes), *praefecti castrorum* (camp prefects) and the *primi pili* (first centurions, each the most senior centurion of a legion). King Agrippa II was almost certainly a trusted ally invited to this group.

Jewish Command

The fractured nature of the uprising, incessant infighting between factions and the dynamic sequence of events meant that a clear Jewish command structure did not exist. De facto peasant leaders also emerged to strive for peace in their region or to lead local militiamen against the Romans. Moreover, not knowing the eventual fate of many commanders confounds our understanding of their roles. Thus, the following command organisation of the Jewish forces must be considered as fluid compared to the rigid Roman system, and coordination between the Jewish leaders was probably limited in many cases. This should not be seen as reflecting a lack of effort on the part of the Jewish leaders involved, rather as being produced by the extraordinarily difficult situation on the ground. Names in **bold** are individuals who played a major role in the later siege of Jerusalem.

Joseph ben Gurion Co-leader of the new coalition government and responsible for home affairs as well as military matters. Fate unknown.[21]

Ananus, High Priest Co-leader with Joseph ben Gurion.[22]

Eleazar ben Simon Supreme military commander appointed in 66 after the new coalition government was formed. Present at the Battle of Beth Horon, he captured Cestius' lost war chest and was leader of the Zealots.[23] One of three leaders during the later siege of Jerusalem from the coup d'état in 67/68 to the fall of the city in 70. Fate unknown.

Eleazar ben Ananias   Captain of the Temple who helped start the rebellion and was likely given a position in the provisional government and troops to lead.[24] Probably a regional general in Idumea.[25] Fate unknown.

Jesus ben Sapphas   Regional general in Idumea, appointed in 66.[26] One of the chief priests. Fate unknown.

Niger the Perean   Existing governor of Idumea, reporting to the two new generals Jesus ben Sapphas and probably Eleazar ben Ananias.[27] Later, one of three generals who commanded the attack on Ascalon.[28]

John ben Sosas   Later Idumean general[29]

Jocab ben Sosas   Later Idumean general[30]

Simon ben Thaceas   Later Idumean general[31]

Phineas ben Clusoth   Later Idumean general[32]

Joseph ben Simon   Regional general in Jericho, appointed in 66.[33] Fate unknown.

Manasseh   Regional general in Perea, appointed in 66.[34] Fate unknown.

John the Essene   Regional general in the toparchy of Thamna with Lydda, Joppa and Emmanus, appointed in 66.[35] Later one of three generals who commanded the attack on Ascalon.[36]

John ben Ananias   Regional general of Gophna and Acrabata, appointed in 66.[37] Fate unknown.

Josephus ben Matthias   Regional general of Galilee and Gamla, appointed in 66.[38] Became a captive of Vespasian and historian whose detailed account of the war has survived.

John ben Levi   Competing unofficial Galilean general who roamed the countryside in 66 before leading the revolt at Gischala and went on to be one of the three leaders during the later siege of Jerusalem.[39] Sometimes referred to as John of Gischala.

Silas the Babylonian   Later one of three generals who commanded the attack on Ascalon.[40]

Simon ben Giora   One of the three leaders during the later siege of Jerusalem.

Jesus ben Sapphias   *Archon* (governor) of Tiberias, not to be confused with Jesus ben Sapphas above.[41] Later a leader of brigands.[42]

Simon ben Gamaliel   Leader of the Pharisees and friend of John ben Levi.[43]

Chares and Joseph   Leaders of the fighters at Gamla.[44]

Roman Forces and Allies

The Roman forces under Vespasian followed the general composition for a major campaign force of our imperial period: namely, the legions formed the central and reserve heavy infantry; non-citizen auxiliaries supported the legions and provided specialised functions; Roman cavalry acted as escorts or harassed enemy flanks and offered pursuit; allied troops reinforced Roman units and did other tasks. Roman legions and auxiliary units were never at full theoretical strength due to illnesses, injuries, deaths, desertions, assignments and other factors. The numbers below include a certain level of attrition to give a realistic estimate of those under Vespasian's authority at the start of the reconquest.[45]

Legions

The complete V *Macedonica*, X *Fretensis* and XV *Apollinaris*, plus two cohorts of XII *Fulminata* from Ptolemais: around 16,000 legionaries.[46]

Roman Cavalry and Auxiliaries

Five Roman cavalry *alae* (wings) from Syria, one of which was the *ala* Gaetulorum Veterana from modern-day Algeria; around 900 cavalrymen each, total around 4,500.[47]
One *ala* from Ptolemais, 900 men.[48]
Ten double-strength and thirteen normal strength cohorts of auxiliary infantry, and cavalry detachments from Egypt; around 12,800 infantry and 2,480 cavalry.[49]
Five auxiliary cohorts (at least one of slingers) and one cavalry *ala* from Caesarea; total around 2,100 infantry and 900 cavalry.[50]

Allies[51]

Kings Antiochus, Agrippa II, Sohaemus: a total of 6,000 foot archers and 3,000 cavalry.
King Malchus: 5,000 infantry (mostly foot archers) and 1,000 cavalry.

Total

Around 55,000 men, of whom around 16,500 were Roman legionaries, plus 8,780 cavalry and 14,900 auxiliary infantry and the rest allied forces. Each legion was assigned an artillery corps, with around sixty bolt-shooting scorpions and ten stone-throwing medium sized *ballistae*, and large stone-throwing onagers when specially commissioned, bringing a total of over 200 artillery machines.[52]

The technological and tactical advantages of the Roman legionaries were key factors in overcoming the local knowledge of their opponents. Legionaries of this period were uniformly equipped from head to toe with standardised, high-quality kit. They wore durable iron or bronze helmets that provided comprehensive protection for the head, cheeks and neck. Their upper bodies were shielded by state-of-the-art, lightweight segmented iron plate armour (*lorica segmentata*), designed to cover the entire torso while allowing flexibility and mobility. They carried large, rectangular, curved shields (*scuta*) made from layers of wood, leather and metal, which provided extensive coverage and could interlock for defensive formations. Sturdy leather shoes (*caligae*) ensured strong footing across a variety of terrains.

In terms of weaponry, each legionary was armed with a *pilum*, a specialised javelin with a long slender shaft designed to pierce enemy shields and armour. This weapon was deployed at the onset of battle, effectively breaking up enemy lines and inflicting serious injuries. The primary close-combat weapon was the *gladius*, a short, thrusting sword, well designed for use in tight formations where stabbing was far more effective than slashing. Together, this combination of advanced equipment, uniformity and the constant application of disciplined training gave the Roman legionaries a significant edge on the battlefield, allowing them to adapt and dominate in various combat scenarios. While auxiliaries were generally well-equipped and provided critical versatility on the battlefield, their armour and weapons were not as uniform in this period as those of the legionaries. The auxiliaries were designed to fulfil different tactical roles, often taking advantage of their regional specialisations, such as archery, cavalry or light infantry. In short, legionaries were the elite arm of the Roman army and auxiliaries more expendable.

The logistical capabilities of the Roman legions and auxiliaries were essential in ensuring the success of their conquests. Among the unsung heroes of Rome's military might were the *muli*, mules, vital pack animals known for their resilience and strength.[53] These hardy creatures could carry up to a third of their own weight and traverse the toughest terrain. The sheer scale of Rome's military operations required an impressive number of mules and other animals. Every eight legionaries had one mule to carry their tent and heavier equipment.[54] Officers would have had more mules for their paraphernalia. Additionally, large items such as siege engine components and artillery pieces necessitated more substantial animals, horses and oxen, to pull wagons.[55] In total, Vespasian's Roman legions and auxiliary cohorts would have relied on approximately 10,000 mules and other animals to support their campaign.[56] Several thousand additional livestock for food, in effect a walking larder, would have also accompanied the campaign force.

The Roman army was much more than just an armed force; it operated as a multi-faceted organisation with medical staff, scribes, engineers and a complex supply chain covering vast distances up to hundreds of miles long. In addition to combatants, each legion was accompanied by a significant number of non-combatants: military slaves, merchants, weapon smiths, contractors and camp followers, totalling in the tens of thousands.[57] In short, Vespasian's army was a mobile city. The crucial supply chain allowed Roman armies to strike far from their central bases. Grain was the staple item but a legion would require many pigs, oxen, sheep, poultry and other animals to supplement the diet along with fruit, vegetables and nuts.[58] Foraging complemented provisions but required the right conditions and seasonality.[59] The supply line was therefore a massive continuous endeavour to bring vast quantities of rations, fodder and other supplies up to the advancing column. Supplies would have come from across the empire after being acquired through edicts issued to certain provinces. Egypt probably played a critical role, sending grain, vinegar, salt and more along the coast into Judea.[60] Without this highly efficient logistical network, the Roman legions were extremely vulnerable, as occurred on Cestius' retreat from Jerusalem because of his weakened supply chain. The fourth-century Roman author Publius Vegetius Renatus, who documented military organisation, described succinctly the importance of supplies in the art of Roman warfare:

> The main and principal point in war is to secure plenty of provisions for oneself and to destroy the enemy by famine. Famine is more terrible than the sword.
>
> *Vegetius*[61]

Jewish Forces

As they lived in a Roman province, the Jews had not maintained an army for many years except the forces of King Agrippa II – and he was closely allied to Rome. The rebel armed forces were an amalgamation of diverse combatants driven by a shared desire for survival or independence from

Rome. Revolting against Rome's military might may appear to have been futile, but the Jewish belief in God's protection and the reality of fighting for their existence were potent motivating factors. At the ends of the spectrum were ordinary people who became fighters willingly or under compulsion, but many seem to have been deeply motivated by the hope of preserving their way of life and protecting their families. At the other end were individuals with varying experience in military operations such as the Temple guards and security personnel, locally trained militia and mercenaries.

The numbers and types of Jewish fighters who took up arms against the Romans are not known. The central Jewish leaders in Jerusalem sought to bolster their regional defences by recruiting militia, providing them with arms and sending them to various districts.[62]

Gross estimates of the Jewish armed forces at the start of the campaign are:

Central government levies sent to regional generals	22,000 infantry[63]
Additional local militia raised by regional generals	36,000 infantry[64]
	1,700 cavalry
	3,000 elite troops
Professional mercenaries	10,000[65]
Jerusalem's mobile reserve	20,000[66]
Idumean army	5,000[67]
Independent local militia	5,000[68]

One can conclude that a total armed force of roughly 100,000 Jewish fighters and mercenaries existed, of whom probably only a fraction were well equipped and trained. Many were just local people drawn into the conflict, picking up arms or makeshift weapons. These forces were not cohesively or centrally commanded and were widely fragmented across the country. Notably, there was very little cavalry and those few were also dispersed – tactically, a major disadvantage. Weapons and armour were not uniform and would have been acquired inconsistently by the vast majority. Generally speaking, the Jewish militia were lightly armed, giving the advantage of agility for skirmishing. However, the use of captured Roman arms during the uprising complemented their repertoire of weapons and armour. Although a minority were paid for their military services, the majority were fighting for their lives, families, friends and freedom.

Roman strategy

Vespasian's principal aim was to shatter the spirit of resistance and instil profound fear in any Jews considering further rebellion. His approach was consistent with the traditional Roman way of waging warfare, where no quarter was given to those who opposed them.[69] To crush an uprising, the Romans would implement a scorched-earth policy that left devastation in their wake. No mercy would be shown and the brutality unleashed by the Roman forces would be relentless. Genocide, pillaging and the utter destruction of towns, villages and the surrounding countryside were intended to petrify rebels into capitulation. In this brutal campaign, women and children would not be spared; many would fall victim to merciless slaughter or be taken as slaves.[70] Vespasian and his legates would rarely hold their forces back; they would give free rein to the soldiers, allowing them to commit heinous acts with impunity: murder, rape and plunder. The atrocities during the Jewish–Roman War would serve as a chilling example of the extremes to which Rome would go to assert its control over a lost province.

To achieve his strategic goal, it was clear right from the outset that Vespasian would adopt a flexible deployment of his forces. Detachments composed of mixed troops would be frequently dispatched to target important Jewish-held positions – divide and conquer.

Jewish Strategy

The Jewish plan was generally aimed at safeguarding key strongholds and strategically important towns across Judea. They undertook the installation or enhancement of fortifications, secured resources to withstand sieges and acquired armaments. Josephus in Galilee fortified nineteen cities, for example. Despite such actions, the new junta in Jerusalem almost certainly recognised the invincible military power of Rome. Josephus alludes to the sentiments of Ananus, a highly respected High Priest and co-leader of the nascent government:

> [Ananus] knew that Roman power was invincible, but when faced with no option but to provide for war, he took care that the Jewish resistance, if they could not come to a settlement, would at least be efficiently managed... there would either be a settlement [with Rome] ... or, if it had to be war, the Jews would have greatly delayed the Roman victory under a leader of his calibre.[71]

In 67 it was therefore quite possible that some of the elder statesmen in Jerusalem such as Ananus may have viewed the rebellion as a potential pathway to a negotiated settlement with the Romans, one that would restore them a measure of autonomy under renewed Roman control. However, the complex political landscape was confounded by violently competing factions in Jerusalem and splinter groups in Galilee and elsewhere. This created conflicting political ideologies and varying degrees of fervour for warfare. In addition, rebel leaders and gangs vied for dominance over civilian populations, though many ordinary people were opposed to the revolt, either because they were pro-Roman or terrified of Roman vengeance. In essence, the rebellion was a patchwork of divergent ideals and contrasting visions of how to exploit the unexpected successes of 66 against Cestius or bring an end to the uprising.

Judea: Environs and Climate

Judea encompassed various administrative divisions and territorial boundaries that are important to understand to appreciate the Jewish resistance efforts and Vespasian's campaign activities. The following list, generally described from north to south, outlines the main regions of the Judean province and adjacent areas in this period:

Galilee bordered the province of Syria in the north-west and included the western shores of the Sea of Galilee. It was a fertile region with many important towns such as Sepphoris, Tarichea and Tiberias.[72]
Tetrarchy of Philip, once ruled by Herod Philip II, a son of Herod the Great, was east of Galilee in the north-eastern region of Judea and included the eastern shores of the Sea of Galilee. It was a Roman client kingdom, separate from the Roman-governed province of Judea, ruled by Agrippa II. Caesarea Philippi was the major metropolitan centre.
Samaria, located between Galilee and Judea Proper had both Jewish and Samaritan populations. The River Jordan delineated the eastern edge. Samaria was part of the Roman province of Judea, but it was politically and culturally distinct. Samaritans were more cooperative with Roman rule than Judeans. Samaria largely stayed out of the revolt, unlike Judea and Galilee.[73]
Decapolis, meaning 'The Ten Cities', formed a region on the eastern side of Judea and encompassed a league of cities known for their Greek-influenced culture and civilisation. The cities of the Decapolis were not under the

same administration as Judea and were largely autonomous under Roman protection. The Decapolis cities remained loyal to Rome during the Jewish revolt.

Perea, part of the Judean province, facing Samaria on the opposite side of the River Jordan, the region stretched down to include the north-eastern shores of the Dead Sea. Its southern boundary met the Nabataean Kingdom.[74]

Judea Proper was the heartland of the Jewish state and held enormous religious and political significance. It corresponded more or less to the ancient Jewish kingdom and included eleven districts: the capital, Jerusalem; Gophna; Acrabata; Thamna; Lydda; Emmaus; Pelle; Idumea; Engaddi; Herodium and Jericho.

Coastal regions included important trading cities along the Mediterranean coast, such as Joppa (modern-day Jaffa) and Caesarea Maritima to the north.

Idumea was part of the Judean province to the south of Judea, with the Dead Sea on its eastern boundary. It was incorporated into the Roman province of Judea after AD 44.

Geographically, and again generally described from north to south, Galilee featured fertile landscapes and valleys suitable for varied agriculture. The Sea of Galilee provided a large source of fresh water and fishing activities. Samaria and Judea Proper had coastal plains and shores along the Mediterranean and were primarily characterised by the Judean hills and mountains as one moved eastward. The central highlands were a dominant feature, and these areas included both arid and fertile zones due to varied topography. Then, as now, the River Jordan flowed from the Sea of Galilee to the Dead Sea, providing a water source that was crucial for the irrigation of arable areas. Perea and parts of southern Judea Proper were challenging areas due to their barren and dry terrain. The Dead Sea region, famously the lowest point on the Earth's surface, was characterised by desert landscapes.

Climatically, the region experiences two seasonal patterns: a cool and rainy winter stretching from October to April and a dry and warm summer spanning from May to September. Along the western coastline, the Mediterranean climate prevails, offering temperate conditions. Inland, the hills offer a moderate climate, while areas to the east and south succumb to desert conditions. Jerusalem witnesses long, warm summers marked by arid conditions, with temperatures soaring above 30 °C. Such conditions underscored the vital significance of fresh water for both the Jewish rebels and Vespasian's army. This importance was amplified by the little precipitation experienced in numerous areas, such as Jerusalem, throughout the summer.

Roman Offensive Campaign, 67

When Vespasian arrived in Antioch in February, his primary activity would have been the crucial, albeit unglamorous task of establishing a secure supply chain for his army's advance. Weeks were dedicated to meticulously securing necessities and ensuring operational logistics were in place for the constant flow of provisions into predefined forward operating centres.[75] Only when all elements were firmly in place did Vespasian embark on his offensive campaign.[76]

Prior to departing, an important rite called the *Suovetaurilia* sacrifice was usually performed, a religious ceremony to purify the army.[77] During this ritual, Vespasian, alongside senior officers, standard bearers and select troops, presided over the offering of a boar, a ram and a bull. This ceremony sought divine favour from Mars, the god of war. Purified and well supplied, Vespasian marched his army in March to the coastal Phoenician city of Ptolemais (Acre), a journey of around three weeks.[78] The city had been made a colony by Claudius and many Roman veterans had settled there, making it an important centre for romanisation in the region and an excellent base for operations.

While Vespasian travelled to Antioch and mustered his troops, the Jewish forces made some poorly coordinated attacks while also fighting among themselves. A figure of considerable consequence emerged onto the scene: Simon ben Giora. Driven by contempt for the provisional government and the affluent classes, ben Giora rallied a substantial contingent of radicals and pillaged wealthy estates in the district of Acrabata.[79] Responding to this turmoil, Ananus and the magistrates in Jerusalem swiftly dispatched a military contingent to defeat the insurrection and ben Giora fled to the formidable mountain stronghold of Masada, held by the entrenched *sicarii*.

Meanwhile, emboldened by their position in Jerusalem, the newly installed leaders of the Jewish government embarked on a daring offensive against Ascalon (Tel Ashkelon), a coastal city beset by persistent conflict between the Romans and the Jewish population.[80] Marshalling their precious mobile reserve of 20,000 troops, the government leaders advanced directly towards the city. However, the Roman infantry cohort and a squadron of the cavalry garrison under the command of Antonius sallied out fearlessly against the Jewish army. In an encounter that underscored the distinction between disciplined and disorganised forces, the hugely outnumbered Roman garrison pierced the unruly ranks of the Jewish army, leading to a chaotic retreat. Over the ensuing hours, a grim scene of carnage unfolded, resulting in the staggering loss of 10,000 Jewish combatants. It was nothing short of a bloodbath. This battle illustrated starkly the prowess of a disciplined Roman cavalry cohort against vulnerable and disorderly infantry on open ground. Heavily armoured in mail and each armed with a lance, several javelins and a long sword for slashing at infantry, the Roman cavalry tore through their enemy.

Remarkably, the following day saw the Jewish forces return to the fray, perhaps driven by desperation or unyielding resolve. However, they stumbled into deadly ambushes orchestrated by Antonius along all the approach routes. The merciless slaughter persisted, claiming another 8,000 lives among the Jewish ranks.[81] The repercussions of this calamitous defeat would have reverberated through Jerusalem. The news must have struck the new war government very badly. Out of their army of 20,000, a mere 2,000 returned, a catastrophic toll after an ill-conceived campaign.[82]

Vespasian's strategy for the campaign of 67 was retribution first by regaining control of Galilee through brutal offensive action against rebel strongholds. Once secure, the region would serve as a rear bastion for action further south. Moreover, the wealthy and prosperous region would provide much needed produce to help sustain his army. Titus had marched XV *Apollinaris* and V *Macedonica* from Alexandria to unite with his father at Ptolemais, probably using a section of the Via Maris. The journey would have taken around twenty-five days.[83] Ptolemais served as an apt coastal launching point and the general and his son and the other officers consolidated forces and again ensured supply lines were open and operating efficiently. Presumably large amounts of intelligence were received daily about the rebellion and Vespasian's *consilium* would have played a key role in the interpretation of dispatches to form a picture of the uprising across Judea.

Before the Battle of Beth Horon in 66, the legate Gallus had negotiated an important peace agreement with the city of Sepphoris (now Tzipori National Park) in Galilee and garrisoned it with various detachments. It was a prosperous and strategically important metropolis and the city's authorities had rejected the revolt. Keen to preserve their peace agreement and seeing no sense in joining a rebellion they still viewed as detrimental and hopeless, the city sent envoys to Vespasian in Ptolemais to express their allegiance. The city feared retaliation from the rebel forces in Galilee under Josephus so the representatives requested additional military support from Vespasian, who agreed to send a detachment of 1,000 cavalry and 6,000 infantry, under a competent tribune called Placidus.[84] His orders were to protect the strategically important centre and attack surrounding communities. Constant sorties were executed and Placidus devastated towns and hamlets, 'capturing and killing large numbers of Galileans'.[85] In response, Josephus, the rebel governor and general defending Galilee, ordered his mobile reserve to attack Sepphoris, but the Romans repelled the counter-offensive successfully.

Placidus now realised that many rebels were evading his sorties by slipping in and out of various fortified centres across Galilee. Doubtless with the approval of Vespasian, Placidus led a force against Jotapata (Yodfat), which was considered one of the toughest of these towns.[86] The tribune may have perceived the defences as weak and decided to make a quick assault. However, the Jews had word of the Roman advance and set an ambush presumably on the northern approach that was the more accessible side of Jotapata. They were able to rout the Romans and killed seven of Placidus' men.[87] This exemplifies the discipline and superior armour of the Romans; they seem to have been caught out but still able to retreat in good order with few casualties.

After receiving a report from Placidus, the Roman general decided his main army would be needed to tackle Galilee.[88] In May, Vespasian ordered his forces to make their first advance to the border of Galilee. A marching Roman army was a sight to behold and normally formed up in the following order:[89]

Scouting troops Lightly armed auxiliaries and archers with cavalry support.

Vanguard A detachment of heavily armed Roman troops, both legionaries and cavalry troopers.

Camp planners Ten men from each century with instruments to map out the camp ahead.

Corps of engineers Assigned to clear the path ahead of major obstacles, as well as level and straighten the route.

Officers' baggage   Vespasian and the senior officers' personal effects, under a strong cavalry guard, would arrive in advance to be arranged and ready prior to their owners' arrival.

Command group   Vespasian, escorted by an elite selection of legionaries and cavalry and his personal guard of mounted lancers.

Legionary cavalry   All the troopers from each legion.

Siege material etc.   Metal and wooden components and ammunition, all packed on mules.

Senior officers   Legates, prefects and tribunes, with an escort of selected soldiers.

Standards   The legion's eagle standards surrounded by all the cohort standards.

Trumpeters   All the signallers grouped together.

Main army   Six abreast if space permitted, the main body of troops with the centurions alongside their centuries to keep order.

Military slaves   All grouped together and leading the pack animals that carried the various paraphernalia and tents of the troops.

Auxiliaries and allies The main body all grouped together.[90]

Rearguard   Mixed detachments of light and heavy troops and a large cavalry force.

The column length would be considerable, even at six abreast. A single legion, including its baggage and non-combatants would have stretched almost two kilometres and taken about twenty-five minutes to pass a point. Thus, the entire army may have stretched up to twenty kilometres. Essentially, the head of the column could arrive at the next selected camp site as the rearguard was leaving the previous camp.

Moving further into Galilee, Vespasian ordered an assault on Gabara.[91] Scouts or deserters may have informed the Roman general that the town was poorly garrisoned and therefore a low-hanging fruit for an immediate direct attack. Artillery, archers and slingers ranged against the city wall to deliver a barrage of missiles to pin down defenders, infantry brought up ladders and other scaling tools, and the wall was stormed.[92] A lack of defenders meant the town was seized after the first attack.

To deter resistance in future, Vespasian allowed horrific pillaging and a total massacre of men, women and children.[93] Gabara was set ablaze and the surrounding villages and hamlets also torched. In some places, there was no one left to kill; in others some of the captured were enslaved and the rest slaughtered. The abandoned areas were a sign that refugees were fleeing for their lives before Vespasian's army.

At this point, Josephus realised that all was nearly lost. His forces were in disarray due to mass desertions.[94] Refugees swelled the remaining fortified centres. Vespasian and his army would stop at nothing in this mission for retribution. In desperation, he wrote to the provisional government in Jerusalem asking for permission to begin peace negotiations if no reinforcements could be sent.[95] Josephus would have known there were no new troops, so he was clearly in favour of the former plan. He received no reply and was left on his own.[96]

The Siege of Jotapata

In May, aware of the refugees massed in Jotapata, as well as its strategic value as a fortified point of resistance, Vespasian marched his enormous army against the comparatively minute town.[97] Situated on a mountainous out-crop, steep ravines provided natural protection to the town on its eastern, southern and western sides.[98] The built-up area within the walls, covering around 46,000 square metres, used terracing to accommodate rows of buildings. Josephus had improved the defences in 66 with the addition of new walls, particularly on the approachable northern side.[99] The residences of Jotapata represented the diverse population of Galileans at the time: wealthy property owners able to decorate their homes with fine frescos; a middle class of olive-oil producers, weavers and potters; and the impoverished. The town's population was normally around 2,500 but had been swelled by the intake of refugees and rebel fighters to 6,000–9,000.[100] There was no water spring meaning all were dependent on the city's cisterns.

The Roman column required four days of arduous work to clear a route through the poorly accessible mountainous terrain and advance on Jotapata. On the fifth day, Josephus bravely managed to slip into the city ahead of the Romans to take control of the defence. Informed of his presence, Vespasian immediately sent a large advance guard under the trusted Placidus and a decurion cavalry commander called Aebutius to surround the area and prevent Josephus escaping.[101] On the sixth day, the Roman forces arrived and possibly raised a single enormous temporary field camp covering the modern area of Yodfat. This was about half a mile north of Jotapata to benefit from the approach and in clear sight of the town to intimidate the Jews.[102]

To inform his plans, Vespasian would almost certainly have ridden closer to survey the defences with his senior officers, accompanied by his

Aerial view of Jotapata (Yodfat National Park), Israel. The bold line delineates the
town's fortifications. Triangles show altitude in metres above sea level
(400 m = 1,312 ft). The striped box marks the approximate location of the Roman
siege works built up against the more accessible northern defensive perimeter.
The circle marks the location from where the accompanying ground-level picture
(*see plates*) was taken. *Google Earth with author's annotations.*

personal bodyguard of lancers. It is easy to imagine that the general viewed
Jotapata as an easy target and its inhabitants as foolish to resist the might
of Rome's army. He therefore ordered a direct assault and the next day the
attack began. However, Jotapata's strength was underestimated and the
first five days became a test of the town's defences as the Romans attacked
the walls and countered Jewish sallies.[103] Jotapata was not going to be such
easy prey. Vespasian convened his *consilium* to discuss their observations
and he concluded that a ramp should be constructed up against the wall on
the north-western approach.[104] This marked the start of the first siege in the
Jewish war.

As legate of XV *Apollinaris*, Titus would have been present at the war council meeting and learned valuable lessons in the art of siege warfare. Again, logistics played a crucial part in such activities. For miles around, any trees were stripped from the landscape to provide timber and large amounts of stones and earth were gathered. The ramp would be a composite of these materials, layer upon layer, until it reached a height that permitted the Romans to storm the battlements or breach defences more easily with a ram or assault tower.[105] Wicker screens like rows of fencing would provide cover for those building the ramp. In an arching semi-circle around the construction works, numerous artillery pieces, specialised Syrian auxiliary archers and cohorts of slingers would constantly provide lethal covering fire.[106]

The defenders of Jotapata did not stand idly by while the Romans waged their siege warfare. Unable to attack from their battlements because of suppressive missile fire, they launched guerrilla-style attacks to destroy the protective screens, attack the guards and engineers and rip down or burn parts of the growing ramp. Vespasian created a more robust line of screening and reinforced the guards. As a result, the relentless work of the Romans bought the ramp close to its required position against the fortifications.[107] Josephus had to act fast.

The Jewish commander decided to increase the height of the wall. Cleverly devising his own protective screens, his masons worked around the clock to raise the height of the wall to nine metres, including new defensive towers for further vantage.[108] In response to this determined effort, the Romans, known for their resourceful siege tactics, continued to raise their siege ramp to match the new height of the fortifications. Meanwhile, the Jewish defenders, equally unwavering, launched frequent daring sorties to disrupt the Roman works. Recognising the need to tighten the siege even further, Vespasian ordered a temporary halt to the construction of the ramp to bolster the blockade around the town in order to prevent supplies from slipping into Jotapata and cut off any attempts by the inhabitants to scavenge for resources.[109] Assuming finite provisions and dwindling water stores, or perhaps tipped off by deserters, the Roman general hoped that this blockade would accelerate the decline of the defenders' strength and morale.[110]

Despite actually having an adequate supply of corn for a prolonged siege, water remained a critical concern within Jotapata. Josephus had enforced water rationing from the beginning. In a clever ploy to deceive the Romans about their shortages, he ordered clothes to be washed and hung from the walls to create the impression of an abundant water supply.[111] This ruse succeeded and the Romans returned to the construction of the ramp. The wily Jewish foragers then devised another plan. They disguised themselves in animal skins to resemble dogs during the cover of darkness and exploited a blind spot in the blockade located in a particularly rugged section on the western side. The Roman guards soon caught on to the scheme and closed the gap, foiling this initiative.[112]

The strong resolve of Josephus and his men, fuelled by the desperation of their situation and the ever-closing Roman net, next brought about a particularly courageous sally. Benefiting from their agility compared to the well-armoured Roman auxiliaries and legionaries, Josephus' men managed, remarkably, to disperse the line of Roman guards and reach the Roman camp, where some superficial damage was inflicted.[113] It is easy to imagine how this would have shocked Vespasian and his officers, resulting in harsh punishments for any lack of discipline that may have allowed the break-through by the Jews.

Ever adaptive, Vespasian realised that his archers and slingers were a better means of dealing with such attacks and he ordered his infantry to avoid such engagements. He also stepped up the onslaught of missile fire from his array of stone and javelin artillery engines. Literally thousands of missiles a day rained down on the Jewish defences and on any sallies, inflicting many casualties.[114] The true worth of archery is well-acknowledged, yet the crucial role played by Balearic slingers remains undervalued. These remarkable specialised auxiliaries were heralded as the finest in their craft, and their exceptional precision was their hallmark. With great accuracy, they could consistently strike down specific targets, even when positioned at considerable distances. This extraordinary level of skill was the result of a lifetime of training and experience. Launching their lead or stone shots at speeds exceeding 160 kilometres per hour and hitting targets over a hundred metres away, a cohort of slingers held the potential to inflict severe casualties, incapacitate enemy formations or unleash a relentless barrage of suppressive fire on opposing positions.[115] The release of the shot gave out a characteristic snap and the sound of hundreds of snaps must have been terrifying for the intended victims. Their contribution to Vespasian's army, often overshadowed by legionaries and cavalry, held undeniable significance on the battlefield and in siege warfare.

What had initially appeared as a straightforward assault, with subsequent hopes of a swift siege, had evolved into a costly and time-consuming conflict for the Romans, delaying their broader campaign objectives. Vespasian decided to introduce a battering ram into the operation once the ramp had reached a level that would allow pounding of the newly constructed wall.[116] This highly valuable piece of siege machinery featured an immense timber beam capped with a formidable iron ram's head. Both components were carried with much effort up to the battlefront, as no local resources provided the necessary materials. It was suspended beneath a frame that allowed it to swing back and forth in action. Under the cover of a renewed barrage of suppressive missile fire, the ram was brought up the ramp and positioned against the wall. In addition, specially constructed protective covered passageways aided its deployment. It was an extremely dangerous task for the Roman soldiers ordered to push the heavy contraption up an incline under hostile conditions. Once in place, the first strike of the ram shook the fortifications and sent a shockwave through the town, instilling panic amongst the townsfolk.[117]

Josephus had to respond quickly as it was clear the ram would not take long to breach the fresh masonry of the raised wall. Some initial success was achieved by lowering sacks full of chaff on ropes to cushion the blows but this was soon countered by the Romans using sickles lashed to long poles to cut the sacks free. Next, the Jewish defenders turned to fire and stormed out simultaneously from three separate points armed with firebrands of dried wood, bitumen, pitch and sulphur. A slow response from the Romans allowed Josephus' men to ignite the battering ram and surrounding protective screens. In one particularly heroic act, one of the Galilean fighters called Eleazar ben Sameas hurled a large boulder at the ram that broke off its iron head, the connection presumably weakened by the flames. Jumping down, he miraculously retrieved the extremely hot iron head and, presumably with some assistance, climbed back up to the battlements with his trophy before he succumbed to five arrows – quite a feat considering the ram head probably weighed over fifty kilograms.[118]

In the heat of the action, Vespasian was positioned within a mere hundred metres of Jotapata's defences when a notable episode occurred. At a critical instant, a Jewish archer let loose an arrow that struck Vespasian on the boot. Despite the considerable distance, the projectile retained enough force to inflict a superficial wound.[119] The sight of their general's blood and the realisation that he had been exposed to such imminent danger caused alarm throughout the Roman army, not least for Titus who was close at hand at the time and visibly distressed by the incident. Roman soldiers often held deep affection and admiration for their leaders, and Vespasian belonged to this category. Concealing his pain, he called for calm. However, the effect on the troops was dramatic. A vengeful surge coursed through the assembled Roman soldiers, now propelled to new heights of determination by Vespasian's stoicism. With darkness falling, the Roman attack resumed with a heightened intensity while a new ram operated under protective screens.[120]

A fateful night of conflict ensued. Jewish defenders rained down every available object on the screened battering ram – firebrands, recycled Roman projectiles and stones alike. To counter this action, the Romans unleashed the full force of their formidable artillery. Arrow-firing *scorpiones* and *catapultae* and stone-hurling *ballistae* and *onagerae* of varying sizes and designs, relentlessly discharged countless projectiles. The defenders, silhouetted against their own fires, became conspicuous targets. The Jews suffered heavy casualties and the heaviest stone projectiles, weighing several kilograms, destroyed sections of the battlements and towers. The force of one stone missile was sufficient to decapitate a man near Josephus. Another gruesome tale records a pregnant woman emerging at dawn only to be struck in the belly by a projectile that propelled the tragic remains of her child some distance away. Adding to the terror, the Romans fired the dead bodies of slain Jews into the town.[121]

Probably a hundred or more Jewish fighters died during the night due to the relentless missile fire then the wall collapsed the next morning due to the ram's nocturnal battering.[122] The battle for the breach of Jotapata began and Vespasian ordered a structured assault. The front line was composed of three companies of dismounted elite cavalrymen using their long lances, over two metres long, to head the thrust against the breached section of the wall after wooden gangways or ramps were thrown across the broken masonry. For the second line, officers hand-picked their bravest and strongest infantry to support the cavalrymen. The third line in the rear was made up of archers and slingers who would rain down their fire on the breach and beyond. To divert some of the Jewish manpower, squads of Roman soldiers brought up ladders to other parts of the walls.

Josephus prepared for the final battle, aware that it would be a fight to the death. The townsfolk were ordered to remain inside their homes to prevent their fearful screams from distracting his fighters and his soldiers were instructed to block their ears against daunting war cries that were expected from the Roman ranks. The Galilean general selected his most resilient fighters to form a human barrier around the breached region, standing shoulder to shoulder with his men for this last stand.

> This was the ultimate fight for their hometown – not to save it, too late for that, but to avenge its imminent loss. Every one of them should picture scenes which were hardly a moment away – old men butchered by the enemy, children and women put to the sword – then prime themselves with fury at these impending horrors, and vent that fury on the perpetrators.
>
> *Josephus*[123]

Fighting commenced with the sound of Roman trumpets signalling the attack followed by a massive volley of Roman arrows that 'darkened the sky', allowing the Romans to lay out gangways that permitted passage through the breach.[124] A back-and-forth clash ensued, with the two sides locked in a deadly struggle. The Roman infantry in the second line, in a famous formation known as the *testudo* (tortoise) provided themselves with cover by overlapping their shields above and on the sides.[125] The huddled ranks in this protective shell were able to advance against the defenders. In response, the Jewish fighters broke one of these formation by hurling boiling oil over the *testudo* from the adjacent battlements.[126] Additionally, they poured boiled fenugreek, a herb made into a slippery mash by its lecithin content, over the wooden gangways in an effort to thwart the Roman advance.[127] Against the odds and with heavy losses on both sides, the Jews managed to hold out, at least for the time being.

Recognising the need to minimise his own casualties, despite the size of his army, Vespasian chose to abandon a direct assault on the breach. Instead, he ordered the elevation of the ramp and the construction of three attack towers. These tall platforms, mounted on wheels, rose fifteen metres above the ground and were clad in iron sheets for protection against fire. They were equipped with light artillery pieces and manned by numerous auxiliary archers and slingers. After several days of preparation, the towers were wheeled into position and unleashed a persistent barrage of missiles down onto the beleaguered defenders. This missile assault from elevated vantage points forced the Jewish defenders to withdraw partially, limiting their ability to rally against Roman assaults.[128]

Meanwhile, the methodical work of the Roman engineers and construction workers raised the ramp to match the full height of the town wall. This marked the forty-seventh day of the siege. Informed by a deserter that the Jewish defenders were now incapable of mounting any meaningful defence, Vespasian decided to allow Titus, accompanied by tribune Domitius Sabinus and a select group of legionaries from XV *Apollinaris*, to slip over the wall in the early hours of the next day. It was a brave feat for the general's son, and highly unusual for a legate, but presumably the risk was very low given that the defence was all but spent – and a thick mist over the town provided cover. Moreover, tribunes Sextus Calvarius and Placidus were right behind with a formidable contingent of soldiers. Thus, on 1 July, after silently dispatching the sleeping sentries, Titus led the Roman soldiers over the wall and opened the gates to let the Roman army flood in. Jotapata was lost.[129]

The slaughter then began. Throngs of inhabitants were driven downhill at sword point within the citadel and channelled into narrow streets where a massacre commenced. Jewish fighters amongst the crowd were incapable of any defence. Many chose suicide in their helpless condition. Over the subsequent days, the Romans scoured Jotapata house by house and room by room in search of those hidden. Only a proportion of infants and women were spared for slavery; everyone else lay where they were killed in every corner of the citadel.[130] Vespasian ordered the city razed to the ground. Only years later would Jews return to the site and care for the remains of those who had fallen. Since they were unable to identify anyone, many bodies were laid to rest by using the cisterns as mass graves.[131] Jotapata was never re-settled.

Against all odds, Josephus eluded capture by slipping down a concealed passage within the citadel into a deep cave, accompanied by others. This had been prepared well in advance, including being furnished with provisions. Actual escape from the city under the cover of night proved impossible. The group managed to hide for two days until a woman with them was captured, presumably foraging in the ruins above, and revealed their location. Intent on capturing Josephus alive, tribune Nicanor eventually convinced Josephus to surrender. In a tragic turn, everyone except Josephus and one other opted for suicide rather than face the consequences of capture.[132]

When he was escorted into the Roman camp, an enraged crowd of soldiers surrounded Josephus, their jeers clamouring for his execution. The atmosphere was charged with hostility as the fallen Galilean general became the focus of fierce abuse. Amidst the tumult, Titus' voice of reason, skilfully quelled the agitated crowd and cleared a path to Vespasian's field tent. One can imagine a palpable tension when Josephus stood before Vespasian. Titus persuaded his father to spare Josephus' life but Vespasian initially wanted him sent in chains to Rome as a trophy for Nero.

Hearing about his fate, Josephus requested a private meeting with Vespasian, who was in the event accompanied by Titus. The captive spoke:

> Vespasian, you may think that in Josephus you have simply won yourself a prisoner of war: but I am come to tell you of your great destiny. If I were not God's chosen emissary, I would have followed the Jewish tradition – I know it well, and how a defeated general should meet his death. Are you sending me to Nero? Why to him? Do you think Nero and his successors will last long before your hour is come? You, Vespasian, will be *Caesar* and emperor, both you and your son here with us. So chain me tighter now and keep me for yourself, as you, Caesar, are master not only of me but all land and sea and the whole human race.
>
> *Josephus*[133]

The shrewd Vespasian initially dismissed Josephus' prophecy as nothing more than a desperate ploy to save his own skin.[134] After all, many could already see in Vespasian the qualities of a man destined for greatness – his military prowess, discipline, and ability to command loyalty were undeniable, and his growing power hinted at the possibility of a grander future. Josephus' words, while striking, may simply have echoed what others whispered in private. Yet in the following days or weeks amidst further discussions, possibly mediated by Titus, a more useful picture of Josephus emerged as not just a captive but a prospective collaborator, armed with intricate knowledge of Judean defences, geography, culture and military strategies. Josephus was a survivor; Vespasian, a pragmatic strategist. The defeated Jewish general became a valuable turncoat advisor.[135]

The Massacres of Japha and Mount Gerizim

In June, during the later stages of the siege of Jotapata, Vespasian's vast reserve of troops had allowed him to dispatch divisions on special missions. Japha (today part of the city of Nazareth) was approximately fifteen kilometres south of Jotapata and had risen in revolt. Based on Roman field intelligence, the city's defences were considered formidable, with a double ring of walls. Vespasian ordered Traianus, with a detachment of 2,000 legionaries from his X *Fretensis* accompanied by a thousand cavalry, to attack the city.

Completely inexperienced, the garrison of Japha offered battle in front of the town rather than man the battlements. Traianus had once successfully faced the far more formidable Parthians in the field. The experienced commander easily routed the Jewish fighters and was able to force through the first gate right behind the fleeing insurgents. Fearing further blunders, their own people kept the gate in the second wall closed. The Romans proceeded to press the defenders up against the inner wall and in the crushing chaos slaughtered the entire army of perhaps 12,000 men. It was a staggering, bloody defeat.[136]

Well aware of the importance of involving his general's son in the imminent assault on Japha, Traianus sent a messenger to invite Titus to 'crown the victory'.[137] With Vespasian's approval, Titus took command of a thousand legionaries from his XV *Apollinaris*, supplemented by 500 cavalry. The combined force formed up in front of the town. With Titus leading the right flank and Traianus on the left, the Romans easily scaled the under-manned battlements using ladders and subsequently opened the gates for reinforcing troops. The ensuing attack turned into street-by-street close combat, with remaining rebel fighters ambushing the Romans. The conflict intensified as, in a desperate bid to support their men, women joined the fray by hurling objects from housetops. A fierce six-hour battle followed, eventually wiping out all the Jewish fighters. Japha was taken on 20 June. In the aftermath, Titus and Traianus permitted their soldiers to massacre all survivors, except for women and children destined for slavery. The toll was grim: 3,000 killed and over 2,000 taken captive.[138]

Cerialis was not left out of the action and was ordered by Vespasian to lead 3,000 legionaries from his V *Macedonica* against a mass gathering of Samaritans on their sacred mountain called Gerizim, in the central Samaritan highlands. The mount is actually a series of peaks over 800 metres above sea level and has a particularly steep eastern flank. Roman intelligence suggested the gathering showed rumblings of trouble. The Samaritans were generally not involved in the revolt so the risky gathering is hard to understand. Regardless, the Romans did not permit such large gatherings in any of their provinces. Shrewdly, Cerialis surrounded the mountain at first because, at the height of summer and with no water sources, the Samaritan crowd would likely soon disperse. This successfully drove many to descend and, sensing his opposition was crippled, Cerialis and his men advanced up the slopes and offered safe passage if all surrendered. Defiantly, the Samaritans declined and Cerialis had no hesitation in slaughtering the entire gathering. Over 11,000 were butchered, a cataclysmic episode for the Samaritan people.[139] Mount Gerizim was captured on 25 June.[140]

The Fall of Tiberias and Tarichea

Midway through the campaigning season, in July, Vespasian made a strategic decision to station his army in central bases and rest his troops.[141] This allowed the majority of his forces to prepare for a significant push against Jerusalem that would require the complete campaign season of the following year. Garrisoning forces tactically, X *Fretensis* and V *Macedonica* were stationed at Caesarea, while XV *Apollinaris* took position at Scythopolis (Beit She'an) in the Decapolis region.[142] Simultaneously, Placidus led the two cohorts of XII *Fulminata* to Laodicea to rejoin the rest of the legion.[143]

Meanwhile, a considerable number of refugees congregated at the coastal town of Joppa (Jaffa) and restored its defences. They also created a pirate fleet to disrupt the lucrative trade traffic along the coasts of Syria and Phoenicia. This would have greatly alarmed Vespasian as it almost certainly interrupted his supply lines along the Eastern Mediterranean waters, as well as threatening Rome's corn supply. He acted swiftly and sent a detachment of infantry and cavalry, likely from Caesarea, sixty kilometres south to Joppa.

When they realised the Romans were approaching, the insurgents fled Joppa in their flotilla of ships. With Joppa now deserted, the Romans secured the town the night they arrived. Rather than get away, the maritime rebels suffered an ill fate the following dawn when a fierce storm struck their anchored fleet. Those who survived drowning or being dashed to death on the rocks and made it to the shore were finished off by the waiting legionaries. The casualties were staggering, over 4,000 killed. Not a single person survived. Joppa was razed to the ground, and the Romans retired to Caesarea.[144]

At this time, Agrippa II invited Vespasian to visit him in Caesarea Philippi (now the Banias Nature Reserve).[145] Nestled in a region of natural beauty at the south-western base of Mount Hermon in the Golan Heights, the city was idyllically positioned near a spring that served as a primary source for the River Jordan. At this scenic location, Agrippa had erected an expansive palace featuring pools, a basilica, a throne room and opulent reception areas. Vespasian accepted the invitation in early August, and accompanied by Titus and an escort of troops, they spent an uninterrupted twenty days in palatial surroundings where they learned more about Agrippa's kingdom.

Queen Berenice, Agrippa's sister and a princess of the Herodian dynasty known for her extraordinary beauty, wealth and considerable influence, was very likely also present during their stay. Not to be underestimated, she was joint ruler with Agrippa and extremely powerful in the region.[146] Titus had met Berenice previously, and whether at that time or now he found himself captivated by her charm and character. She was in her late thirties, eleven years older than Titus and neither of them was married at the time. During their stay at the palace, a lasting affair between Titus and Berenice began to unfold, with the palace providing a conducive environment for their relationship to flourish.[147]

Berenice has enthralled past and modern imaginations, a mysterious eastern queen whose allure clearly attracted Titus. Born in 28 to King Herod Agrippa I and his wife Cypros, she was the great-granddaughter of Herod the Great. Married three times for political purposes, with her first marriage occurring when she was as young as thirteen, she remained single from the age of twenty-two. Rumours, almost certainly false, circulated of an incestuous relationship with her brother Agrippa who never married.[148] It is essential to understand that Berenice and her brother were Jewish but also Hellenised and romanised, meaning that the multi-lingual, multi-cultural Berenice possessed much more than her famed beauty and fabulous wealth. Alas, no coin portraits or statues identified as Berenice have survived, so her appearance can only be guessed at. With so little certain about her, the myth and intrigue around Berenice will never be resolved but Titus certainly seems to have bonded with the queen emotionally and physically.

Titus' involvement with Berenice had to pause when news arrived that the city of Tiberias was threatening to revolt and Tarichea had already rebelled.[149] Both cities were very important urban areas within Agrippa's kingdom and were well situated on the western banks of the Sea of Galilee to profit from the fishing industry. They were not part of Vespasian's province of Judea, but the situation needed to be dealt with to avoid them becoming rebel centres.

Vespasian sent Titus to Caesarea with orders to bring forward V *Macedonica* and X *Fretensis*. The plan was to rendezvous at Scythopolis, where Vespasian would muster the quartered XV *Apollinaris*. The Roman general then led all three legions to a camp within five kilometres of Tiberias, conspicuously positioned in full view of the city to intimidate the inhabitants.[150] Believing that the city had been coerced into rebellion by a small faction, and hoping to spare Agrippa's important centre from destruction, Vespasian opted for a diplomatic approach. He chose Valerianus, a decurion cavalry officer, presumably known for his negotiating skills, and sent him with a squadron of troopers to hold peace talks. Dismounting to parlay, Valerianus found himself confronted unexpectedly by Jesus ben Sapphias, the governor of Tiberias turned faction leader. He and his fighters forced Valerianus and five of his men to flee on foot and then led their captured horses triumphantly back into the city.[151]

In a desperate bid to save Tiberias, the city elders sought refuge in the Roman camp, where Agrippa facilitated an audience with Vespasian. Despite his anger over the loss of precious horses, the Roman general agreed to spare the city, honouring Agrippa's kingdom.[152] Recognising his untenable situation in Tiberias, Jesus ben Sapphias retreated swiftly to Tarichea, about five kilometres north along the lakeshore. Vespasian moved his field camp up halfway between Tiberias and Tarichea and, during the construction of its earthen ramparts, repelled an audacious attack by Jesus ben Sapphias before the rebels retreated on boats.

Reports next reached Vespasian of a significant force gathering in the plain outside Tarichea. With limited cavalry himself, the general recognised the distinct advantage his few mounted troops had over the insurgents in open fields and dispatched Titus with 600 troopers. However, the size of the Jewish force had been underestimated so reinforcements were called up in the form of Traianus and 400 more cavalry. In another example of his bravery, arguably a reckless move, Titus gave a rallying speech to his men before spreading out his troopers in a thin line in front of the Jewish fighters. Titus then ordered a charge and spurred his own horse to lead the attack. Using shock tactics, the charging cavalry slammed into the rebel lines. The clash knocked many of the defenders to the ground and their weapons were no match for the long Roman lances. The Jews soon broke into a chaotic retreat. Hunted as they fled by Titus and his men, the insurgents managed to find refuge behind the city walls.[153]

While the battlements of Tarichea were robust, the Achilles heel of the defences was the oddly unprotected waterfront. Presumably now joined by Traianus and his reinforcements, Titus personally led the cavalry division into the water and rode into the city from the seafront. A frenzied action followed, in which Titus attacked fleeing rebels trying to make their escape in boats and non-combatant townsfolk who could not easily be distinguished from the fighters. Eventually satisfied that the rebels were all killed, Titus stood his troopers down and sent a message to his father that Tarichea was captured; it was 8 September.[154] Slipping into the countryside, Jesus ben Sapphias evaded capture, but Vespasian was pleased at the daring success of his son.[155]

The next day, Vespasian ordered the construction of a fleet of rafts to pursue the fighters who had escaped on fishing boats. The abundance of wood and the skilled craftsmen at hand allowed large sturdy platforms to be created that would carry the weight of several Roman soldiers. When ready, Vespasian gave the order for the rafts to be launched and encircle the rebels who remained nearby. With a small mast and oars, the Jewish fishing boats were likely around eight metres long and two and half wide.[156] They were not designed for naval warfare. It is hard to understand why the rebels did not simply sail away across the sea of Galilee but they decided to hold their position. Feeble attempts to throw stones at the rafts or run alongside to swipe at the Romans met with disaster. Roman arrows and spear thrusts claimed many lives and Vespasian's men leapt from their rafts into the rebels' boats to fight with their swords. The solid rafts were also able to capsize or crush some boats. Those who managed to break through the line of Roman rafts were swiftly killed on the shoreline. Thousands of insurgents were killed and the waters turned red around Tarichea. In the aftermath, the shoreline was littered with wreckage and the bloated bodies of the dead.[157] Vespasian took the ruthless decision that no distinction should be made between the local inhabitants and the hostile groups.[158] The captives were escorted to the stadium in Tiberias where the old and frail, around 1,200, were brutally executed. Some 6,000 of the young and able were segregated and sent to Greece to toil on the canal of Corinth. The rest, over 30,000 were sold as ordinary slaves.[159]

The Siege of Gamla and Surrender of Gischala

As planned, the Roman atrocities brought about the surrender of virtually all the revolting Galileans – except for those at Gischala (Jish) and Mount Tabor. Within Agrippa's kingdom, the hilltop town of Gamla, on the other side of the Sea of Galilee in the Golan Heights, was also identified as a hot-spot for rebels. About ten kilometres from the shoreline, the buildings of Gamla sat on a narrow rocky spur enclosed on all sides by precipitous ravines, except to the north-east where the ridge was connected by a slim saddle to the plateau above. This meant that access was only possible from the south-west, across the 35-metre-wide ridge. The town itself covered around 38,000 square metres on a raised section of the ridge, and partially down the southern side. Terracing supported rows of houses, a synagogue hall and, unusually, a basilica.[160] The northern slope was far too steep for any practical construction with a slope of around 45 per cent. Unlike Jotapata, a spring within the walls provided fresh water.

Gamla was not a purpose-built fortress, however. In 66, Josephus had commissioned fortifications at Gamla and presumably provided useful intelligence to Vespasian on the matter. On the eastern side where defences were needed, a large round tower probably built in the Hellenistic period, stood directly over the approach ridge. The patchwork of pre-existing buildings along the eastern perimeter had also been converted into battlements; gaps between houses were filled and the buildings themselves were reinforced and given thicker walls. In other places, rooms were filled in with stones. The haphazard fortifications nevertheless created a stone barrier 5–7 metres thick. Two towers may have already existed to guard the town entrance about mid-way down the eastern barricades.[161] To strengthen the whole arrangement, a large trench was dug out in front of the walls from the saddle down to the stream at the bottom of the southern ravine, a length of around 240 metres. Even though the Romans could simply have descended to the bottom of the gorge to skirt around the eastern fortifications and trench, it would then be unnecessarily risky to clamber back up to attack the town; the steep southern slope would have left them breathless and over-exposed. There were no fortifications built from the round tower at the northern end of the eastern perimeter but the steep northern slope, which included some cliffs, was too treacherous to venture across.[162]

As testament to the daunting nature of the defences, Agrippa's army had failed to break Gamla despite a seven-month siege started earlier in the year.[163] In response, at the end of August, Vespasian marched his three legions, auxiliaries and supporting units to Gamla and camped in the mountains surrounding the Gamla ridge. It was an enormous overkill to bring the might of three legions against a small town, and perhaps the exaggerated strength served Vespasian's need to portray himself as a formidable foe.

The siege works were divided up between the legions: XV *Apollinaris* was tasked with raising earthworks against the north-eastern round tower; X *Fretensis* began the construction of a ramp facing the fortress centre and V *Macedonica* began work to fill the defensive trench to allow access from the saddle area. During this time, Agrippa II tried in vain to convince the inhabitants to capitulate and was struck by a stone missile on his elbow while attempting to negotiate. This enhanced the Roman resolve to press ahead with the siegeworks.[164]

Vespasian's vast manpower completed the ramps and commissioned battering rams for action.[165] The town leaders of Gamla, Chares and Joseph, positioned their fighters along the eastern fortifications and only kept the rams back for a short period until suppressive Roman missile fire forced the defenders back into the town. At least one ram quickly breached the wall at its weakest point, where the original thickness was two-thirds of a metre and it had only been thickened to two metres.[166] It is possible that Josephus had remembered this weak spot and passed the information on to Vespasian.[167] In any event the fortifications of Gamla were clearly no match for Roman siege warfare.

A concentrated barrage of missiles targeted the breach to repel any defenders; over 300 arrowheads and 180 *ballista* balls were recovered from that area during archaeological studies.[168] The blaring of trumpets signalled Roman soldiers to flood through the breach. Insurgents and residents retreated west and to the higher part of the town in the face of the rush. In a tactical misstep, the Romans pursued them instead of first consolidating the lower areas. Consequently, the rebels gained the upper hand as the Romans struggled on steep streets, compounded by narrow alleyways hindering line formations. Seeking escape from the crushing mêlée, Roman troops climbed up to low rooftops accessible due to the terraced layout. The weight caused one building to collapse, triggering a domino effect that claimed many Roman casualties as several other buildings also caved in. The resulting dust clouds obscured visibility, leading to Romans inadvertently attacking each other in the confusion, and the enemy counter-attacked.[169]

Remarkably, Vespasian was in the midst of the chaos and had even advanced beyond the collapse zone. Since he had only a few guards, this marked the most perilous moment in his military career. He kept his composure and ordered his elite guards to create a shield wall. Gradually, they 'retreated step by step' until they reached the breach and made their escape. Overnight, it became evident that the Romans had suffered significant casualties relative to the scale of the Gamlan opposition. Morale plummeted further when news quickly spread about the perilous situation their general had faced.[170] Shame indeed for them to have let their beloved general to have been so isolated. Presumably many a centurion's vine rod dealt out punishment.

In the aftermath of the disastrous assault, the Gamlans had mixed sentiments. Some were motivated to continue the fight, while others despaired at the realisation that no negotiated settlement would ever be reached. As the Romans prepared for a renewed assault over the next days, many inhabitants lost faith and deserted the town down the steep slopes and through gaps in the Roman encirclement. Their despair was confounded by the prioritisation of the last remaining rations for the fighters. At this stage, a much more cautious Roman side was being kept at bay by the defenders. However, one night three legionaries of XV *Apollinaris* crept up to the base of the round tower. Under the cover of darkness, they prised out five load-bearing stones. The tower had no foundations, so the action caused its complete collapse while the brave legionaries jumped back.[171] In the confusion that followed, defenders withdrew from their posts thinking the Romans were attacking or tried to escape over the rubble of the collapsed tower only to be butchered by Roman guards. Joseph was shot by an arrow during an escape attempt. Elsewhere, the other leader, Chares, had expired in his sickbed. Lacking any leadership, the last inhabitants withdrew with the dwindling number of fighters to the highest part of the town for a last stand.

Given the anticipated imminent return of Titus from his diplomatic mission to speak with the new Syrian governor, Gaius Licinius Mucianus, and mindful of the recent setback, there was a one-day pause in the Roman action.[172] When Titus arrived, he was understandably furious to learn about the near miss to his father during the first assault. One can picture a heated debate amongst the officers in a field tent to understand how this could have happened to a general of Rome. Taking matters into his own hands but with Vespasian's approval, Titus selected 200 crack cavalrymen, accompanied by infantry support. Like at Jotapata, this was only allowed by the general because by now it was clear that the rebels were on their knees due to exhaustion and lack of provisions. In the quiet predawn hours, they stealthily infiltrated the town before any sentries could sound the alarm.[173] As Titus' detachment advanced, panic seized the remaining Gamlans. Vespasian ordered reinforcements into the town. Those inhabitants not felled by Roman weapons were trampled in the chaos. The more agile were able to tumble their way down the northern slope to the gorge below.[174] In the midst of the horror, infants were horrifically hurled down the slope to their demise by Roman troops.[175] So ended the siege of Gamla on 23 October and, as with so many other Roman assaults, the trapped innocents were shown no mercy.[176]

After the fall of Gamla, Vespasian turned his attention to the town of Gischala. The rebel leader John ben Levi had managed to fire up the community into revolt and it was the last rebellious town in Galilee to tackle. The insurgent gathering at Mount Tabor had been dealt with during the siege of Gamla by a detachment of cavalry under the trusted command of Placidus.[177]

While deciding what course of action to take, Titus would have briefed his father about his mission to Mucianus in Syria.[178] The newly appointed governor had probably arrived in Antioch in early October.[179] Relations between Vespasian and Mucianus were initially strained but there were no deeply rooted issues.[180] Mucianus had on occasion been jealous of the Vespasian[181] while for his part Vespasian scorned Mucianus' 'notorious homosexuality and theatrical manner'.[182] However, both recognised the need to be allies given their immediately adjacent jurisdictions and their command of many legions. In acknowledgement of Titus' astute diplomacy skills, first honed during his imperial education next to Britannicus, Vespasian had trusted his son with the mission to ride to Syria to manage the relationship between the two governors.[183]

Titus probably addressed several topics with Mucianus. First was the sensitive topic of overlapping authority, given that Vespasian had started his operations in Syria. They would have also discussed the general political issues of the period and the progress made to date against the rebels in Judea. Supplies from Syria for Vespasian's massive army were almost certainly a key point. It is thought that Titus brought positive news back to Vespasian that Mucianus had been receptive to his overtures.[184]

Returning to the action needed against Gischala, Vespasian decided to deploy Titus with a thousand cavalry against the insurgents. At the same time, to rest his men at the close of the campaign season, he sent V *Macedonica* to Scythopolis and he took the other two legions to Caesarea. The journey north-west from Gamla to Gischala would have taken Titus around two days. On his arrival, the legate realised that the town could easily be taken by direct assault. However, revealing a part of his character open to clemency, Titus opted for diplomacy.[185] Perhaps he was worn out with all the fighting during the year. Speaking from the battlements, John ben Levi told Titus he accepted the call to surrender and offered to persuade his fellow revolutionaries to step down. However, he asked for time in observance of the Sabbath. Titus respected the request and withdrew his cavalry detachment about a day's ride north to Kadasa (Kedesh). During the night, John ben Levi made a dash for Jerusalem, taking his fighters and numerous residents with him. When Titus returned the next day to find he had been fooled, he immediately sent his cavalry in pursuit. They failed to find John ben Levi but killed 6,000 and escorted around 3,000 women and children back to Gischala. Titus then ordered a section of the town wall to be pulled down and posted a garrison to ensure peace.[186]

All of Galilee was now brought to heel. Vespasian and Titus returned to Caesarea, arriving at the beginning of November, and together they would have reflected on the year's campaigning. Progress had been slower than expected but they had achieved the strategic goal of securing Galilee prior to taking on Jerusalem. Beginning with Jotapata, a formidable fortress defended fiercely by Jewish rebels, the Romans had persisted for the forty-seven days it took to capture the citadel. The massacres at Japha and Mount Gerizim showed no hesitation by the Romans in committing acts of genocide. The clashes with fortified towns like Japha and Tarichea had showcased the challenges of urban warfare, with the Romans adapting their tactics to navigate narrow streets and defend against surprise attacks. The capture of Tiberias, though not without complications, underscored Vespasian's attempts to balance military objectives with the conservation of Agrippa's kingdom. Titus had displayed his military acumen and, on several occasions, shown his bravery during daring, sometimes reckless, assaults. The campaign had also shown on two occasions that Vespasian's life had been in real danger from his close involvement in the fighting. As in all conflicts across the ages, Roman warfare was a perilous business.

CHAPTER 5

BELLUM JUDAICUM: THE JEWISH WAR, CAMPAIGN OF 68-69

The Disrupted Campaign of 68

During the winter of 67, Vespasian rested his army in its bases and the majority of his time was occupied with planning for the new campaign season. At this time numerous reports of infighting between Jewish factions in Jerusalem begged the question amongst the Roman officers as to whether an immediate attack on the capital was warranted.[1] Convening his *consilium* to debate the opportunity, the Roman general decided to wait; better for now to let the Jews continue their self-destruction.[2] His strategy for the coming year was also devised during this period. The initial design was to quash the possibility of other rebels interfering in the Roman assault on Jerusalem.[3] Thus, at the start of the campaign season in 68, Vespasian marched on Gadara, where an insurgent faction was stirring up discontent. Unbeknown to the renegades, the city authorities had sent a delegation to Vespasian offering their loyalty. As the vast Roman army approached the city, the rebels fled when they realised the scale of their internal and external opposition.

On 4 March, Vespasian and his forces were welcomed by the Gadarenes with acclamations and the general dispatched his most trusted tribune, Placidus, on a mission to pursue the fleeing dissidents while he returned to Caesarea.[4] With 500 cavalry and 3,000 infantry, Placidus pursued them into the village of Bethennabris in the Jordan Valley and, after a fierce battle, routed them. The Romans slaughtered all the residents before pillaging the village and burning it to the ground. Escapees were able to disperse and rallied large numbers of agitated followers en route to Jericho. However, confident of the major tactical advantage his cavalry had over the insurrectionists in open areas, Placidus was eventually able to pin them against the bank of the River Jordan where the Romans easily slew them all. Over several weeks, the tribune led further attacks against all the surrounding villages as far as the Dead Sea, such that the whole of Perea was subdued. Once again, the talented Placidus must have greatly pleased his general, Vespasian.

In Caesarea, in mid-April, Vespasian received a crucial message from Rome. Back in March as he had begun his campaign, the governor of Gallia Lugdunensis, Gaius Julius Vindex, had declared a revolt against Nero. Many senators were deeply troubled by Nero's incompetence and his murderous purging of statesmen and Vindex could no longer tolerate the situation. Though Vindex had the support of Gallic chieftains, the news that Vespasian received may not have caused him much alarm, since Nero himself appeared unfazed by the uprising. Perhaps the emperor had been aware the revolt was brewing and not taken it seriously.[5] Besides, Vindex had no legions. Vespasian's response to the news was a pragmatic one; he decided to press on with his campaign – he could not yet have predicted that the fall of Nero was imminent.

At the springtime, Vespasian mustered a large proportion of his army and commenced a sweep through Judea, heading south out of Caesarea. He marched first towards Antipatris (Tel Afek) then Thamna, Lydda (Lod) and Jamnia (Yavne).[6] To reimpose control over these areas, he pillaged and torched the whole territory. Satisfied with his progress, the Roman general issued an important order to control the district surrounding Emmaus (Kiriath Yearim).[7] The location was around fifteen kilometres west of Jerusalem. Here, Vespasian ordered the construction of a fortified camp and posted V *Macedonica* there under the command of Cerialis.[8] This allowed the Romans to tighten the noose around Jerusalem by controlling many major approaches to the city.

Continuing on his roundabout route, Vespasian marched his army south to Bethleptenpha, in the toparchy of Judea, before sweeping into parts of Idumea – again implementing a scorched-earth policy. Turning north through Samaritis and past Neapolis, he set up a camp at Corea on 2 June.[9] Jericho was next in Vespasian's sights. The famous 'City of Palms' was one of the oldest cities in the world, with settlements dating back as far as 9,000 BC. Situated in a barren region around thirty kilometres north-west of Jerusalem, it was blessed by numerous springs that allowed productive irrigation. Many inhabitants had already abandoned Jericho for the hill country facing Jerusalem before the Romans arrived. Vespasian rendezvoused with Traianus and his X *Fretensis* at Jericho on the following day and found the city deserted. Nevertheless, he hunted down many refugees who had failed to make it far from the area.[10] After an odd detour to the Dead Sea, where he threw bound captives into the water to test its reputation for buoyancy, Vespasian returned to the serious work of limiting access around Jerusalem by garrisoning additional locations, including placing X *Fretensis* at Jericho and other troops at Adida.[11] Each was manned with a mix of Romans and auxiliaries.

Vespasian next returned to his main base at Caesarea, where discussions with his *consilium* led him to conclude that conditions were suitable for an attack on Jerusalem. Order had been restored in most areas, the capital was effectively surrounded, allies remained supportive and established supply chains were in place. Plans were therefore prepared for imminent action. However, a dispatch reached Vespasian at the end of June informing him of an event that would change the Roman world – the death of Nero. This would trigger the civil conflict to follow: *bellum Neronis* (Nero's war). Titus was made privy to the news either immediately or soon after. He is not mentioned at all in accounts of the start of the campaign in 68 and had continued his diplomatic dealings with Mucianus, shuttling back and forth between Caesarea and Antioch.[12] Understandably, Vespasian called an immediate halt to the campaign against Jerusalem, as his mandate to command had expired with the death of Nero, who had granted it. In real terms his authority persisted, but his prudent nature was to await orders from Nero's successor.

What had led to Nero's death? When Vindex revolted against Nero back in March, he had won the support of the governor of Hispania Tarraconensis, Servius Sulpicius Galba, who commanded one legion. Vindex urged Galba, an elder statesman, to claim the Principate and, after some hesitation, he declared his hand on 3 April. Marcus Salvius Otho, the governor of Lusitania and quaestor of Baetica, sided with Galba. Nero was now alarmed and summoned forces to Northern Italy under Petronius Turpilianus.

From mid-April, the sequence of events is blurred, and to complicate matters, Clodius Macer, legate of Africa, rose in revolt but did not side with Galba or Vindex. Verginius Rufus, governor of Germania Superior, intervened – initially on behalf of Nero – and he had the might of three legions at his back. However, Verginius appears to have struggled to control his army who urged him to claim the Principate for himself. At some time in May there was a confused negotiation between Verginius and Vindex, during which Verginius dropped his loyalty to Nero. In the end, though, there was a battle and the Vindex's revolt was crushed; Vindex took his own life. Verginius refused his army's calls to become emperor and deferred to the Senate's authority. Next, in a further complication, rumours reached Rome that Nero's general in northern Italy, Petronius, was at best doing nothing – or, worse, had abandoned his fealty to Nero.[13]

Galba, *denarius*, struck *ca.* July 68–January 69, Rome mint. Reverse, *diva* Julia Augusta (Livia). *Sear I, no.2012v.*

Nero was distraught and falsely believed that all his armies had defected. He might have been able to rally certain legions but he lacked the leadership qualities to do so and his support in Rome was dwindling.[14] In panic mode, he made a feeble and abortive attempt to flee Rome for Alexandria. Shortly after, rising in the early hours in his palatial Golden House, Nero realised that his bodyguards had deserted him. He fled with a few faithful freedmen to one of their houses outside Rome. The Praetorian Guard were persuaded by one of their prefects to declare for Galba and the Senate seized the moment by declaring Nero a public enemy. On 9 June, aware of approaching Praetorian Guards who had tracked him down, Nero committed suicide with the aid of Epaphroditus, his private secretary.[15] His demise, after a reign of thirteen years, marked the end of the great Julio-Claudian line of emperors.

Civil War and the Flavian Bid for Empire

Vespasian and Titus received further details of Nero's demise and the new Principate under Galba as more messages arrived from Rome. The reconquest of Judea remained on hold. The subjugation of an entire lost province, requiring three legions and allied forces, would benefit from endorsement from the new emperor to proceed.[16] Meanwhile, the situation in Jerusalem continued to deteriorate due to class and sectarian conflicts, exacerbated by the burning of the city's enormous grain stocks in the ensuing chaos. Several months passed without instructions from the new emperor, making Vespasian increasingly impatient. Finally, the removal of his brother Sabinus from his post as prefect of Rome prompted Vespasian to send Titus to Rome, accompanied by Herod Agrippa. Titus, now recognised as an astute diplomat, was told to judge how the Flavii stood with Galba and to solicit instructions for the war. Another reason for Titus to travel to Rome was the opportunity for him to canvas for a praetorship because his approaching twenty-ninth birthday on 30 December would make him eligible.[17] He embarked on his journey late in 68 with plans to sail by the coastal route passing Phoenicia, Cilicia, Lycia, Greece and finally across to the heel of Italy. Envisioning a 6–8 week journey, assuming no requirement to stop for bad weather, Titus had ample time for reading correspondence and contemplating the critical assignment that awaited him in Rome.

While the voyagers sailed along the Greek coastline in early February, unnerving news reached them: the Emperor Galba had been assassinated in the forum in Rome on 15 January 69. Galba's brief reign, fraught with ill-advised decisions and unpopular policies, had sown deep discontent. The legions from Germania had quickly abandoned him, declaring Aulus Vitellius emperor two weeks earlier on 2 January. Galba's desperate efforts, including adopting Lucius Calpurnius Piso Licinianus as his son, had failed to quell the turmoil. Otho, the co-mutineer, was deeply vexed at being passed over and had orchestrated Galba's assassination by a group of Praetorian thugs. The new heir, Licinianus, was also murdered. Otho then delivered a speech to the Senate, falsely claiming to have been called on in the street by the Praetorian Guard and taken to their camp where he accepted the Principate, a choice which the Senate ratified despite the distant claims of Vitellius.[18] Rome and its empire were in turmoil.

Otho, *denarius*, struck 15 January–8 March 69, Rome mint. Reverse, *Securitas*. Otho is known to have worn hairpieces as can be clearly seen on his bust. *Sear I, no.2163v.*

Amidst this imperial tempest, Titus faced an important decision. Should he go ahead and lobby Otho or return to his father in Judea to avoid the instability in Rome? He decided on the latter, while Herod Agrippa, who saw no threat to himself personally, continued to the capital. Part of Titus' reasoning was almost certainly based at this time on the realisation that his father could make a bid for the Principate. The Praetorian Guard and the legions were emperor-makers and the pedigree of claimants was less important than before. Titus might have been one of the first to consider his father's opportunities.[19] Moreover, his dealings with Mucianus might have provided a sense that the Syrian governor could be won over. With the Egyptian forces as well, Vespasian could potentially rally eight legions.[20] In addition, Titus' uncle in Rome may have discreetly conveyed the sentiment that many senators would unite behind Vespasian, given the chaotic situation and the poor reputations of Otho and particularly Vitellius.[21] Lastly, Titus would have calculated that Otho's chances against the hardened Rhine legions were poor unless he rapidly secured support from the majority of the Danubian legions.[22]

During Titus' return trip, guided by a superstitious impulse, he sought reassurance from the oracle of the Paphian Aphrodite in Cyprus, a deeply religious centre, on the future of the Flavii.[23] Then, on reaching the Syrian coast, he almost certainly detoured to Antioch for a crucial meeting with Mucianus.[24] Their relationship had solidified over several months following Titus' efforts to engage and build trust. Private conversations would have reflected on the turmoil in Rome and Titus would have probed Mucianus' view on the possibility of his father claiming imperial power. Putting aside the prior differences and tensions between the Judean and Syrian governors, Mucianus sensed Vespasian's potential to restore Rome's imperial dignity. He may have also appreciated that an Eastern revolt would have a good chance of rallying the Danubian legions. This tête-à-tête was arguably a major turning point in Rome's history, and Titus' diplomatic skills seem to have tipped the delicate balance of power within the Empire.

Eventually back in Caesarea, Titus found that the legions had declared for Otho, a move that would later lend legitimacy to Vespasian should he move against Vitellius.[25] Titus had much to discuss with his father and he possibly played an essential role in persuading him to think more actively about seizing the Principate.[26] He would have conveyed his private conversations with Mucianus, and Vespasian, fully in charge of the situation, brought trusted senior officers such as Traianus and Cerialis into the secret fold.[27] Vespasian had to consider a complex series of interrelated factors during such confidential conversations. First and foremost, he needed to secure all eight of the Eastern legions, so the news that Mucianus appeared receptive was fundamentally important and moreover the Syrian governor seemed to like Titus. The prefect in Egypt, Tiberius Julius Alexander (hereafter Tiberius Alexander), with his two legions, could be firmly counted on.[28] Not to be forgotten, the support of key allies such as Herod Agrippa II and Antiochus IV of Commagene was a crucial source of additional military power.[29] King Antiochus IV may have personally led the last Hellenistic pikemen during the Jewish War.[30] Secondly, Vespasian needed to ensure he had sufficient cash to pay his troops and secure the necessary supplies for any large military operation. Third, he needed to engage clandestinely with Danubian legion commanders he fully trusted to know how they would respond to his move. Vespasian could count on the loyalty of III *Gallica*, which had been transferred from Syria to Moesia, and he expected the other Balkan legions would follow its lead.[31] Fourthly, his brother had been reinstated as prefect of Rome and through him Vespasian needed cautiously to gauge the atmosphere in the Senate. Last but not least, Vespasian had the novelty of two adult sons who would offer a unique dynastic stability to the Principate not seen before.[32] Vespasian's judicious nature required all these aspects to be set up before he would give the order for action.

In March as these contemplations matured, Vespasian ordered limited military operations in Judea and Idumea, although the main campaign remained on hold. Simon ben Giora had managed to destabilise the district of Acrabata, north of Jerusalem, and parts of Upper Idumea.[33] Vespasian led detachments of his army into the former region and quelled the situation. Cerialis, with a cavalry and infantry division, stormed through northern Idumea to restore order.[34] Simon ben Giora managed to evade capture and ended up in Jerusalem. Throughout this period, sedition and carnage continued to plague the residents of Jerusalem due to the incessant infighting between various factions unable to settle their bitter ideological and political differences.

In early May, Vespasian returned to Caesarea, where bulletins reported the grim consequences of civil war. Otho had rallied legions to his side and his outnumbered army clashed with Vitellius' troops on 14 April east of Cremona in Cisalpine Gaul (Northern Italy) at the first Battle of Bedriacum (Calvatone).[35] Neither Otho nor Vitellius were present at the battle; they relied on their generals. Otho's legions were no match for the battle-hardened Rhine veterans and Vitellius' men were victorious, but there were enormous casualties on both sides.[36] Otho committed suicide on

16 April after a reign of only three months. The Senate proclaimed Vitellius emperor on 19 April, although he was never acknowledged across the whole Roman Empire. Titus' uncle, Sabinus II, in Rome had no choice but to swear his Urban Cohort's allegiance to Vitellius. After the Battle of Bedriacum, Vitellius went to see the scenes of conflict

> It was a revolting and ghastly sight: not forty days had passed since the battle, and on every side were mutilated corpses, severed limbs, rotting bodies of men and horses, the ground soaked with filth and gore, trees overthrown and crops trampled down in appalling devastation.
>
> *Tacitus*[37]

Up to this point, Vitellius appears to have been vigorous in his efforts and displayed excellent organisational abilities to have rallied so many legions behind him and defeated Otho.[38] However, his unnecessary decision to march his entire army of 60,000 towards Rome at a leisurely rate, plundering communities in their path, revealed his true character.

Vitellius, *denarius*, struck *ca.* May–July 69, Rome mint. Reverse, *Libertas*.
Sear I, no. 2198.

These harrowing outcomes of civil war were a turning point for Vespasian, who by now had squared away all he needed to move robustly against Vitellius. He would not make the same mistakes as Galba, Otho and Vitellius and would seek a deeper military and political level of support. Further assurances of support from Mucianus, through secret correspondence and Titus' diplomacy, would have been an essential requirement. Lacking subtlety, even some of his officers and soldiers now pressured Vespasian to seize the Principate.[39] Thus, with a limited number of his most trusted advisors, Vespasian convened a special *consilium* in Caesarea with Titus, Traianus and Cerialis, and now decided on revolt.[40] Nevertheless, a summit was required with Mucianus to ratify all the details because a final agreement between the two powerful governors had not been made. Mount Carmel was selected as the venue for this alignment in the first half of June.[41]

Despite these decisions, the Eastern legions declared for Vitellius, at least for the moment, though many officers and soldiers were aware that the tide might well turn.

Mount Carmel is in a coastal range north of Caesarea within the province of Syria not far from Galilee. The actual location was close to a mysterious altar to a pagan god with no image or temple, and presumably a legionary field camp hosted the attendees. It is not clear why this site was selected, although its central position and spiritual significance may have played a part, since Vespasian made a sacrifice on the enigmatic altar.[42] The *Praetorium*, the commander's field tent, may have been the scene where all the major stakeholders gathered for the summit: Vespasian, Mucianus, Titus, Traianus, Cerialis, Tiberius Alexander and several senior officers representing the Syrian legions.[43] The most trusted client kings would have also been present. The highly prestigious event would have been a series of private discussions that reviewed and agreed the process by which the eastern legions would proclaim their allegiance to Vespasian. The climax of the conference was a compelling speech delivered by Mucianus. He asserted Vespasian's virtues over Vitellius and made it clear he was not a rival but an avid sponsor, prepared to share the risks and dangers of the civil war that lay ahead.[44] Mucianus was indeed Vespasian's most essential partner. They complemented each other extremely well. Vespasian was the battle-hardened military leader who led by example. He was down-to-earth, frugal and 'hardly differed from the common soldier'.[45] By contrast, Mucianus was more flamboyant and better-known. He was a competent orator and an astute civil administrator and statesman.[46]

Vespasian moved on from Mount Carmel to Caesarea and, in the second half of June, Titus was again sent to Antioch to meet Mucianus and fine-tune details of the Eastern revolt. With everything in place, the precise process of the Eastern legions swearing allegiance to the new Emperor Vespasian began in Alexandria on 1 July.[47] Tiberius Alexander administered the oath of allegiance to III *Cyrenaica* and four cohorts of Legio XVIII. Two days later, on 3 July, the Judean legions – V *Macedonica*, XV *Apollinaris*, and X *Fretensis* – swore their loyalty. On 15 July, all the Syrian legions – IV *Scythica*, VI *Ferrata* and XII *Fulminata* – followed suit. Mucianus spoke to crowds in a theatre in Antioch to express his support for Vespasian.[48] Rome had two emperors again: Vitellius in the West and Vespasian in the East.

The clandestine planning and choreography of these events was not the image Vespasian wanted to project to the Roman world. Through propaganda and allowance for popular rumours, Vespasian implied that the devoted Eastern legions were greatly dismayed by Vitellius' actions and spontaneously took matters into their own hands by hailing him emperor to save Rome and that he accepted the burden of power reluctantly.[49]

In late July, a regal assembly was convened in Berytus (Beirut), where Vespasian hosted provincial delegates, regional embassies and dignitaries.[50] This grand council served as a display of stately splendour and, more importantly, a platform to fortify Vespasian's new authority. Mucianus, accompanied by senior officers, distinguished centurions and selected legionaries, stood by the new emperor's side. Herod Agrippa, who had discreetly left Rome, graced the occasion along with Berenice and other key allies. Amidst military parades to display the might of Vespasian's armed capabilities, pivotal decisions were made. When Vespasian's position was secure, Titus would assume command of the Jewish War, with Tiberius Alexander as his chief of staff; Mucianus would lead an expeditionary force against Vitellius in the West, while Vespasian himself would journey to Alexandria.[51] Vespasian wanted only to get involved as a last resort; he intended to take as little part as possible in the horrors of civil war; and his presence in Egypt offered strategic control over Rome's crucial grain supply if the need arose.[52] In reality, the Jewish War paled in significance at this point for Vespasian, on the cusp of becoming the Emperor of Rome, if Vitellius could be removed.

Preceding these next moves, a flurry of activities unfolded in late July and early August: veterans were summoned; towns were mobilised for production of arms; bullion was minted in Antioch and a modest financial incentive was pledged to the troops. Deputations were dispatched to Armenia and Parthia to ensure peace. Letters also went to all armies and commanders, signalling Vespasian's open arms for the disbanded Othonian Praetorian Guard.[53] Having now gone to Antioch himself, Vespasian, almost certainly accompanied by Titus, attended to the last details of Mucianus' campaign before his departure. By mid-August, news from Rome painted a chaotic picture of the Vitellian army flooding the streets, taverns and brothels, plunging the city into anarchy. The behaviour of the new emperor mirrored the prevailing pandemonium. Encouraging reports indicated that III *Gallica* in Moesia had declared for Vespasian and other Danubian legions were poised to follow suit.[54]

At this juncture, it is essential to comprehend the circumstances in Rome for Titus' younger brother, Domitian, who was now charting his own course towards imperial power as a potential heir. Eleven years and ten months Titus' junior, Domitian had not received an education at the imperial court and had limited contact with close relatives during his formative years. Despite later historians' vilification of Domitian, it is more plausible that he was a very capable young man. In the summer of 69, at the age of seventeen, he was still a few years away from qualifying for a vigintivirate position to initiate his senatorial career. After Vespasian's proclamation, Domitian was held under house arrest by Vitellius, serving as a hostage and a bargaining chip.[55] His uncle, Sabinus II, would conduct negotiations on behalf of the Flavii in Rome.

Back in the East, Mucianus set out in mid-August on the overland route to Italy with VI *Ferrata*, 13,000 veteran reservists, 2,000 legionary detachments from each Judean legion and various auxiliaries – a total force of around 30,000 men.[56] The fleet in the Black Sea was ordered to concentrate at Byzantium (Istanbul).[57] The expeditionary force was relatively small but it was known by then that other legions could be collected en route through the Balkan provinces. The long march over two months was uneventful and Mucianus reached Moesia in mid-October. However, back in early September, Antonius Primus, legate of VII *Galbiana* in Pannonia, with support from Cornelius Fuscus, the procurator of Illyricum, had decided not to wait for Mucianus, despite Vespasian's instruction to hold off. Primus, joined by Arrius Varus, made a dash into northern Italy and occupied the region of Patavium (Padua). They were then joined by two Pannonian legions as the army went on to control Verona by the end of September.

In response, Vitellius sent his general Caecina towards Cremona with detachments from several legions, cavalry and auxiliaries. Many of the troops were a shadow of their former selves after months of leave and indulgence in Rome. Valens, another of Vitellius' generals, would follow later due to a sickness.[58] In early October, Caecina arrived at Hostilla (Ostiglia). Caecina had an overwhelming numerical advantage with which he could have crushed the limited Flavian forces under Primus, but instead he set up a base at Hostilla and deployed two legions to defend Cremona. Evidently, Caecina was planning to betray Vitellius, having witnessed the shambles of his Principate in Rome. This crucially allowed the additional Moesian legions under the governor, Aponius Saturninus, to join Primus by the middle of October at the time when Mucianus was arriving in Moesia. Next, a series of defections seriously undermined Vitellius' position. The large Adriatic fleet at Ravenna went over to the Flavians on 17 October and the next day Caecina abandoned Vitellius.[59] However, the defecting general failed to bring his forces over with him before loyalists captured him and put him in custody.[60] The Vitellians then moved their whole army to Cremona and Primus reacted by moving his forces to within forty kilometres of Bedriacum.[61]

The stage was set for a second Battle of Bedriacum within six months of the first. Mass graves and the devastation from the first battle were still evident in the area. Over two intense days, 24 and 25 October, the clash between Flavian and Vitellian forces took a brutal toll, with Cremona caught in the crossfire. The Vitellian forces had no commanding general: Vitellius was in Rome, Valens ill and Caecina under arrest for conspiracy. Primus emerged victorious but lost control of his troops, who were hell-bent on retribution and pillage, resulting in the sack of Cremona. The once great Italian city paid a heavy price for its perceived allegiance to the Vitellians, its inhabitants slaughtered by the victorious forces.[62] At this point in the civil war, Italy was essentially divided between the two opposing armies by the Apennines, with Vespasian in Alexandria and Vitellius in Rome. Recovered from his illness, Valens sailed to Gaul to raise a new army. Fate had different plans, as a storm led to his capture and subsequent execution.

Refusing to acknowledge the grim reality, Vitellius posted Praetorians and marines to guard the Apennine passes, attempting to stem the tide of attrition in Italy,[63] but support still ebbed away from him, and he saw his dominion reduced to Rome and the surrounding region of Latium.[64] In the heart of Rome, Sabinus II, oddly still allowed to oversee the city cohorts and night watchmen, hesitated to attack the remaining Vitellian troops. Impaired by age and motivated by a desire for negotiation, he rather sought to persuade Vitellius to surrender. After private negotiations, the City Prefect convinced Vitellius to capitulate, only to abandon his surrender later under pressure from advisors.[65] In reality, there was no viable retirement path for the embattled emperor who had played his part in dragging the empire into civil war.

The possibility of Vitellius' abdication backfired on Sabinus. As he descended the Quirinal Hill, escorted by an armed retinue, he encountered fervent Vitellian supporters who may have heard about the negotiations. Seeking refuge, he led a retreat up the Capitoline Hill, a defensible position centred around the Temple of Jupiter. As the poorly coordinated Vitellian siege progressed, Sabinus' sons and Domitian managed to join the besieged. Botched communications between Sabinus and Vitellius failed to establish a solution; by now Vitellius' remaining military and civilian supporters were a mob beyond his control. The following day, 19 December, witnessed intense fighting, culminating in a fire that consumed the glorious Temple of Jupiter. This ignominious event, seen once before, during the civil war between Marius and Sulla in 83 BC, would have stunned those who witnessed the ominous glow of the fires from various corners of Rome. The gods had abandoned Rome. Sabinus was captured and dragged before Vitellius, who was unable to save the prefect. The enraged throng mutilated and beheaded him, hurling his headless body down the Gemonian stairs. It was a tragic and ignoble moment for the Flavii for Sabinus to have perished in such a manner after thirty-five years of statesmanship. Domitian, very fortunate to escape the besieged Capitoline in what must have been a cunning disguise, found secret refuge within the city.[66] Sabinus' sons also escaped.

On the following morning, Primus arrived at the gates of Rome and his legions stormed the city to purge all Vitellian resistance. Fierce street fighting ensued, house to house and temple to temple, until the Praetorian Camp was the last refuge for Vitellian soldiers. It was the scene of bitter fighting to the last Vitellian standing.[67] Finding himself completely abandoned within the imperial palace, Vitellius was apprehended and his hands bound behind his back. His clothes were stripped and zealous captors assaulted him. He was forced to watch his statues being torn down and was then dragged to the spot where Galba had been killed in the forum. Excrement and other filth were thrown at him and he was tortured by numerous little cuts. Finally, at the Gemonian steps where Sabinus' body had so recently been discarded, a volley of blows ended the macabre episode, Vitellius' body being mutilated long after he was dead.[68] It was 20 December and Vitellius had reigned for only eight months.

It was impossible for the Senate to convene and manage the situation because the members were scattered and in hiding. Nevertheless, Domitian emerged from his concealment and was hailed '*Caesar*' to recognise his status as an heir to the Principate. Soldiers swarmed around him for his protection.[69] The prefecture of the Praetorian Guard was awarded to Arrius Varus and central authority in Rome was exercised by Antonius Primus while Mucianus approached Rome.[70] On 21 December, the Senate voted Vespasian all the honours and privileges usually given to the emperors.[71] The devastating civil war was over.

Mucianus reached Rome when the Senate was proclaiming Vespasian and found the city in great disorder. He was empowered by the new emperor to take control and was authorised to act on his own initiative. Symbolically, Mucianus was given a ring with the new imperial seal and, in collaboration with Domitian, they made senatorial appointments, including consuls.[72] This was an extremely important activity in which Flavian loyalists and supporters were rewarded and the process would gradually convert representation in the Senate towards Vespasian's principles.[73] Mucianus also had to deal with an acute situation related to the Praetorian Guard. The Othonian Praetorians, dismissed by Vitellius, were demanding their lucrative positions back. Select Flavian legionaries earmarked to become Guards were vying for the same positions. Moreover, a decision was required regarding the Vitellian Praetorian Guards. To resolve the issue, Mucianus mustered all the Guards and claimants, and each soldier was assessed one at a time to whittle down the force to a suitable number of the best Praetorians. It is probable that nine cohorts were created, each with 1,000 men.[74]

Far away in Egypt, Vespasian learned before the close of 69 of Primus' victory at Bedriacum in November but not yet the news of his brother's and Vitellius' deaths and the Senate's recognition of him as emperor.[75] Titus was probably still with his father in Alexandria at the time.[76] In a pre-arranged move that assumed victory had been achieved, on 1 January, Vespasian and Titus were proclaimed as Rome's two consuls, *in absentia*, a highly symbolic move to begin solidifying the Flavian dynasty. It was a monumental moment for Vespasian, master of the Roman world, ruler of the superpower of its day. Titus is not known to have held the praetorship typically required before a consulship but that role was now superfluous.[77] Titus and Domitian shared in the historic occasion as designated heirs and coins were churned out at mints showing the two Flavian sons on the obverse as *Caesares*.[78] The turbulent Year of Four Emperors was over.

Vespasian, *denarius*, struck January–June 70, Rome mint. Reverse, bare heads
of Titus and Domitian as *caesares*, each with a short beard.
RIC II 16; RSC 5; BMCRE 368.

CHAPTER 6

THE DESTRUCTION OF JERUSALEM

After experiencing an early imperial period spanning several decades marked by the relative stability of the Julio-Claudian successions, the Roman Empire fell apart in 69. In that single tumultuous year, four emperors had grappled for the Principate, reawakening the spectre of the devastating civil wars that had once torn at the very fabric of the hegemony following the collapse of the Republic. In the midst of this chaos, Vespasian had emerged as the new emperor, ascending to the purple and restoring order. Titus and his brother Domitian were designated heirs, and Titus as the elder was the likely immediate successor.

Vespasian remained in Alexandria until the summer of 70 when favourable conditions permitted a safe crossing to Rome.[1] Besides, he was in no apparent rush to return to Rome and more concerned with settling strategic issues in the East prior to departing. Again, we see that Vespasian wanted to be in charge until he was fully satisfied with the situation. The veteran Traianus, now a highly trusted confidant of the new emperor, had been relieved of his legionary command in 69 and joined Vespasian in Egypt. He would later accompany Vespasian back to Rome as a *comes*, companion of the emperor.[2]

In the meantime, in the spring of 70, Titus had travelled to Caesarea where he mustered an army for the capture of Jerusalem, postponed during the civil wars.[3] The young general had the complicated task of assembling the force he needed by marshalling together legions of varying strengths and detachments from others.[4] With his senior officers in attendance, he promptly set about the crucial organisation of supplies and the initiation of military plans for the campaign ahead.

Roman Command

The command of the campaign in 70 against the heavily defended city of Jerusalem was a defining moment in Titus' military career, a pivotal conquest that would characterise the start of the Flavian dynasty and a historic crisis for the Jews, who had suffered innumerable losses in the preceding years. As before in earlier campaigns, the Roman command structure for the attack on Jerusalem was typical of a large force of the period and the senior officers would have been carefully hand-picked jointly by Vespasian and Titus:

Titus Vespasianus   General of Roman forces in Judea and overall commander of all the armed forces. All strategic decisions and, where possible, all major tactical decisions, required his approval.

Tiberius Alexander Camp Prefect and chief of staff to Titus. Previously procurator of Judea and as prefect of Egypt the first to hail Vespasian emperor as an old trusted friend. This was possibly an appointment by Vespasian, perhaps wary of fully trusting his son and wanting Tiberius Alexander to assist closely.[5] He was effectively second-in-command.

Sextus Vettulenus Cerialis

Legate of V *Macedonica*, taking orders from Titus and with a direct commission from Vespasian to command the legion. Cerialis had led V *Macedonica* during the earlier campaigns of 67 and 68.

Larcius Lepidus Sulpicianus

Legate of X *Fretensis*, taking over from Traianus probably in the second half of 69.[6] A quaestorship in Crete and Cyrenaica immediately preceded this post, either in 67 or 68.[7] He was well known by the Flavii and belonged to a group of officers who were promoted rapidly under Vespasian.[8]

Marcus Tittius Frugi   Legate of XV *Apollinaris*, taking over from Titus.[9] Little is known about Frugi but he was possibly a trusted colleague of Titus rather than of Vespasian.[10]

Unknown

The tribune in charge of XII *Fulminata* is unidentified, perhaps because no senator wanted to lead the disgraced legion until it had redeemed itself.[11]

Unknown

An unknown tribune was in charge of detachments from IV *Scythica* based in Zeugma.

C. Aeternius Fronto   Tribune in charge of detachments from III *Cyrenaica* and Legio XVIII, from Egypt.[12] A friend and client of Titus.[13]

Notable officers

Ti. Julius Celsus Polemaeanus, tribune of III *Cyrenaica*.[14]

Gaius Velius Rufus, *primus pilus* of XII *Fulminata*, previously a highly decorated centurion in XV *Apollinaris* during the Japha assault.[15]

Nicanor, tribune.[16]

Domitius Sabinus, tribune.[17]

Consilarii

Senior commanders and the procurator of Judea, Marcus Antonius Julianus.[18] Josephus may have earned a place by now. Similar to Vespasian's *consilium* there were almost certainly representatives of the *tribuni militum* (military tribunes), the *praefecti castrorum* (camp prefects) and the *primi pili*. Herod Agrippa II and other senior allied commanders were almost certainly trusted advisors invited to this group.

Jewish Command

After months of bitter infighting, three individuals – Eleazar ben Simon, John ben Levi and Simon ben Giora – emerged as leaders responsible for the defence of Jerusalem. Each commanded a section of the city, and their factions engaged in open conflict. The internal strife between them knew no bounds, and the futile hostilities led to a large number of casualties, the destruction of areas around the Temple and the transformation of the entire city into a 'desolate no man's land'.[19] In short, the absence of a central, coordinated command and the relentless partisan infighting played into the hands of Titus.

Eleazar ben Simon   Military commander appointed in 66 after the new coalition government was formed.[20] Present at the Battle of Beth Horon, he captured Cestius' lost war chest and was leader of a Zealot group.[21] Eleazar and his Zealots had seized control of the inner courts of the Temple and the sacred facade above the Holy Gates.[22] Fate unknown.

John ben Levi   Unofficial Galilean general who roamed the countryside in 66 before leading the revolt at Gischala.[23] After his arrival in Jerusalem, he tried to seize control of the city but was challenged by Simon ben Giora in April 69. In turn they were both challenged by Eleazar ben Simon. John controlled much of the city as well as the outer parts of the Temple complex and the immediate surrounding areas, including the Ophel.[24]

Simon ben Giora   Called in by the people of Jerusalem, he had control of the Upper City, parts of the First Wall and sections of the Lower City.[25]

Jacob ben Sosas   One of the Idumean leaders whose fighters made a significant contribution towards the defence of Jerusalem.[26]

Simon ben Cathlas Like Jacob, one of the Idumean leaders.[27]

Roman Troops

Making an assault on Jerusalem, while also policing the region against any resurgence, necessitated a large Roman force and sufficient reserves. The estimates below have considered attrition and other factors to arrive at a realistic strength for Titus.

Legions

V *Macedonica*, X *Fretensis*, XV *Apollinaris*	around 8,600 legionaries because detachments sent with Mucianus were still in the West.[28]
XII *Fulminata*	5,700 in total.[29]
Detachments from III *Cyrenaica* and Legio XVIII in Egypt	a total of 2,000 men to make up for shortfalls in detachments mentioned above.
Detachments from IV *Scythica*	3,000 men, also to help make up numbers.[30]
	Total legionaries around 19,300.[31]

Cavalry and Auxiliaries

A selection of auxiliary infantry cohorts and cavalry squadrons were pooled from Syria, Judea and Egypt, comparable to the prior campaigns. Additionally, 'substantial numbers of Syrian auxiliaries' were mustered.[32] In all, around 16,000 infantry and 9,000 cavalry.[33]

Allies

The contribution from allies was increased compared to the previous campaigns and further expanded by a strong Arab contingent. Around 25,000 troops in total.[34] Herod Agrippa II and King Sohaemus accompanied their own troops.

Titus' Total Force

The above give a grand total of around 69,000 armed men, made up of 19,300 legionaries, 9,000 cavalry and 16,000 infantry auxiliaries and the rest allied forces. Each legion was assigned an artillery corps, organised in the same way as at Jotapata (*see above*), with a total here of around 240 artillery machines.[35]

Jewish Forces

These included:

> 10,000 armed followers of Simon ben Giora, combined with 5,000 Idumeans
> 6,000 armed adherents of John ben Levi
> 2,400 Zealots under Eleazar ben Simon.[36]

This suggests a total of around 20,000 armed fighters garrisoning the city's defences. Many weapons had been taken from fallen Romans and they possessed the missile artillery captured during Cestius' retreat in 66.[37]

Roman Strategy

After much discussion with his father before leaving Alexandria and further debate with his own *consilium*, as well as reviewing countless military intelligence reports, Titus decided on a traditional siege strategy. The first objective would be to camp his forces in elevated positions surrounding Jerusalem and to clear the vicinity of obstacles to improve access. The western third wall protecting the New Town would be the target for the first breach to avoid the precipitous slopes that protected the walls around the old quarters of the Upper and Lower City. Absolutely no mercy would be shown and there would be no concern for the preservation of the city nor the Temple.[38] Negotiations would be offered only if they spared Roman resources and accelerated the capture of the capital.

Jerusalem

It is crucial to understand the layout of Jerusalem, as it was to the Romans, to appreciate the magnitude of attacking and defending the city.[39] It is important to note that, balancing all available historic, archaeological, topographical and modern interpretations, it is assumed here that the Antonia Fort was not a small attachment to the Temple, as traditionally presented, but rather the site of the fortress is where the Temple Mount is today. The following description, proceeding broadly from north to south, outlines the general structure and topography of the city and accompanies the map included in the plate section:

General location: Jerusalem is nestled in the Judean Mountains on a series of limestone hills. The northern half of the capital, called the New Town, had evolved to house the growing population and spread out over an area that lacked any natural protection, necessitating the construction of two walls. The older districts, called the Old City, occupied the lower, southern half of the city and straddled two elevated areas divided by the Tyropoeon Valley, running through the urbanised part from north to south. The higher, south-western lower half was called the Upper City and the south-eastern half the Lower City. Natural rocky defences surrounded the entire southern half with the Hinnom Valley to the west and south and the Kidron Valley to the east. The Mount of Olives, standing over 800 metres above sea level, lay directly east of the Temple, on the other side of the Kidron Valley.

The New Town and the Third Wall: The most recently urbanised area, not yet densely inhabited, covered a little over three-quarters of a square kilometre. Large areas remained in ruins since October 66 following Cestius' torching of the region during the initial uprisings.[40] This area was surrounded by a wall around two metres thick. The wall included numerous towers and ran north for around 750 metres from the large Hippicus Tower (generally identified with the foundations of the Tower of David located near the Jaffa Gate entrance to the Old City) to the formidable octagonal Psephinus Tower, standing thirty-two metres high, which defended the north-western corner of the New Town. Here, this Third Wall turned east for about 1.3 kilometres before turning south for around a kilometre to link up with the Antonia Fort.[41] Overall, the Third Wall was of varying levels of quality and finish along its course but there is evidence of solid foundations.[42]

Second Wall: The Second Wall aimed to protect a newer district north of the older boundaries, enclosing a quarter of the New Town. Starting from the First Wall in the vicinity of the Gennath Gate, it arched around and joined the Antonia Fort.[43]

First Wall: The oldest wall ran in one direction from the Hippicus Tower to the Xystus (a colonnaded area used for gymnasts and for public assemblies) and terminated at a vaulted bridge across to the Temple's western portico. In the other direction it ran from the Hippicus, south past Herod's Palace to the Essene Gate, where it turned east and along the southern end of the city before turning north around the Siloam Pool and reservoir to join up with the perimeter of the Temple.[44]

The Second Temple: As much a fortress, as the religious epicentre for the Jewish faith, the Temple covered a precinct area on the south-eastern side of Jerusalem near the Gihon Spring.[45] Tall high-quality walls had been built on enormous elevating foundations and surrounded the outer courtyards with towers in the southern corners. Built against the walls, elegant white marble colonnaded porticoes thirteen metres deep supported roof ramparts around the entire outer perimeter. Several entrances allowed access from numerous locations. The outer courtyard, the Court of Gentiles, was the outer public area, the place described in the New Testament from where Jesus expelled the throngs of moneylenders and traders.[46] A latticed railing demarcated the elevated inner courts from which any non-Jew was strictly forbidden. In the centre of the whole complex stood the three-storey-high Temple that the Jews considered the House of the Lord from which his divine presence emanated from the Holy of the Holies. Surrounded by its own fortified walls, one could enter from the east past a vast Corinthian Bronze Gate into the Court of Women, where Jewish women were permitted. Next steps led up to the largest gate into the Court of the Israelites, reserved for ritually pure Jewish men, beyond which a parapet marked the Court of Priests. This spiritual space had a sacrificial altar and areas where priests could make offerings. Here one could gaze up at the magnificent Temple tabernacle fronted by dazzling bright white marble and gold relief on all its surround, beyond which the inner sanctuary preceded the innermost chamber, the Holy of Holies. This was screened by curtains and no one was allowed to enter except the High Priest. It is thought the Second Temple was built on the site of the First Temple constructed by King Solomon to house, amongst other treasures, the Ark of the Covenant. The First was destroyed by

Nebuchadrezzar II of Babylon and was seen as the fulfilment of a prophecy that strengthened Jewish monotheism. This history partially explains the fanatical defence of the Second Temple.

Antonia Fort: Constructed by Herod the Great to protect the Temple and named after his patron, Mark Antony, the fortress was located north of the Temple. The formidable structure on a raised area had housed the Roman garrison and the 'overall design was that of a tower with four further towers rising from it, one in each corner'. Reaching over thirty metres in height, it would have dominated the skyline of the city.[47] It occupied a considerable area given that it contained military quarters, palatial accommodation, cloisters, baths, barracks and an open courtyard where soldiers could camp. Its southern end may have been around 180 metres away from the northern walls of the Temple perimeter and the two were possibly connected by bridge walkways and stairways, as well as an elegant plaza in-between known as the Ophel (*see below*).[48]

Herod's Palace: Constructed on an elevated area up against the western wall of the Upper City, the fortified palace had provided luxurious accommodation for Herod the Great. North of the complex, Herod had built three defensive towers into the First Wall, the Hippicus, Phasael and the Mariamme, to fortify the entire area. The *praetorium*, the residence of the Roman procurator when in Jerusalem, was in the palace.

Upper City: Covering the south-western proportion of Jerusalem, this part of the Old City was on higher ground than the rest of the city, even than the Temple Mount, and was home to more affluent residents. It boasted elegant homes, open spaces and public buildings. Herod's Palace was within the Upper City.

Lower City: Occupying the lower, south-eastern part of Jerusalem, it was traditionally considered the location for poorer neighbourhoods, but it was not without large edifices.[49]

City of David: The original citadel founded by King David was the ancient centre of Jerusalem, situated on a ridge in the south-eastern quarter, west of Kidron Valley and east of the Tyropoeon Valley.

Ophel: A poorly understood zone between the Temple Mount and the Temple, it was a raised royal plaza area. The Ophel is mentioned in ancient sources as being close to the Temple complex.

Defensive Summary

The sheer scale of Jerusalem posed a daunting challenge for Titus and his legions. The lower half of the city, characterised by steep rocky ravines and well-constructed sturdy walls, presented a near-impenetrable barrier to siege engines. The Temple complex, boasting massive walls and enormous foundations, benefited from additional protection in the form of the imposing Antonia Fort. The city's strategic water supply, using tunnels to access the Gihon Spring, plus an array of cisterns within the city, added to its resilience.[50] However, the Achilles heel of the city defences was the western section of the newer Third Wall. Here, there was no natural protection and careful surveying of the fortifications would glean some weaker spots to attack. Roman knowledge of the Antonia Fort and its location relative to the Temple necessitated taking the former before the latter.[51] For example, even if the Second Wall was taken, the area between the Antonia and the Temple was a 'killing zone', given the elevated protective position of the fortress over that area.

While the extent of the defences was daunting for the Romans, the Jews faced their own set of challenges. The need to secure and defend a large perimeter, coupled with internal conflicts preventing any cooperation, made the task extremely arduous. Moreover, the substantial population swelled by Passover pilgrims posed a humanitarian crisis due to the lack of provisions. The defenders recognised the pivotal role of the Temple and Antonia Fort as bastions of resistance, envisioning retreat to these strongholds if walls were lost. Finally, the absence of any outside relief force marching to Jerusalem's rescue was a major disadvantage to the Jewish defenders. The intricate balance between imposing fortifications and tactical vulnerabilities would become a defining feature of the conflict.

The Siege

In April, confident in the readiness of his forces and supply lines, Titus set out from Caesarea with his legions, auxiliaries and allies, heading towards Jerusalem. V *Macedonica* and X *Fretensis* were directed to rendezvous with Titus just outside the city.[52] Titus ordered the establishment of a field camp for his troops in the Valley of the Thorns, approximately five kilometres north of the city.[53]

Eager to survey Jerusalem's defences, Titus decided to take 600 of his elite cavalry south towards the city for a reconnaissance. As he led the column of troopers up to the northern face of the Third Wall, lulled into a false sense of security by the absence of any visible defenders, he turned his column west off the road towards the Psephinus Tower. However, observant guards had seen the approaching column and waited for this moment to spring an attack. Surging out of a gate in the Women's Tower, a fierce group of Jewish fighters was able to break through the turning Roman column and block the road, isolating Titus and a handful of troopers at the front. This was arguably the most dangerous situation Titus had encountered since the start of the war, underscoring his rash nature. Moreover, he could not escape along the wall because the garden terracing and dividing borders were impassable on horseback. Surprisingly, to make matters even worse, the main Roman column retreated up the road, seemingly unaware their general had been isolated.[54]

Left with no other option, Titus wheeled his horse around and cried at his few cavalrymen to follow his charge directly through the mass of fighters. Titus had no breastplate or helmet, having considered the trip a scouting exercise, so the move was extremely bold. Miraculously, none of the innumerable missiles fired struck him, and he slashed his way masterfully through the mass and used his mount to barge past others. Somehow, amongst the throng of fighters, he managed to keep sufficient momentum on his mount to force his way out. It really was a near miss: two Roman cavalrymen were overwhelmed and killed in the mêlée. It seems possible that the main column that had pulled back realised by this time that Titus had been separated and were charging back to intervene when they met him in retreat.[55] This incident was a very dubious start for Titus' campaign, as well as a humiliating event for a general and his elite bodyguards. It would have prompted major changes in the way Titus was protected during the campaign and it further highlighted that the insurgents should never be underestimated. Ironically, the rebels had no idea how close they had come to killing their enemy's general and the son of Rome's emperor.

That night, V *Macedonica* arrived, and the following morning the legions built a vast field camp on an elevated area known as Mount Scopus, just over a kilometre north-east of Jerusalem.[56] As the camp took shape, X *Fretensis* also arrived and began to set up camp on the Mount of Olives. The view of these expansive camps under construction, teeming with tens of thousands of troops, must have been a sight to behold. The impact on the rebels served as a wake-up call, forcing a stark realisation that cooperation between them was an imperative.[57]

Temporarily putting aside their violent partisan differences, rebel leaders orchestrated an attack on X *Fretensis*. Emerging from various gates on the eastern side, they descended and ascended the Kidron Valley, or may have been aided by a bridge that spanned the valley.[58] During the construction of a Roman camp in a hostile environment, it was common practice for a portion of legionaries to face the enemy's direction on watch while their comrades worked on the camp. Therefore, X *Fretensis* was almost certainly not caught off guard, but rather overwhelmed by the enormous number of Jewish fighters. Despite the Jews being breathless from running across and up the slopes of the Mount of Olives, their overwhelming numbers, coupled with the irregular formation on the Roman side due to construction work, forced X *Fretensis* to abandon their campsite.[59]

Alerted to the battle, Titus led a relief column from his position on Mount Scopus and struck against the flank of the Jewish fighters.[60] This action rallied X *Fretensis* into a counter-attack. Suffering numerous casualties, the Jews were forced to retreat down the valley but held their ground on the opposite slope. The stream running through the valley became the battlefront until around midday. At that point, Titus misjudged the situation and decided to let X *Fretensis* return to camp construction. Interpreted by the Jews as a sign of retreat, this brought a massive wave of fresh fighters surging out. Despite the discipline of the Roman army, the troops defending the valley bottom broke their line and fled up the ravine, shocked by the staggering numbers of Jews swarming down on them. Despite the previous day's lesson when Titus narrowly avoided death, the retreating Roman line threatened to leave Titus isolated halfway up the ravine slope. Those close to Titus urged him to pull back with the others, but the general managed to halt the retreat and commanded a strong line on the incline. The higher ground afforded them an advantage.[61] Word spread across X *Fretensis* that their general was vulnerable, and presumably Sulpicianus gave the order to abandon camp construction again and advance down the Kidron. The height advantage eventually enabled the Romans to rout the Jews. Sensing that the rebel offensives were finally exhausted, Titus again ordered X *Fretensis* to return to camp construction while he remained with the original relief column on guard.

In his field tent that night, surrounded by Tiberius Alexander, Cerialis, Sulpicianus, Frugi and other close advisors, one can imagine Titus holding an animated discussion about the day's events. Not least, the lack of Roman discipline would have been a hot topic. Titus had displayed great bravery but, as a Roman general and successor to Vespasian, it was nothing short of recklessness to have exposed himself to such danger. Only Tiberius Alexander may have had the authority and courage to suggest to Titus that he must be more cautious. The attack on X *Fretensis* also served as a frank reminder of the insurgents' numbers and of a tenacity that had been underestimated yet again. The siege had begun with a shaky start for Titus.

Despite the Jewish warriors' success in forcing a Roman legion into retreat, the deeply ingrained hatred between the factions promptly returned. At the start of Passover, Eleazar ben Simon and his men opened access to the Temple to allow the devoted to worship.[62] However, John ben Levi took advantage of this gesture and infiltrated the crowds with a party of his men carrying concealed weapons, causing panic and casualties. Eleazar's Zealots capitulated to John and decided to join his side. The fate of Eleazar is not known, but he was almost certainly killed.[63] Jerusalem was now in the hands of two leaders, John ben Levi and Simon ben Giora.[64]

By this time, Titus, his officers and Roman engineers had completed initial surveys of Jerusalem's defences and identified various weak spots in the Third Wall, particularly on the western side.[65] As a result, Titus made plans to redeploy his legions and other forces to alternative locations adjacent to these weaker points. Before doing so, it was important to improve conditions for any strike, so he ordered all obstacles near the walls to be cleared and the ground to be completely levelled. A screen of infantry and cavalry were posted to protect the engineers and soldiers tasked with this labour.

While the ground-levelling proceeded, a notable episode unfolded. A band of Jewish fighters devised a trap on the northern side of the Third Wall. They staged a scene in which a group of individuals appeared to be banished from the city for causing rebellion. On the ramparts, a crowd pretended to be citizens pleading for Roman peace and offering to open the gates. Suspicious of this out-of-the-blue invitation, Titus, who was in the vicinity, ordered his men not to react.[66] Unfortunately, a group of Roman soldiers, acting without orders, had already taken up arms and rushed at the gates, believing they would be opened by the peace-seekers. The trap was sprung, and those beyond the wall and on its ramparts attacked. Many Romans in the vicinity were killed and nearly all the others were injured during their retreat. Understandably, Titus and the officers were furious at the lack of discipline that led to this action, compounded by the shame of what happened during the X *Fretensis* camp construction a few days earlier.[67]

Titus, *ca.* 79, in a bust found hidden in a cistern on the island of Pantelleria.
The high quality craftsmanship suggests a close likeness to the emperor.

Vespasian, Vatican Museum, Rome. A classic depiction of the Vespasian image: bold, rugged simplicity and the impression of a distant stare, eyeing the future.

Julia, only daughter of Titus, *ca.* 90, Getty Villa, California. Evidently a striking woman, her fashionable hairstyle with tight curls topped by a diadem add to the dramatic image.

Thought to be a young Britannicus (*left*) and Nero. Titus was educated alongside his childhood friend Britannicus, biological son of the Emperor Claudius.

Domitian, bust from Italy *ca.* 90. The emperor was very sensitive about his increasing baldness later in life.

The Roman province of Judea and the surrounding region.

The magnificent palace at Caesarea Maritima that became the official residence of Roman leaders such as procurator Antonius Felix. Built by Herod the Great on the Judean Mediterranean coast and later named in honour of Emperor Augustus.

The palace of Herod Agrippa II, Caesarea Philippi, Israel.
Titus was invited to the sprawling palatial complex inside the city during the Jewish War.

Jotapata, Israel. Picture taken from the north-west (cf. aerial view on p. 61). The steeply sloping western side of the fortress is at right. The left-hand side of the image shows the more accessible northern approach where the Romans built their ramp.

Gamla, Golan Heights, Israel. Picture taken from the north-east with the distant Sea of Galilee visible in the far upper right corner. The fortified town occupied the upper southern side (*left side of the picture*) of the 'camel hump' rock formation.

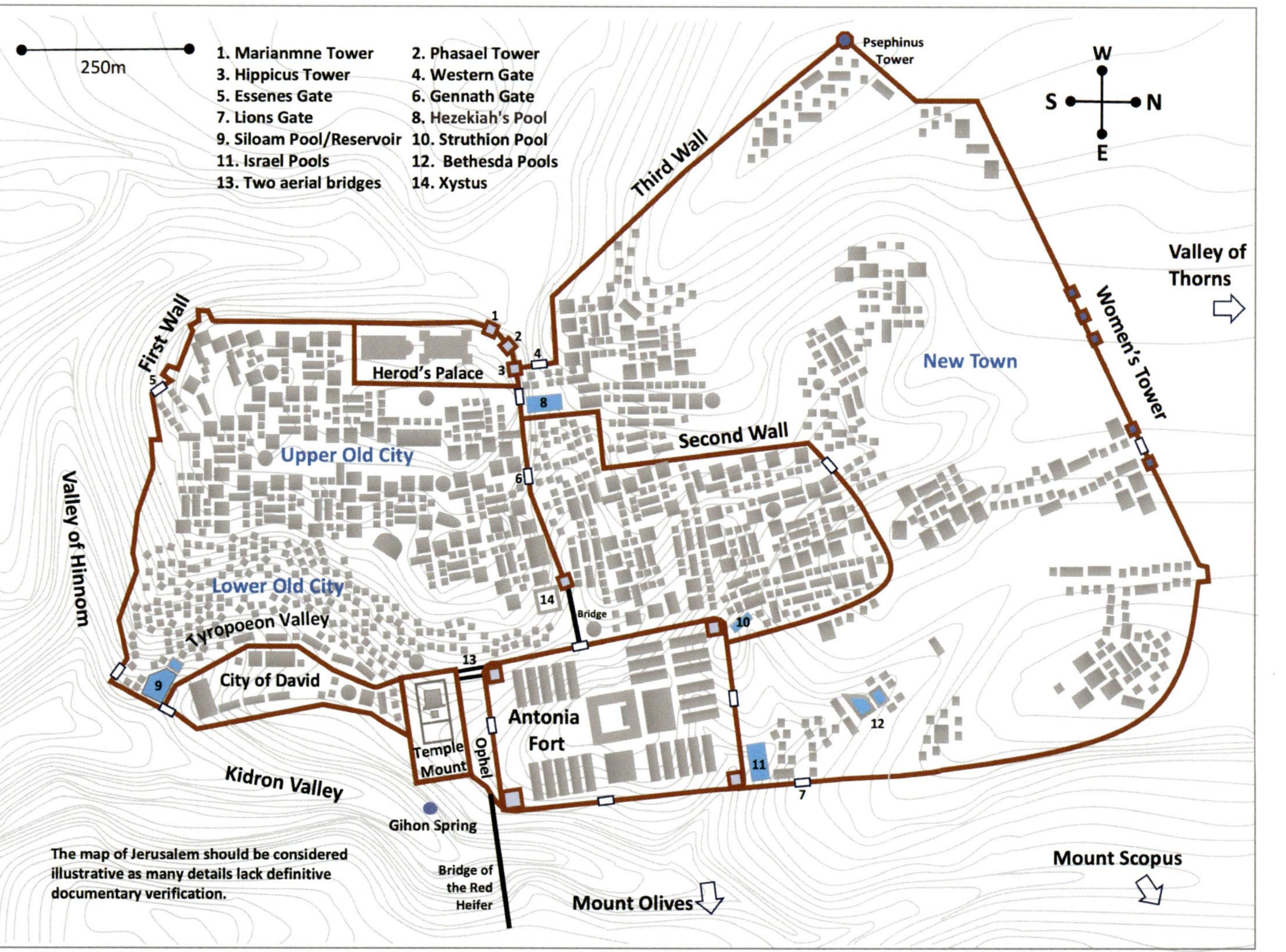
250m
1. Marianmne Tower
2. Phasael Tower
3. Hippicus Tower
4. Western Gate
5. Essenes Gate
6. Gennath Gate
7. Lions Gate
8. Hezekiah's Pool
9. Siloam Pool/Reservoir
10. Struthion Pool
11. Israel Pools
12. Bethesda Pools
13. Two aerial bridges
14. Xystus
Psephinus Tower
W
S N
E
Valley of Thorns
Third Wall
New Town
Women's Tower
First Wall
Herod's Palace
Upper Old City
Second Wall
Valley of Hinnom
Lower Old City
Tyropoeon Valley
City of David
Bridge
Antonia Fort
Temple Mount
Ophel
Kidron Valley
Gihon Spring
Bridge of the Red Heifer
Mount Olives
Mount Scopus
The map of Jerusalem should be considered illustrative as many details lack definitive documentary verification.

Replica Roman battering ram in the National Military Museum, Bucharest, Romania. A principal breaching engine in Graeco-Roman siegecraft.

Model replica of a Roman scorpion, being loaded by three legionary re-enactors. Twisted ropes housed in metal-reinforced casings (left side of picture) provided the lethal torsion force.

Western Wall, Jerusalem. Although traditionally considered as part of the wall of the Second Temple, alternative theories suggest the Western Wall may actually have belonged to the Antonia Fort. The Wall today consists of forty-five stone courses, twenty-eight of them above ground and seventeen underground (accessible through the Western Wall tunnels, dated to the Herodian Period). There are no stones of the time of Solomon at any level, as might be expected if the Wall was indeed part of the Second Temple.

Top left: *The Siege and Destruction of Jerusalem by the Romans Under the Command of Titus,* by David Roberts, oil on canvas, 1850.

Left: *Destruction of the Temple in Jerusalem* by Francesco Hayez, oil on canvas, 1867.

Above: *The Triumph of Titus: The Flavians,* by Lawrence Alma-Tadema, oil on panel, 1885.

Herculaneum ancient beach and vaulted boat houses. Five of the twelve boathouses can be seen directly on the beachfront, still filled with the remains of those who perished.

An ornate solid gold woman's double-headed snake armlet found in the House of the Golden Bracelet, Pompeii.

Plaster casts and remains of the four victims found in 1974 in the House of the Golden Bracelet, Pompeii. Cowered in an alcove near a staircase, two adults – a male and female – and two young male children (all unrelated genetically) had decided to stay rather than flee.

Roman legionary *testudo*, 'tortoise' formation, cast of Trajan's Column, National Museum of Romanian History. Josephus describes this tactical formation being used by the Romans during the Jewish Wars.

Praetorian Guards, marble relief, Louvre-Lens, France. Dated to *ca.* 51–52, from the Arch of Claudius in Rome, the relief depicts three guards in the foreground and two in the background, accompanied by an *aquilifer*, responsible for carrying the sacred eagle standard. Titus was Prefect of the Guard from around the summer of 71.

Arch of Titus, Roman Forum, Rome. Commissioned by his brother, the vault of the arch depicts Titus in the wings of an eagle rising to the heavens as a god. The fine relief in the marble work was originally painted in an array of colours.

Arch of Titus, Roman Forum, Rome. The southern underside of the arch depicts the triumph over the Jews when the spoils of war, including the sacred golden seven-branched *menorah* were carried through the streets of Rome.

Arch of Titus, Roman Forum, Rome. The northern underside of the arch depicts the victor Titus on his ornate four-horse *quadriga* chariot. The goddess Roma leads the chariot, and Victory rides beside Titus.

Colosseum, Flavian Amphitheatre, Rome. Arguably the most iconic structure of the Roman imperial era. Construction began under Vespasian and was completed by Titus. The now missing tiered seating would have covered the intricate network of arches that form the core of the massive structure. At the centre, the underground passageways – once used to house animals, fighters, and stage equipment – are now visible. These passageways were originally concealed beneath a sand-covered wooden arena floor equipped with trapdoors, allowing animals and combatants to be released onto the arena via gangways and elevators.

Temple of Peace, or Forum of Peace, Rome. Built by Vespasian, the colonnade of the western portico has been restored. The seven columns were made from fine pink Egyptian Aswan granite. The foreground of the picture was the open square of the forum and the shrine of the temple is out of shot to the left.

Laocoön and His Sons, also called the *Laocoön Group*, Vatican Museum, Rome. Pliny the Elder reported that this statue was displayed in Titus' home, describing it as one of the finest works of art in the ancient world.

'Villa di Tito', Province of Rieti, Italy, an opulent summer retreat and surrounding estates that may have been the imperial residence constructed by Vespasian in his native region and later inherited by Titus. If indeed this was the Flavian ancestral home, it was the very place where both father and son passed their final days. The residence commanded spectacular views over Lago di Paterno (Lake of Cutilia) and the verdant Apennines. In the foreground, the tops of large buttresses can be seen that fronted the villa to create an elevated terrace on which two storeys of indoor and outdoor living spaces were arranged around a central courtyard.

Titus, Vatican Museum, Rome. The statue portrays a contrasting image from his military persona during and after the Jewish War. Here we see the statesman in his fine toga, an arm extended in a rhetorical posture and a scroll in the other hand.

It was around this time that Titus attempted to negotiate a peace settlement through Josephus, but found no compromise.[68] The tribune Nicanor, who supported negotiations, was shot in the shoulder by an arrow during the parley. This act incensed Titus, whose motives for negotiation were not concerned either with saving Jewish lives or preserving the city; rather, he sought a quick resolution and the avoidance of Roman casualties. Thus, it was time to move the camps and begin the assault.

To guard the baggage trains and non-combatants during the relocation, an enormous protective screen, seven ranks deep, spanned the entire length of the northern and western sections of the Third Wall. It comprised three rows of infantry at the front, followed by three rows of cavalry and a row of archers, involving around 3,000 infantry, 3,000 cavalrymen and 1,000 archers.[69] The deterrent proved successful and the camp transfers proceeded uneventfully.[70] V *Macedonica* relocated opposite the Western Gate facing the Hippicus Tower, the other legions with Titus faced the Psephinus Tower, both reportedly 370 metres from the wall, and X *Fretensis* remained on the Mount of Olives.[71]

With the legions in place and the levelling project completed the Roman attack could commence. On the eve of the initial assault, on or around 21 April, presumably within Titus' *praetorium*, the plan of attack was established and subsequently delegated down the chain of command. Three separate wooden ramps, along with associated earthworks, were to be constructed simultaneously against the western section of the Third Wall. Large numbers of artillery units assigned to centuries of legionaries, or cohorts of specialised missile-firing auxiliary units such as archers and slingers would be stationed between the construction areas. Their primary role was to provide covering fire and protection against any sorties by the Jews.[72]

In anticipation of the Roman offensive, Simon ben Giora organised his men along the Third Wall and positioned captured Roman artillery machines along the ramparts. As his men were not trained in the use of these weapons, their effectiveness against the Romans might have been limited. Nonetheless, other defenders hailed stones and arrows on the Romans as they began work on the ramps, while some executed commando-like raids against the Roman construction workers. Replicating tactics from the siege of Jotapata, Titus and his officers ordered the erection of robust wicker screens to shield their men, and a relentless barrage of Roman counter-artillery fire bombarded the defences and repelled any sallies. Many examples of these *ballista* stones were unearthed recently at an archaeological site that revealed a section of the Third Wall. Most weighed five kilograms, some were up to eleven, and the biggest were twenty-four.[73] Clustered in a relatively small area, speaking to the deadly accuracy of such artillery fire, this onslaught would have devastated the defensive positions on the Third Wall.[74] Adding to their deadliness, the Romans learned to paint the stones black to obscure them during their trajectory against the backdrop of the sky.[75]

The effectiveness of the Roman protection methods allowed the completion of the ramps with minimal incident. Engineers confirmed the ramps were ready for the battering rams and Titus gave the order to proceed. Three rams began pounding the Third Wall simultaneously, while artillery units were brought closer to the action to continue their suppressive fire along the ramparts. The ominous thud of the rams striking the wall was no doubt familiar to any rebels who had escaped siege works earlier in the conflict and would have disturbed even the bravest among them.

In response, Simon ben Giora and John ben Levi agreed on a joint effort to step up their volley of missiles and firebrands and to launch raids along the Roman lines. However, Titus was prepared for this and was personally close at hand, as his father had been during the siege of Jotapata, and he successfully directed cavalrymen and archers posted as guards against these Jewish strikes.[76]

At this juncture, the Third Wall still remained intact but the Jews needed a desperate act to stave off collapse at vulnerable points. Rallying a substantial force, their leaders coordinated a strike, surging out from a concealed gate near the Hippicus Tower. A fierce skirmish erupted between the rebels and the Roman guards surrounding the siegeworks nearest to the tower. The Jews gained the upper hand, setting fires in the wooden frameworks of the earthworks that threatened to destroy the progress made by the Romans. However, the valour of legionaries from III *Cyrenaica* and Legio XVIII held a line against the onslaught. Their distinguished courage bought sufficient time for Titus, in close proximity, to charge into the mêlée with a cavalry division. Disregarding advice to consider his safety yet again, the young *Caesar* was said to have personally cut down twelve Jews. He was clearly determined to be at the heart of this combat. Perhaps by now new measures to better protect their general meant that his guard detail was always formed up to provide rings of security around him. Eventually the combined action of legionaries and cavalrymen tipped the balance, forcing the Jews to retreat behind the Third Wall. The fires were controlled, saving the works and, as a grim warning, a lone captured Jew was crucified in front of the wall, on Titus' orders.[77]

To gain a tactical advantage over the Jews defending the Third Wall, Titus directed the construction of three attack towers, each over twenty metres high. Such towers typically featured a wooden framework covered in metal plates to prevent fires. The interior was segmented into different floor levels, serving as platforms for missile firing or the positioning of gangways to reach onto the enemies' defences. The roof also functioned as an offensive podium. Moved on wheels, the towers were positioned close to the Third Wall, where Roman archers, slingers and scorpion artillery machines initiated a devastating barrage of missile fire onto the Jewish defenders manning their rampart. This suppressive fire compelled the Jews to abandon their positions, allowing the Roman battering rams to continue their pounding unhindered.[78]

Ultimately, the Third Wall succumbed to the largest battering ram, nick-named the 'The Conqueror'. The breach permitted the first wave of Romans to enter the New Town and secure various gates for the army through which to advance. The New Town was found deserted, as the Jews had withdrawn to the First and Second Walls. This Roman milestone was achieved on or around 7 May, only the fifteenth day of the siege, which suggested swift progress despite the doubtful start.[79] A substantial portion of the Third Wall was demolished and a significant part of the New Town was destroyed, reminiscent of Cestius' actions in 66 during the initial uprising. Following this action, Titus decided to clear a large area in the New Town to relocate his camp there, positioned out of bow range from the Second Wall. This effectively converted the area of the New Town into a Roman military zone. The move, undoubtedly intimidating, would have instilled despair in many Jewish fighters and citizens witnessing an enormous Roman camp being established within their sacred city.[80]

The stage was meticulously set for the next phase of the siege, and Titus gave the go-ahead to start a direct assault on the Second Wall. John ben Levi and Simon ben Giora assumed defensive positions, with the former orchestrating resistance from the Antonia and the northern colonnade of the Temple and the latter commanding defences along the Second Wall.[81] Presumably, the Romans attacked several points with ladders, ropes with grappling hooks, and siege towers, but the Jews held their defensive positions.[82] With no need for any earthworks, a battering ram was deployed against a central tower in the northern section of the Second Wall. Roman missile and artillery fire effectively subdued the defenders and the ram's relentless pounding resulted in a breach after only four days.

The speed of this success would have pleased Titus, but the Roman assault went wrong. Titus and his officers allowed their soldiers to file through the breach without widening it. There was an ambush waiting on the other side as the Jewish fighters had not retreated to the next line of defences. Instead, they had concealed themselves among the wool and metal workshops that characterised this quarter of the New Town. The first Romans through the breach were hampered by the narrow streets – and their subsequent retreat through the narrow breach was also difficult.[83] Once again, Titus was in close proximity, with his trusted tribune Domitius Sabinus by his side, reminiscent of their collaboration when breaching Jotapata together. They directed a detachment of archers who pinned down the Jews effectively, allowing all the soldiers to pull back through the breach.[84]

The Roman retreat was not easily avenged as a dogged fight at the breach ensued over several days.[85] The Jews defiantly defended the gap around the clock but in the end were driven back. This time, once the wall was secured beyond the breach, Titus ordered the immediate demolition of the entire northern section of the Second Wall and manned the towers along its western side.

At this point, Roman progress had exceeded expectations and Titus devised an event to wage psychological warfare against the Jews. Taking advantage of the regulation payday for his army, a massive military parade was organised in which individuals were paid during the ceremony. Titus' army was displayed in full splendour, with polished armour, crested helmets, dressed-up horses and other pageantry. Many Jews crowded along the First Wall and the fortifications of Antonia to observe the event, which lasted four days.[86] Among the rebels, there were doubtless mixed feelings, ranging from indifference to scorn and, in cases, utter despair.

During the assaults to capture the Third and Second Walls, Titus was multitasking to devise subsequent military plans. An important question still needed to be addressed: once the Second Wall was under Roman control: should the offensive directly target the Temple? The answer was no. Any attempt to assault in the northern or north-western sections of the Temple perimeter would have left the Romans heavily exposed to the Antonia Fort defences directly behind them. The area between the Temple and Antonia Fort, both in Jewish hands, was a killing zone for raining down missile fire and carrying out counter-offensive sallies. Thus, pragmatically,

Titus needed to capture the Antonia Fort first to mount an unhindered attack on the Temple subsequently.

On 12 May Titus issued orders to create two legionary divisions to build two pairs of siege ramps for the next offensive phase.[87] The first division made up of V *Macedonica* and XII *Fulminata* would each construct a ramp close together against the Antonia Fort on its northern side. The second division, X *Fretensis* and XV *Apollinaris*, was ordered to build its ramps close together, presumably against the First Wall near the pool of Amygdalon (Pool of Hezekiah) and the Tomb of John Hyrcanus to allow for an assault on the Upper City and then a pincer attack on the western side of the Temple.[88] With options dwindling, Simon ben Giora's men and the Idumeans sallied out to raid the earthworks, and John ben Levi's fighters, along with the Zealots, manned the Antonia Fort. The Jewish defenders, increasingly adept in the use of captured Roman artillery, inflicted more significant losses on the soldiers building the ramps.[89]

Sensing an opportunity to negotiate a Jewish surrender, considering the Romans were attacking some of their last lines of defence, Titus again employed Josephus to communicate with the rebels.[90] As before, Titus' primary concern was not preserving Jewish lives but saving Romans and their resources. Despite Josephus' appeals, the negotiations proved futile. Nevertheless, the combined impact of psychological warfare, the Romans' proximity to the heart of the city and Josephus' petitions together heightened desperation among the citizens. Tens of thousands were trapped in the uncaptured parts of Jerusalem, many having entered the city for the Passover festival.[91] With provisions exhausted, famine set in, leading to a human catastrophe. Insurgent thugs with no regard for their fellow Jews raided homes in search of food, indiscriminately torturing and killing in the process.[92] The price of any available food skyrocketed and fortunes were traded for minimal amounts of grain. Josephus vividly describes the horrors:

> Famine overpowers all human feelings, and decency is the main casualty – at a time of famine what would otherwise have guaranteed respect is cast aside. So, wives would snatch food from their husbands, children from their parents, and, most pitiable of all, mothers would take the food from the very mouths of their babies and not scruple when their dearest ones were wasting away in their arms, to rob them of those drops of nourishment which could keep them alive.[93]

People began deserting in droves and stories circulated of individuals swallowing gold to avoid losing it to the Romans when capitulating. Deserters who managed to evade ben Giora's and ben Levi's men were scrutinised by the Romans to identify any rebels hidden among them. Titus may have allowed a minority to pass freely, while others faced enslavement or death.[94]

The famine also drove hopeless rebels and citizens to forage beyond the city walls into the Hinnom and Kidron valleys. Patrolling cavalry captured upwards of 500 people a day, subjecting them to ruthless torture and crucifixion in front of the walls:

> The [Roman] soldiers … felt nothing but anger and hatred, and amused themselves by nailing up their captives in all sorts of different positions, until the numbers were such that they ran short of space for the crosses and of crosses for the bodies.[95]

These deaths were another tragic episode amidst the countless atrocities of the war. Like so many conflicts before and since, the innocent bore the greatest humanitarian costs.

As construction on the Roman ramps progressed and the desertions continued, the son of the king of Commagene, Antiochus Epiphanes, arrived with a large army of heavy infantry and a crack bodyguard called the 'Macedonians'. These guards were not from Macedonia but they were an impressive sight: all young, tall and trained to emulate the famous Macedonian phalanx. Titus and his senior officers would have greeted Antiochus in a Roman camp in a manner befitting a royal ally. However, somewhat discourteously, Antiochus questioned why the Romans were hesitant to attack the First Wall. Titus' response, rarely preserved, humoured him:

> Well, many hands make light work![96]

Presumably affronted, the pompous new arrival decided to charge at the wall at the head of his Macedonian guard, which simply resulted in many of his bodyguards being wounded to no avail.[97]

After seventeen days of gruelling construction work, four colossal Roman terraces were completed on 29 May. With this accomplishment, a host of siege engines were brought forward. This was the moment John ben Levi had been anticipating. With great ingenuity, his sappers had tunnelled beneath the Roman ramps adjacent to the Antonia Fort. The wooden rafters supporting these tunnels were now set ablaze, causing a booming crash as the ramps and siege engines above collapsed into the void. The wooden materials in the earthworks eventually caught fire amongst the smouldering remains creating a towering blaze – a triumph for the Jews.[98]

Two days later, Simon ben Giora launched a daring assault against the ramps and siege engines in his sector. Three courageous individuals, armed with firebrands, succeeded in igniting a battering ram and its surrounding wicker shields. Efforts by the Romans to extinguish the flames or retrieve the ram proved futile. As the fire spread to the earthworks, the legionary guards and supporting auxiliaries were compelled to retreat. X *Fretensis* probably withdrew to a safe distance to await orders and XV *Apollinaris* returned to their camp in the New Town.[99]

Recognising an opportunity, Simon ben Giora and his leaders mobilised large numbers to attack the Roman camp. Fuelled by pent-up fury and emboldened by their recent successes, the Jews clashed with the Roman forward guard tasked with protecting their camp under the threat of death for desertion. A fierce battle developed and more Jewish fighters joined the mêlée giving 'their aggression free rein'.[100] Titus, abandoning his inspection of the Antonia Fort, led his elite mounted guard against the eastern flank of the Jewish warriors. The tide began to turn in favour of the Romans and the Jews retreated to their defences.[101]

To assess their setbacks, Titus convened his *consilium*, attended by Tiberius Alexander and his three legates, senior tribunes and other key figures.[102] The exhausting work on the ramps was all undone and the precious materials used in their creation were lost. Two views emerged in discussions on the next course of action. The more aggressive of these advocated for an all-out assault on the First Wall, engaging the entire army. Up until then, only relatively small contingents had been deployed to establish and force breaches. The second, more cautious approach proposed implementing a blockade to starve the rebels into submission. Titus' own views give us an important insight into his military thinking and his practical reasoning.[103] Concerning a blockade, he was reluctant to keep such an enormous Roman force inactive and underused. He also acknowledged the operational challenges of cordoning off a large city surrounded by difficult mountainous terrain and hindered by the scarcity of timber for an encircling wall. At the same time, he understood that fighting the Jews unified them, whereas they were prone to self-destruction when left to their own devices. The Roman general was clearly well informed and cognisant of the various pros and cons of any tactical approach. Eventually, he opted for a compromise that would begin with the construction of a blockading palisade to destroy any last Jewish hopes for escape and to prevent provisions from being smuggled in. The Romans would then return to active siege warfare, rebuilding ramps with the classic Roman determination seen throughout the war in the face of setbacks. Time was on *Caesar's* side as supplies continued to flow into the theatre of war, while the Jews were on borrowed time and enduring famine.

To motivate his army to build the palisade in the sweltering summer heat, a competitive spirit was instilled between legions, cohorts, officers, centurions and legionaries. Titus personally umpired the competing progress between his legates and toured the works several times a day to inspire his men. Wood was stripped from miles around and transported to the sites on a massive scale.[104] The wall started at the Roman camp in the New Town and ran across to the eastern side. Starting again beyond the city, it crossed the Kidron Valley up to the Roman camp on the Mount of Olives. Here, it headed south along the higher ground on the eastern side of the Kidron before presumably turning westward along the southern side of the Hinnom Valley. It then turned north past Herod's Tomb and back to where it started at the Roman camp. The herculean feat of engineering and effort, nearly seven kilometres in length, had thirteen forts spaced along the circuit and the whole enterprise was manned around the clock.[105] Such a wooden wall required an estimated 20,000 cubic metres or more of timber.[106] To put this into perspective, this is equivalent to the volume of around 500 modern shipping containers.

With Jerusalem now in a stranglehold, the level of famine escalated further. To envision the abhorrent scenes inside Jerusalem at this time, one must appreciate that starvation by now had claimed the lives of the most vulnerable: the youngest and oldest and those with existing comorbidities. Alongside these deaths, casualties mounted from infighting between factions, battles with the Romans and rebels killing in search of provisions. The appalling conditions probably led to outbreaks of infectious disease, further raising the death toll. Many thousands were dead and burying them was impossible.[107] Corpses covered every street and corner across Jerusalem, decomposing rapidly in the summer heat; the stench of death was everywhere. In other instances, the dead were thrown over the walls into the ravines below.[108]

When Titus on his rounds saw the ravines clogged with corpses, and pools of putrid matter oozing out from the decomposing bodies, he groaned aloud and raised his hands to the heavens, calling God to witness that this was not his doing.[109]

For the besieged with only their faith to sustain them, nothing to do but despair, grieve and suffer terrible anguish, days and nights would have seemed endless. The rebels, imposing martial law over the population with little or no pity, were increasingly enfeebled as there was no more food to steal from the people. Their leaders, ben Levi and ben Giora, appeared to make no effort to inspire their followers and chose instead to descend into further thuggery.[110]

Individuals no longer able to bear the torment continued to flee and the majority were rounded up by the Romans to be enslaved or executed. One surviving deserter was caught in the Syrian auxiliary camp picking gold pieces out of his excrement, causing a sensation among the soldiers who began cutting up deserters for their swallowed treasures. In one night, almost 2,000 of the wretched refugees were cut open. Titus got wind of the activity, a serious lack of discipline from his perspective, and issued stern orders to desist immediately.[111]

In the meantime, the Romans sourced more wood from up to ten miles away, felling every available tree to provide materials for the construction of four ramps against Antonia. Bigger than before, they were completed towards the end of June in twenty-one days. John ben Levi's followers sallied out before the siege engines were brought up but failed to set fire to the ramps, thanks to the discipline and bravery of the Roman guards supported by artillery fire. Under constant bombardment from all manner of rocks and missiles from the Jewish defenders in Antonia, the battering rams were moved into position and commenced their pounding. While the battering continued through the first day, a group of legionaries formed up into a *testudo* and were able to reach the base of a wall, prising out four foundation stones with crowbars. That night, weakened by the battering rams, the removal of foundation stones and the tunnels dug by John ben Levi's sappers, the northern wall collapsed.[112]

The next morning, 3 July, a second, newly constructed wall was revealed. Ben Levi had built it secretly as a contingency.[113] It would only delay the inevitable because the new wall could be scaled from the debris of the collapsed Antonia wall. A brave Syrian auxiliary infantry soldier named

Sabinus distinguished himself by volunteering to be the first to scale the wall after Titus delivered a rousing speech to troops assembled in the vicinity. Sabinus made it over the wall but was outnumbered and killed, and eleven others who followed him were either killed or abandoned the assault.[114] In the past, Titus and his father had shown great concern for even a minor number of casualties despite the vastness of their armies. Thus, this suicide mission appears irrational and rather counter-productive in motivating others to go over the wall.

Nevertheless, a couple of days later, under the cover of darkness in the early hours of 5 July, twenty Roman forward guards enlisted the help of a standard bearer from V *Macedonica*, two auxiliary cavalrymen and a trumpeter, to scale the new wall at two o'clock in the morning. After they stealthily dispatched the sentries, the trumpeter blasted out a rallying call to give the impression that a large Roman force was in the Antonia Fort. The desired effect was achieved and the remaining Jewish sentries fled in panic. Titus would have been aware of the plan and was ready with a contingent of troops and his elite guard to storm into the Antonia Fort over the wall and also through the tunnels dug by John ben Levi.[115] As a result, the Jews abandoned the fortress, falling back to the Temple to defend from the high walls on the colonnade roof ramparts and to block the connecting narrow walkways and stairs between the Antonia Fort and the Temple complex. The bottleneck of these areas and the plaza area south of the fortress became the scene of a fierce battle, with heavy casualties on both sides.[116]

After eleven bloody hours of hand-to-hand combat, the determined spirit of the Jews eventually overcame the Roman troops. Legionaries and auxiliaries were masters of close combat, stabbing with their *gladii* from behind their large shields. In the cramped spaces, however, their skills were hindered. Titus decided not to send in reinforcements and had the signal given for his men to pull back into the Antonia Fort. The Jews were victorious for now and both sides stood down to consolidate their respective defensive positions. At this moment, a remarkable episode occurred in which an auxiliary centurion called Julianus decided to make a lone attack on the Temple. Julianus was renowned for his bravery, strength and swordsmanship and was standing next to Titus in the Antonia Fort before he leapt into action. He probably noticed an opportunity in one of the connecting walkways, perhaps a wavering in the Jewish line, and was able to dash across and fight his way down into the outer courtyard of the Temple.[117] Displaying his elite fighting skills, he single-handedly fought a path to the corner of the Inner Temple court. The superhuman performance stunned the Jewish rebels who had fled before Julianus until he slipped on the court stones, dispelling his invulnerable status. Titus and other cheering Romans were observing the scene from the elevated position of the southern Antonia walls as Julianus was surrounded. Fighting to the bitter end, he was overwhelmed and killed. Titus was apparently greatly moved by Julianus' courage and admired his tenacity even when on his knees at the last.[118]

On 17 July, approximately halfway through the campaign season, Titus ordered the Antonia Fort to be razed to its foundations, except for the south-east tower, which would serve as an observation post. The demolition would improve access for a larger proportion of his army to engage in the assault on the Temple.[119] On the same day, the Jewish religious officials were unable to maintain their sacred twice-daily lamb sacrifices to God and the cessation caused great distress amongst the people.[120] While the demolition work commenced, Titus appointed Cerialis to lead an elite force to attack the Temple: thirty of the best legionaries selected from each century and formed into detachments of 1,000, each under a tribune.[121] Presumably the best centurions were also included. This force was the largest engaged at one point against the rebels since the start of the siege: over 6,800 legionaries.[122]

The attack on the Temple started before dawn to catch sentries off guard.[123] The objective was probably to attack gates in the northern and western walls.[124] The connecting walkways may not have been included because their narrow access had proven to be a bottleneck. Alternatively, the walkways had been pulled down by the entrenched Jewish fighters. The attack did not start well for the Romans as the sentries were fully alert and a multitude of Jewish fighters rushed up in support. Moreover, in the darkness the Roman formations were disorientated. As the light grew, better formations were achieved on both sides but neither side gained any ground. After many hours, a Roman retreat was eventually signalled.[125]

With the Antonia Fort razed in seven days and a wide access road completed into the vicinity, the legions had a better approach to the perimeter wall of the Temple complex. The improved access allowed the legionary engineers to direct the construction of several earthworks against the northern and western outer walls.[126] Harvesting at an even greater distance from Jerusalem was required to gather the necessary timber and presumably timber from previous ramps was recycled. These earthworks were a defining moment for the Roman siege, finally building up access that would allow a decisive assault on the Temple. It was also an indication that Titus wanted to take a cautious approach in which large numbers of troops could be more safely ranged against the precinct.[127] Battering rams would not be used on the northern side; it was rather a case of constructing earthworks to provide a route for the Romans to move en masse onto the colonnaded roof and then down into the outer courtyard.

As before, the rebels never gave up their sallies against the earthworks. In addition, they had some success with several sorties that captured Roman horses, presumably for food.[128] In response Titus threatened harsh punishments for any cavalryman who lost his horse. In desperation for provisions, the insurgents even dared to raid the X *Fretensis* camp on the Mount of Olives but they were successfully intercepted by the guards.[129]

As the Roman earthworks approached completion, the rebels in the Temple realised that the colonnaded rooftops were becoming a liability. They would allow the Romans to storm onto this platform and use the stairwells to descend to the courtyard. They therefore decided to burn the northern and western sections opposite the ramps.[130] Now the Romans would have the much harder task of climbing down from the top of the ruined perimeter into the courtyard. Shortly after, on 24 July, the Romans realised they needed to respond to this because the remaining adjacent sections of the portico rooftops would serve as vantage points for the rebels to fire missiles at the Romans coming off the ramp onto the wall and moving down. Thus, the Romans burned those sections and the Jews were forced to pull them down to prevent further spread.[131]

Still seeking to ensnare the Romans where possible, the defenders laid a trap in the rafters of a remaining section of the western colonnade. The cavity was filled with flammable materials and the rebels pretended to abandon the section due to fatigue. Many of the Roman guards in their eagerness to finish the siege were tricked into climbing onto the rooftop of the portico with ladders. The whole section was then set alight and a horror scene unfolded.

> Completely surrounded by fire, some threw themselves down into the city behind them, others straight into the hands of the enemy in front of them; many hoped to save their lives by jumping back down among their own men, and broke legs and arms; but for most the fire was too quick for any attempt to escape, and some pre-empted it with their own swords; even those already facing some other form of death were caught by the rapid spread of fire.[132]

The disaster claimed many Roman lives and the fires consumed a considerable section of the western colonnade. The next day, again to remove a vantage point for the Jews, the Romans burned the remaining section of the northern colonnade.

On 2 August, the fateful moment arrived for the Jews holed up in the Temple. In what appears a change of tactics, Roman battering rams were brought up on the western earthwork and commenced their pounding. For six days the quality and strength of the wall resisted the unrelenting hammering. Many had heard this foreboding sound before and it surely unnerved those within the Temple complex. On 8 August, even bigger rams were wheeled into place but they too failed to breach the wall, testament to the robust quality of the defensive stonework.[133] A party of Roman soldiers even tried to collapse the foundations of the northern gates but the removal of the outer stones had no effect given the strength of the inner foundations.[134]

Titus and his senior officers now ordered a different attack on the Temple perimeter from two earthworks. Ladders were used to escalade the western and northern perimeters from the ramps up against the walls and then to descend into the courtyard below.[135] Artillery fire from the Antonia Fort site had a height advantage to help pin back the Jewish forces and protect the Roman scaling parties. Even for the well-protected Roman soldiers, storming fortifications from ladders was a highly hazardous task. Both sides suffered heavily in the mêlée and the Romans were unable to establish a position in the outer courtyard of the precinct.[136]

In response to this setback, Titus next ordered the burning of the western gates to add another point of attack and split up the rebel defence further.[137] The heat melted the ornate silver panelling and the thick wooden beams behind subsequently caught fire. As the fire spread, it took hold in the colonnades and probably consumed the last sections of portico on that side of the Temple perimeter. As it burned all day and through the night, the glow in the darkness was a terrible warning for all the defenders of Jerusalem.[138] With nothing left of the gate the following day, the Romans needed to prepare the ground for the legionaries to advance through the debris into the outer courtyard. A simultaneous assault from the Antonia ramp was no doubt also prepared. In Titus' *consilium* of 9 August, the deliberations addressed whether to preserve the inner courtyards and the sacred Sanctuary of the Temple. Titus concluded that it should be spared if possible. He had no interest in the cult or sacred nature of the Temple nor in the political ramifications; he was undoubtedly concerned solely with preserving its priceless contents for capture.[139]

On 10 August, the climax of the Roman siege arrived. At first light, the Romans surged into the outer courtyard of the Temple precinct and formed up in disciplined lines to attack. The remaining rebels had spent the night behind the walls of the inner courtyards and they poured out of the bronze eastern gate. It was their last stand and doubtless John ben Levi and Simon ben Giora called on their fury and faith.[140] The battle ebbed and flowed for several hours. Despite their exhaustion and starvation, the Jewish fighters put up a remarkable fight against the Roman units. Observing from the remaining Antonia Fort tower, Titus spotted the opportunity to send in his elite cavalry through the destroyed western gate and their charge broke the Jewish lines. By around 11 o'clock that morning, the Jewish positions had crumbled and they retreated behind the walls of the inner courtyards. The Romans were called off and Titus sensed the need to stand down his men until the next day, when a fresh attack would aim to encircle the inner Temple structures completely.[141]

As Titus retired to his headquarters, a group of Romans continued trying to extinguish the remaining fires in the western sections of the perimeter. The Jewish defenders, still with remarkable determination, probably saw an opportunity to strike this vulnerable party and rushed out to attack. The Romans managed to defeat the sortie, however, and the attackers slipped back again through the eastern gate. To punish the Jews for this action, an unnamed Roman soldier called on a comrade to hoist him up so he could throw a firebrand through the gold-plated window of one of the northern antechambers lining the Sanctuary. A fire caught in the room and began to spread. It was an extraordinary moment in history that has reverberated through time.

The Jewish fighters detected the fire swiftly but lacked the means to control it. News rapidly reached Titus who made his way immediately to the Temple with a retinue of officers and guards. Drawn into the excitement, many legionaries followed suit. Chaos erupted in the Roman ranks as Titus and his officers struggled to contain their men's euphoria and rage. The Jews were unable to control the fire and many fled into the outer courtyard where they were butchered by the Romans. Frenzied Roman soldiers charged into the inner Courts, amid horrible scenes of bloodshed.

Most of the victims were ordinary citizens, unarmed and defenceless, slaughtered wherever they were found. Corpses piled up round the Altar [Court of the Priests] as blood cascaded down the Sanctuary steps and the bodies of those killed on the upper level slithered to the bottom.[142]

Although the fire raged out of control in the rooms lining the Temple, Titus was able to lead his officers through and up into the Sanctuary. There he observed its generously gilded interior, fine tapestries, golden doors and gateways, the priceless gold menorah and numerous other treasures and precious relics. No doubt concerned about the enormous value of the contents, the general attempted to assemble a party to save the Sanctuary building from the fire. He ordered a centurion from his bodyguard, called Liberalius, to control insubordinates. However, amidst the pandemonium of Roman troops dashing in every direction, seeking loot and vengeance, a torch carried into the building ignited another fire.[143]

Realising that time was running short, Titus ordered his officers and guards to rescue as many treasures as possible to be packed off back to Rome for his triumph. He then withdrew to safety, away from the burning structures. The monumental Temple was engulfed in flames. First built over a thousand years before when King Solomon laid its great foundations, it was once reputedly the home to the Ark of the Covenant, placed inside the Holy of Holies. Destroyed once before, by the Babylonians, and rebuilt under the decree of the Persian King Cyrus, it had stood for another 600 years until this moment on 10 August 70.[144] An attempted third construction by the Emperor Julian (331–63) was aborted.[145]

With many areas of the Temple burning, the massacres and atrocities continued throughout the complex. Ben Giora, ben Levi and some of their men were able to escape into the Old City, but many others and large numbers of citizens remained trapped by the fires or the Roman soldiers. Seeing no reason to hold back, the Romans torched all the remaining structures. One horrific incident stands out from among the many. The southern colonnade had remained intact up until that point and many civilians had taken refuge in the upper storey basilica. They all perished in the flames. The Romans also burned the treasury storerooms after extracting vast sums of money and valuable objects banked there by the wealthy for safe keeping.[146]

Even with fires still burning, the legion eagle standards were set up opposite the remains of the eastern gate of the Inner Courts by the legions' aquilifers and sacrifices were dedicated to the emblems. As general, Titus led the ceremony. Turning afterwards to the gathered officers and legionaries he was hailed as *imperator*. Typically reserved for the emperor, this acclamation would have been a sign of rebellion were it not offered to his son and heir. The Roman soldiers were triumphant, and had taken large amounts of loot. The value of gold trading in Syria would later halve because of the flush of bullion into circulation as they spent their booty. Paradoxically, a section of sanctuary wall had survived the fires and several priests remained defiantly on top. It seems strange that Titus did not have them dragged down but, in the end, they were forced down by hunger and thirst. They were executed without mercy.[147] Their deaths marked the end of the killings in the Temple that was now a smouldering mass of debris.

After fleeing, ben Levi and ben Giora found themselves in the totally desolate Old City. Famine and disease had claimed countless lives and stories of cannibalism circulated.[148] Lifeless masses of civilians with no hope and no means of escape waited to die. Though a combination of faith, fanaticism and anger had thus far sustained the courage of the rebel leaders, John and Simon were now broken and offered surrender talks. Titus agreed to talk and a bridge that connected the destroyed Temple perimeter to the Upper City was selected as the location. Titus, surrounded by his guards and accompanied by his officers and a translator, allowed the two rebel leaders to approach after doubtless having them frisked and put under close watch. Crowds were permitted to mass around the area adding tension to the occasion. *Caesar* initiated the parley, recalling the rebels' defiance, their losses and questioning their motives. In response, the warlords claimed they could never surrender because of their oaths but pleaded for safe passage away from Jerusalem with their families. It was not the unconditional capitulation that Titus expected and he had no hesitation in stating that he would 'apply all the rules of war'.[149] Respecting the truce talks, he dismissed the rebels and granted his troops permission to burn and sack what remained of Jerusalem.[150] Such were the brutal rules of ancient warfare.

The following day, the horrors of the war recommenced, starting with the torching of public buildings such as the Records Office and the Council of Chambers. The City of David was burned as was the Adiabene Palace of Helena and the Ophel region south of the Temple. A large group of rebels, not yet ready to give in, stormed Herod's Palace and routed some Romans in the vicinity and subsequently slaughtered thousands of their fellow countrymen who had taken shelter in the palace. Like the Temple treasury storerooms, the wealthy had deposited their important possessions in the palace, believing they were safely guarded, but the rebels looted the contents.

With fires raging and smoke billowing over Jerusalem, the Roman army flushed insurgents out of the Lower City and no doubt pillaged, raped and murdered their way through the streets and houses. The area as far as the Siloam Pool in the south-east corner of the Lower City was torched. The Upper City was a harder prospect to sack because it occupied an elevated area and was protected by the First Wall and Herod's Palace. On 20 August, Titus approved a two-pronged approach. His legions would focus on the construction of ramps against the western walls of the palace. Simultaneously his auxiliaries would mass opposite the north-east section of the Upper City and prepare earthworks against the First Wall, where John ben Levi was ensconced with his remaining followers.[151]

During this period, the Idumean leaders saw the absolute futility of continuing to support Simon ben Giora and sought to surrender. Titus reluctantly agreed through emissaries, but ben Giora uncovered the betrayal, executed the messengers returning from Titus and decapitated the Idumean leadership, including Jacob ben Sosas. However, ben Giora was not able to prevent massive waves of deserters – Idumeans and others. The sheer numbers posed a colossal logistical challenge to the Romans who triaged the masses for execution, slavery or release.[152] Economically, the eastern slave markets were by now over-supplied because of the conflict so there were diminishing returns for enslaving feeble deserters and refugees. Two notable individuals, a priest and the Temple Treasurer, managed to secure their freedom in exchange for handing over the whereabouts of fabulous amounts of treasure and relics from the Temple.[153]

The earthworks against the western side of Herod's Palace were completed without incident after eighteen days on 7 September and siege engines were dragged into position. The rebels were now a spent force. Demoralised and weak due to prolonged starvation, many retreated into the Old City. A feeble defensive line had no hope against the Roman onslaught and the wall was breached on the same day without any Roman blood spilt. It is probable that the majority of remaining Jewish fighters dispersed at this time to take their chances amongst the surviving civilians. A last group of diehards was holed up in the extremely well fortified northern Herodian Towers but their hunger drove them to flee. Sneaking their way to a ravine in the Kidron Valley, they attempted to break through the Roman siege wall but were repelled by the guards. Their last refuge was in the sewers below the city.[154]

With the last organised resistance in the city broken, Jerusalem was officially captured on 7 September.[155] Dispatches to Rome would have been sent claiming an end to the revolt and announcing that all the districts of Jerusalem were under Roman control.[156] The sacking of the city would continue for many more weeks. As a symbol of capture, legionary standards were mounted on the Herodian towers to the triumphant cheer of all the soldiers in the area. Elsewhere, the Romans continued to loot and the grim circumstances of the besieged were evident.

> They poured into the streets, sword in hand, slaughtering indiscriminately all they came across and burning houses with those who had fled there still inside. In their ravages they would often burst into houses in search of loot, only to find whole families dead and rooms filled with the corpses of famine victims: horrified at the sight, they would then leave empty-handed. They might pity those who had died like that, but they felt no such pity for the living. They ran through anyone they met, choked the alleyways with corpses, and set the city awash with blood.[157]

That night, the fires took hold across large areas of the Upper City and the dawn light was mixed with the glow of the Old City in flames. Titus, the conqueror of Jerusalem, surveyed the last of the areas to have fallen and was notably impressed by the robustness and defensive qualities of the Herodian Towers. As the slaughter of the population abated, the Roman soldiers literally exhausted by days of carnage, the more able individuals captured were instead marshalled into the wreckage of the Temple where Fronto was appointed by Titus to oversee their assessment.

Those identified as insurgents were executed. Persons in their prime were separated for transportation to Rome to be paraded at the future triumph and the remainder were either packed off in chains for hard labour in Egypt or destined for gladiatorial sports in the Eastern Roman amphitheatres. The youngest were sold into slavery. The large numbers meant the process took a considerable time during which many thousands perished from starvation.[158]

The search for loot and survivors continued across the city and even the sewers were eventually investigated. The hope of booty overcame the appalling conditions in the drains and cesspits. The stench of decay must have been overwhelming because more than 2,000 dead bodies were found amongst the refugees underground. John ben Levi and his brothers were found in a sewer and spared execution to be taken to Titus. The fallen leader would be spared and sent to Rome for life imprisonment, an unusual fate for an enemy leader. Perhaps Titus wanted the living testament of the rebel leadership as a trophy.[159] Simon ben Giora was still missing.

With the sacking at an end in the second half of September, Titus issued orders to raze the burnt city to the ground. Nothing should be spared. Even the magnificent Herodian Towers, which he initially thought should remain as a symbol of what Rome had conquered, were in the end destroyed. The ancient grand foundations of the Temple complex were torn out to eradicate its elevated position and to obliterate any evidence of its existence.[160] These colossal tasks, with around one million tonnes of masonry and other materials to be pulled down or displaced, required a very large proportion of the Roman army to engage in the demolition work for several weeks.[161] With the demolition completed, Lepidus and X *Fretensis* were posted to garrison the Jerusalem area.[162] Although archaeological evidence is lacking it is thought that X *Fretensis* selected the Upper City for the site of their permanent camp. A Roman fortress rising from the ruins of Jerusalem was a visible assertion of their victory, showcasing the overwhelming power of the Roman Empire. The city, sacred to the Jews, was transformed into a stark emblem of conquest and imperial authority.

The last act for Titus before he departed was to conduct a ceremony to issue military awards. A magnificent event was organised with a large platform erected in the temporary Roman camp in the north of the city. With officers, standard bearers, legionaries, cavalry and auxiliaries assembled in full military display, Titus delivered his victory speech; those close by could have heard his voice, while others relayed his words across the mass of troops gathered. Military honours were distributed to awardees along with financial rewards. An enormous sacrifice of oxen was offered to the gods in thanks for the victory and the meat distributed to his men. It would have taken weeks in advance to organise, including the transportation of livestock to Jerusalem for the offering. Over fifty oxen would have been required to provide a ration of meat to every soldier for the celebrations.[163] Three days of festivities followed and Titus mingled with his officers amidst the revelry.

From the start of the siege, the dogged determination of the Jewish fighters had made it apparent that a Roman victory would require the destruction of one of the ancient world's most significant religious and cultural centres. For the Jewish population, Jerusalem was the heart of their religious life and worship. It was also a symbol of their national identity and heritage. Its rich history could be traced back to first settlements now dated to around 3,500 BC; King David had conquered the city and declared it the capital of the Jewish Kingdom around 1,000 BC. It had been captured five times, but only the Babylonians had destroyed the city so thoroughly before. Now, over a thousand years after King David made it the capital, it lay in total ruins. Yet the loss of life far eclipsed the physical destruction of Jerusalem. It is difficult to judge how many Jewish fighters and citizens were killed during the siege, or subsequently enslaved. However, one can estimate in an order of magnitude that tens of thousands perished and perhaps the same number were sold into slavery. For those who escaped the catastrophic event, there was nothing to return to and their displacement led to a widespread Jewish diaspora.

In the tumultuous account of the siege of Jerusalem in 70, the Roman legions, led by the daring Titus, engaged in a protracted and arduous campaign against the deeply entrenched Jewish forces defending their sacred city. The chronicle progressed with the construction of massive siege works, including ramps, towers and battering rams, as the Romans pressed relentlessly against the formidable walls of Jerusalem. The defenders, under the divided leadership of Simon ben Giora, John ben Levi and others, displayed fierce resistance, employing guerrilla tactics and calculated strikes. Each side was responsible for unspeakable atrocities. The breach of the Third Wall signified the beginning of the end for the beleaguered city. The tragic zenith was reached with the destruction of the sacred Temple, a historic climax to the relentless conflict. The narrative bore witness to a staggering loss of life, predominantly innocent souls caught in the fighting to suffer famine and the brutalities of war. Ever defiant, the rebels and their followers displayed unwavering resistance but their efforts could not forestall the fate that awaited Jerusalem. The aftermath left the city in total devastation, its once-thriving streets and magnificent public buildings irrecoverably lost.

TITUS' EASTERN TOUR

In a period of 140 days, Titus had orchestrated the historic siege of Jerusalem, resulting in the city's complete destruction and the annihilation of its population. It was now early October 70, just two months shy of his thirty-first birthday. The victorious *Caesar*, heir apparent to the Emperor Vespasian, needed to disband his colossal army. X *Fretensis* would not return to Syria; instead, it was posted amongst the ruins of Jerusalem to protect Judea. XII *Fulminata* was dispatched to Melitene on the western banks of the Euphrates, a new strategic position for a legion on the border of Cappadocia. XV *Apollinaris* and V *Macedonica* were tasked with escorting Titus during his remaining time in the East.[1] The detachments from III *Cyrenaica*, Legio XVIII and IV *Scythica* headed back to their respective bases. The winter conditions were unfavourable for Titus to return to Rome, and he had agreed with this father to remain in the region, primarily for an important diplomatic mission to be discussed shortly.[2] Vespasian had finally returned to Rome probably arriving by the end of September 70, having maintained his court in Alexandria while politics settled at home and having dealt remotely with the Batavian revolt on the Rhine through Mucianus.[3] Vespasian was not the first Roman leader to take his time in the Hellenistic urban masterpiece that was Alexandria.[4]

Accordingly, Titus chose first to go to Caesarea, where he deposited the treasures seized from Jerusalem and left his prisoners, presumably in make-shift detention centres.[5] Without further delay, he next headed north-east to Caesarea Philippi – around a week's march – escorted by XV *Apollinaris* and V *Macedonica*. He had been invited by his closest eastern ally, Herod Agrippa II, but the lure of Herod's sister Berenice was an added attraction.[6] The exquisite palatial surroundings detained Titus for several days and he sponsored numerous games. Many of his prisoners of war were savaged by wild animals and others killed in staged battles between opposing groups.

During his stay, a message arrived from the new commander of X *Fretensis* in Jerusalem, Terentius Rufus. The Zealot leader Simon ben Giora had been captured following a bizarre attempt to escape.[7] During the last days of resistance, ben Giora had slipped away with trusted friends and sappers into a secret underground passageway in the Upper City. They had intended to burrow their way hundreds of metres to freedom. The foolish plan was an impossible task due to the limestone bedrock and their limited provisions. Abandoning the scheme, ben Giora decided to dress up in a white shirt and purple shawl, in a vain effort to appear like some sort of imperial authority. He surfaced somewhere in the Old City and sneaked into the location where the Temple once stood. He presented himself to perplexed Roman soldiers and refused to give his name, demanding to see their commander. Terentius Rufus was sufficiently intrigued to interview ben Giora personally and soon exposed his true identify after which he was thrown into chains. Titus' reply to the news was to have him brought to Caesarea Maritima where he would await transfer to Rome to be executed during the planned triumph.[8]

Concluding celebrations at Caesarea Philippi, Titus returned to Caesarea on the coast. On 24 October, he had a good excuse to lay on further festivities for his brother's eighteenth birthday. Observing Domitian's birthday had a serious purpose: to promote the new Flavian dynasty. In a series of public spectacles, Titus used thousands of his Jewish prisoners in all manners of morbid entertainment for the bloodthirsty crowds, including mass burnings at the stake.[9] This level of inhumanity was entirely normal for the period during gladiatorial games. Three weeks later, Titus travelled north to Berytus (Beirut) to lay on even more extravagant

Vespasian, with Titus as *Caesar, tetradrachm*, struck 69/70, Antioch mint.
Obverse, laureate bust of Vespasian. Reverse, laureate bust of Titus.
Prieur 107A; McAlee 329.

and lavish celebrations for his father's sixtieth birthday on 17 November. Again, large numbers of prisoners were used as fodder for the macabre taste of the crowds.

During Titus' extended visit to Berytus, the outgoing governor of Syria, Gnaeus Collega, sent word to *Caesar* of escalating unrest in Antioch directed against the sizable Jewish community residing in the city. In preceding years, anti-Jewish sentiments had intensified in the Syrian capital, where the Jewish community was falsely blamed for a recent catastrophic arson attack on the city centre. Collega managed to quell hostilities against the Jews but cautioned Titus that those tensions persisted. Titus, in the midst of planning a tour of Syria after Berytus, chose not to take any action.

Stopping in several Syrian cities to host entertainments, Titus neared Antioch towards the end of 70 and large crowds gathered outside the city to welcome him. Representatives amongst the masses called for the expulsion of the Jews. However, Titus seemed unmoved by these demands, probably recognising the substantial contributions of the Jewish population to Antioch's economy and discerned no compelling reason to disrupt this established order.[10]

Titus' journey through Syria served as a pretext for a significant ulterior motive. His destination was the neighbouring kingdom of Commagene, where he would employ his diplomatic skills to appease the Parthians and advance his father's ambitious plans to fortify Rome's eastern borders. Before Vespasian's ascent to power, the Eastern Empire comprised a patchwork of provinces and client kingdoms. To the north, the provinces of Pontus, Galatia and Cappadocia lacked permanent legionary garrisons and relied on auxiliary forces for defence.[11] Four legions were stationed in Syria, with an additional two in Egypt.[12] Following Corbulo's campaign against Parthia over Armenia, IV *Scythica* remained stationed at Zeugma, west of the Euphrates. Although this city fell within the independent kingdom of Commagene, the legion provided a lone bastion supporting Roman interests in that region. Despite the distant location of IV *Scythica*, the actual depth from the frontier regions of Syria to the major metropolitan areas was precariously limited.[13] As a result, the system of defence and security in the East was largely reliant on the ability of client kingdoms to diminish the impact of incursions and provide troops while Roman mobile forces were dispatched from Syria or Egypt.

Within this organisation, Armenia was regarded as a neutral buffer state between Rome and its traditional enemy, the Parthian Empire – the only empire capable of putting Rome in its place.[14] Armenia was not a true independent buffer state: during Augustus' reign, it had been agreed that client kings independent of Parthia would rule Armenia.[15] However, this situation unsettled both empires, each of which considered Armenia to be within its zone of authority and the unease led to conflict.[16] Stability was eventually restored in 66 with an amendment to Augustus' policy such that Parthia would henceforth nominate a candidate for the Armenian throne and Rome would endorse the selection prior to any coronation.[17]

The stability of the eastern regions faced multiple challenges, including widespread pillaging along the Pontic coast by brigands and insurgent attacks on major cities like Trapezus. Compounding the issue was Rome's inability to dispatch *vexillationes*, legionary detachments, to aid the province. In 70, the available pool of *vexillationes* was tied up in various conflicts, including the siege of Jerusalem, the Batavian revolt and the Sarmatian invasion of Moesia. This predicament prompted consideration of the annexation of Lesser Armenia, including the deployment of a legion to secure the region and extend the zone of Roman influence into the Caucasus.[18]

Overall, the Eastern military doctrine was dependent on centralised offensive–defensive legionary forces. This entailed the launch of pre-emptive campaigns to defend a region's stability and security from areas where legions were concentrated.[19] Rather than waiting for enemy forces to invade Roman territory, the legions were prepared to engage perceived threats beyond the empire's borders or within its provinces. However, the volatility of the Roman East exposed several disadvantages: over-centralisation leaving vast areas under-defended; slow reaction time in remote areas; vulnerability to attacks on multiple fronts; and the need some-times to fight prolonged conflicts. Combined with the precarious status of Armenia as an independent entity, as well as the Pontic coast brigandage, a restructuring of Roman defences was needed. Recognising the need for change in the East, Vespasian sought to re-distribute his legions after the fall of Jerusalem. His reforms were to be implemented gradually. In the short term, as already described, X *Fretensis* was posted in Judea and in the autumn of 70 XII *Fulminata* was ordered to relocate to Melitene (Malatya, Turkey) in Cappadocia, about ten kilometres south-west of the Euphrates at a critical crossing over the river at the foot of the Taurus mountains.[20] This action allowed the development of Cappadocian *limes* (open frontier networks of roads, paths, watchtowers and forts) with a legion in reserve for special operations.[21] Meanwhile, IV *Scythica* remained stationed at Zeugma, bolstering Roman military influence opposite northern Mesopotamia. In Syria, a reshuffle reduced the number of legions to two in the core of the province, with VI *Ferrata* returning from Italy to Syria and possibly joining III *Gallica*, now back from Moesia, at Raphanaea.[22] In terms of leadership, Vespasian needed a highly trusted and experienced new consular governor for Cappadocia and he may have appointed his friend Traianus after his suffect consulship in September–October 70.[23] It is possible that Traianus arrived at Caesarea (Kayseri) in Cappadocia before the end of 70 and served as Vespasian's principal agent in the reorganisation of eastern security.[24] In such a role, he may have been the architect of the unification of Cappadocia and Galatia into one consular assignment. In the meantime, Caesennius Paetus, married to Titus' cousin, Flavia Sabina, was en route to Syria to replace Collega as governor.

Presumably in close communication, Traianus and Paetus would oversee the next phase of Vespasian's plans. Under the pretext of dealing with the instability along the Pontic Coast, a significant step would be taken in 72 to annex Lesser Armenia following the probable abdication of King Aristobulus. This region was then incorporated into the Cappadocia–Galatia complex and, again, *limes* were developed further.[25] To bolster defences, the newly formed XVI *Flavia*, established in 70, was sent to garrison Satala in the heart of Lesser Armenia, roughly fifty kilometres from the uppermost reaches of the Euphrates, opposite Armenia. XVI *Flavia* probably arrived in the region in 71 in advance of the absorption of Lesser Armenia.[26] Around the same time, in 72, Paetus would annex Commagene under the false pretext of collusion between Antiochus IV and the Parthians.[27] The kingdom would be amalgamated into the province of Syria, with VI *Ferrata* stationed at Samosata (Samsat) to complete the defences along the upper Euphrates.[28]

All these actions effectively established a new military zone in the vicinity of the Upper Euphrates. It was apparent that the arrangement with Armenia was no longer trusted and that Cappadocia, Galatia and Pontus required this additional protection.[29] The evolution of these changes would result in a frontier less reliant on client states, with a line of four legions spanning a position along the western banks of the upper Euphrates at Satala, Melitene, Samosata and Zeugma. The configuration formed a defensive screen from north to south across Rome's eastern domains, extending from Pontus in the north to Judea in the south, poised to defend the fertile regions, trade routes, principal cities and road networks of the east against insurgents or

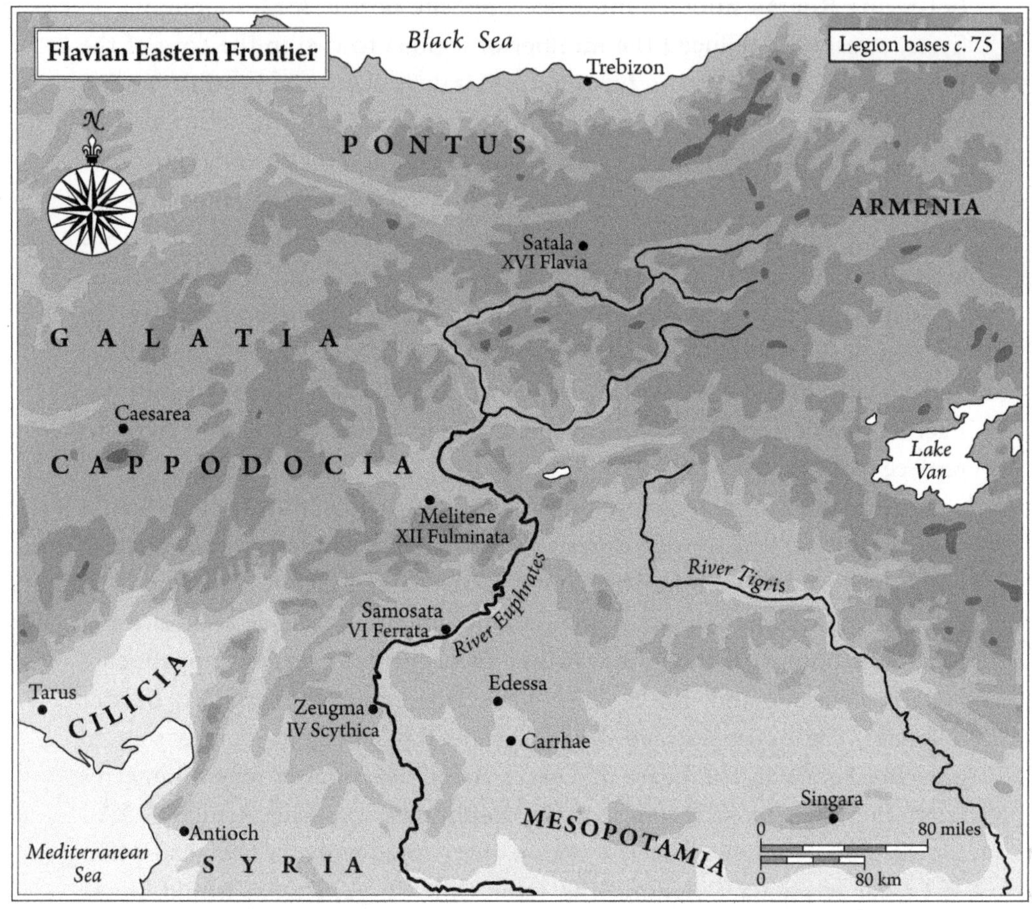

incursions, with the Euphrates serving in part as the backbone of the new frontier. These strategic adjustments laid the groundwork for Vespasian's longer-term plans to extend Rome's military control into the kingdoms of the Caucasus, which would become protectorates under the Roman Cappadocia–Galatia–Lesser Armenia plans.[30]

From the Parthian perspective, Vespasian's refusal of the offer of 40,000 cavalry from King Vologeses in 69 was significant.[31] Instead, he redirected the king's envoys to the Senate in Rome to ratify peace terms.[32] In reality, Vespasian did not want to be indebted to a Parthian king, a fact not lost on Vologeses. Another point of concern for Vologeses was the capture of King Izates of Adiabene's sons and his half-brother successor during the final stages of the Jerusalem siege.[33] Adiabene was a Parthian client kingdom in Northern Mesopotamia. Given that the captives were Jewish converts and supporters of the uprising, Titus had kept them in custody and later packed them off to Rome as hostages.[34] Izates was a Parthian vassal, so the situation was embarrassing for Vologeses. Additionally, the new deployment of XII *Fulminata* at Melitene near the Euphrates, reinforced by IV *Scythica* further south, almost certainly raised Parthian concerns. Vespasian's appointments of Traianus and Caesennius Paetus, along with the unification of Cappadocia and Galatia, would have also been monitored by the Parthians. They were not yet aware of Vespasian's medium-term vision for 72 and beyond, and when changes later occurred the Parthians would be distracted by internal conflict and an Alani invasion.

Aware of the immediate plans, mindful of his father's broader vision, and anticipating the Parthian reaction, Titus' mission was to reassure Vologeses' envoys that Rome sought peace and regional consolidation under its new emperor's leadership. Probably in early 71, Titus met ambassadors from King Vologeses at Zeugma, a highly symbolic location that secured a vital bridge over the Euphrates.[35] Accompanied by his two legions and joining IV *Scythica* on location, Titus projected significant power with over 10,000 troops on display.[36] Ceremonial announcements and military parades probably preceded discussions, and the Parthian delegates presented Titus with a golden crown in recognition of his victory over the Jews. Titus accepted the crown and hosted the delegates at a lavish banquet, where he continued his overtures for peace between the two ancient superpowers.[37]

Accepting the crown may have raised eyebrows back in Rome. The practice of Roman officials receiving crowns from Eastern dignitaries was a controversial matter due to Rome's historical aversion to kingship. Rome had a long-standing custom of opposing monarchy, traditionally dated to the expulsion of the last Roman king, Tarquin the Proud, in 509 BC, and emperors were usually cautious about how they presented themselves in Rome to avoid arousing suspicions of aspiring to be a monarch. Eastern cultures, particularly the Hellenistic and Persian influences, had a different perspective on regal symbolism. In the East, particularly in the Hellenistic kingdoms, the act of offering crowns or other royal symbols was often a gesture of respect and acknowledgement of authority rather than a literal declaration of kingship.

Roman generals and emperors, when involved in eastern campaigns or diplomatic missions, sometimes received honours and gestures that were traditionally associated with monarchs. Indeed, Greek-speaking people often referred to Roman emperors as βασιλεύς (king) and the term was used interchangeably with αὐτοκράτωρ (emperor) in the Greek East.[38] Titus would have been aware of such cultural matters and his acceptance rather reflected his vanity and a confidence that his father would understand the cultural symbolism.

After the banquet in Zeugma, Titus promptly returned to Antioch, where he surely contemplated the outcome of his diplomatic efforts and sent messages to his father describing the event. There were no immediate signs of warmongering or retaliatory actions from the Parthians. Even the later Roman annexations of Lesser Armenia and Commagene, coupled with the deployment of two additional legions near the Euphrates, would occur without any apparent Parthian response. In this regard, Titus' diplomatic overtures left a lasting legacy, earning him recognition as a successful negotiator. Arriving back in Antioch towards the end of January 71, having fulfilled his primary mission, he prepared to return to Rome. Accompanied by his legions, he travelled first to Jerusalem, presumably to oversee the duties of X *Fretensis* in maintaining post-war order in the region. During his visit, the city was still being searched for loot as prisoners continued to reveal hidden stashes.[39]

Titus next departed for Alexandria but travelled via Memphis, where he blessed the sacred Apis bull, a deity worshipped in that part of Egypt. There was a degree of syncretism in Egyptian and Roman religious practices. The Romans paid respect to Egyptian gods, especially after the annexation of Egypt as a province in 30 BC. The cult of Isis, for example, became popular throughout the Roman Empire and temples dedicated to Egyptian gods were built in various Roman cities.[40] Thus, Titus' detour to Memphis was an act motivated by political and religious considerations. By honouring Egyptian gods and customs, Titus aimed to demonstrate respect for the local religious beliefs and gain the favour of the Egyptian population. Additionally, by participating in an important religious ritual, Titus may have sought to portray himself as a legitimate authority in the eyes of the Egyptian people, thus solidifying Roman control over the region.

During the sanctified proceedings at Memphis, Titus wore a diadem, sparking rumours in Rome of a planned revolt.[41] Once again, we witness Titus taking the precarious step of wearing a crown, this time more poignantly on Egyptian soil. However, Vespasian's trust in his son does not seem to have been affected; once more, his father appears to have grasped the cultural representation. After Memphis, Titus probably reached Alexandria in the second half of March 71. It was time to send V *Macedonica* to its posting in Moesia and XV *Apollinaris* to Pannonia. The very best of his remaining Jewish prisoners, around 700 individuals in their prime, were sent in chains to Rome for the upcoming triumph.

The emerging spring weather permitted Titus to leave for Rome on a naval vessel, with two stops, at Rhegium and Puteoli.[42] He would never return to the East, where he had arguably made his greatest impact on the future of the Roman Empire. It had provided the opportunity for his military conquests. He had even been appointed a consul of Rome alongside his father, both *in absentia* while in Alexandria on 1 January 70.[43] And in his private life, he had an ongoing relationship with a powerful and wealthy eastern sovereign, Queen Berenice. As Titus sailed towards Rome, leaving the East behind him, he carried with him the profound legacy of his experiences in those distant lands.

CHAPTER 8

AUGUSTI FILIUS IN ROME

In the summer of 71, Titus returned to Rome, a city he had left five years earlier as an obscure figure. At the time of his departure he was an undistinguished junior senator having held only a quaestorship and possessing limited military experience as a *tribunus laticlavius*. Now he returned transformed, a celebrated ex-consul of Rome, *Caesar*, heir apparent to the Principate and the triumphant conqueror of Jerusalem. Rome had also changed. The tyranny and extravagance that defined the final years of Nero's reign had given way to what was being heralded as a new era of pragmatism, stability and peace under the rule of Vespasian. There was some truth to this narrative, though much of it was shaped and amplified by the Flavian propaganda machine, eager to solidify the legitimacy of the new dynasty and distance it from the turmoil of the recent past.

As soon as Titus landed at Ostia, swift messengers were sent ahead to rally crowds for his imminent arrival in Rome and the cheers were their loudest when he greeted his father and brother in the capital, a set piece for the image of imperial stability under the Flavian patriarch and his sons.[1] Titus was united again with his daughter, Julia Titi, now aged seven. She would not have recognised her father after his absence.

Months prior to Titus' return to Rome in June, meticulous plans were laid for the triumphant celebration of the Jewish War.[2] Notably, the Senate had granted individual triumphs for Vespasian and Titus, but as a powerful symbol of their unified dynastic position, they chose to hold a single grand event.[3] On the eve of the triumph, the soldiery marched out of their camps on the outskirts of Rome and it is thought that they mustered in and around the grounds of the Villa Publica, a prominent two-storey building set in its own park on the Campus Martius.[4] These troops were selected from cohorts distinguished for bravery during the war and were individuals awarded military crowns to represent their units.[5] The *porticus triumphi* may have been the large colonnaded arcade surrounding the Villa where the procession could find shelter while they waited for the event to start the following morning. Close by, the soldiers may have also assembled in the Saepta Julia, a building that had long lost its political significance as a venue for assemblies to elect the republic's magistrates. Used subsequently by some emperors for games, it was a large piazza, 30,000 square metres, surrounded by porticoes that may have also served as the *porticus triumphi* for the large procession to gather within.[6] Close by, Vespasian and Titus slept the night before in the Temple of Isis.[7] It was a curious choice, despite the acceptance of the Egyptian goddess in Rome and elsewhere. It could have been a practical decision relating to the auspicious surroundings in the Campus Martius or perhaps a nod to the support that had come from Egypt as a Roman province during the Jewish War.

At first light, the victors emerged from the temple crowned with laurels and wearing robes of traditional purple, the colour of imperial power reserved for emperors.[8] Their first formal act was to meet with the Senate at the Porticus Octaviae, a complex of buildings including temples, a library and a meeting house.[9] The complex was a short walk south of the Temple of Isis and they both mounted a tribunal erected in front of the main cloisters and sat on ornate ivory chairs. Gathered behind the distinguished guests, soldiers dressed in silk garments and crowned with laurels applauded their emperor and *Caesar*, requiring Vespasian eventually to signal for silence. As a traditional gesture of reverence, Vespasian pulled a fold of his toga over his head and offered prayers, followed by Titus who also gave prayers to the gods. Vespasian delivered a short speech to the dignitaries and soldiers before dismissing the latter to take a breakfast provided for by him.[10]

Vespasian and Titus next partially retraced their path through the Campus Martius to the Porta Triumphalis, Triumphal Gate. The free-standing arch is lost today and the location remains unknown.[11] At that time, it might have referred to the Arch of Claudius over the Via Lata. Here, they ate breakfast and were dressed in the full triumphal attire, a suitably ostentatious gold-embroidered purple toga over a similarly adorned purple tunic.[12] They then gathered their required paraphernalia: in their right hands, laurel boughs; in their left, sceptres topped by eagles. *Laurus nobilis*, bay laurel, was featured frequently during the event because it symbolised victory and triumph. Finally, their faces were painted red, the colour of Mars, god of war.[13] After sacrifices were offered to the gods by the Porta Triumphalis, they both mounted their spectacular ornate chariots, each pulled by four immaculately groomed horses. They were ready to start the triumph and presumably the procession of several hundred metres was assembled before and behind them along the Via Lata.

The following list proposes an order and participation for the assembled triumphal column:[14]

1st: Trumpeters, heralding the advance.

2nd: Members of the Senate.

3rd: A display of precious 'arts, riches of all sorts, rarities of nature' to represent the reach of the Roman Empire.[15] Enormous quantities of gold, silver, tapestries and ivory artworks and artefacts were carried as if a flowing river of treasure.

4th: A plethora of animals dressed in ornamented trappings.

5th: Images of Roman gods made from rare materials and crafted by the finest workmanship. All the bearers of these and other parts of the procession were adorned with purple garments, interwoven with gold.

6th: Sacrificial white bulls or oxen, adorned with decorations and led by priests.

7th: Jewish prisoners and probably a display of their arms. The captives were dressed up to obscure any malnutrition, injuries or other deformities as a result of captivity. Simon ben Giora and John ben Levi, bound in chains, were the highlight of the prisoner section.

8th: Magnificent floats, towering three to four stories high and adorned with golden carpets, showcasing intricate scaled models and figurines portraying pivotal moments from the war. Among these depictions were scenes of besieged towns and the engulfed Temple of Jerusalem in flames. Additionally, statues immortalising Jewish commanders and their conquered cities were featured prominently, capturing the manner in which they were vanquished. Much like Trajan's Column, these elaborate displays reflected the Romans' appreciation for visually immersive representations of military triumphs.

9th: Ships, presumably meant to depict the fleet of enemy vessels destroyed during the battle on the Lake of Galilee.[16]

10th: A display of war spoils from Judea and Jerusalem, including a pageant of the most prized treasures taken from the Temple of Jerusalem, including the golden table, the golden seven-branch menorah and a pair of trumpets.

11th: The Laws of the Jews probably represented on tablets or large parchments.

12th: A large group carrying statues of Victory made from gold and ivory.

13th: Lictors of the Emperor, symbolic state bodyguards.

14th: Vespasian followed by Titus on their chariots and accompanied by Domitian on an impressive horse. According to one ancient source, such a triumph may have involved a slave holding a golden Etruscan jewelled crown over Vespasian's head, constantly whispering a warning into his ear, 'Respice post te. Hominem te memento' ('Look behind you. Remember that you are a man'), just in case Vespasian lapsed into thinking all this display of power made him a god.[17]

15th: On horseback, a selection of senior officers representing the forces involved in the triumph.

16th: Last, the long column of soldiers, their javelins adorned with laurels, singing songs or jesting in verses at Vespasian's and Titus' expense in a unique moment where such freedom of speech was allowed.

The detailed route of the procession is not known and one cannot assume that the same course was used by different victors.[18] However, it is probable that the spectacle first wove across Campus Martius to make a circuit inside the Circus Flaminius, giving a chance for many seated spectators to view the column. Exiting the Circus, the parade passed around the Theatre of Marcellus and filed through the Forum Holitorium to pass around the southern slope of the Capitoline then proceed north along the Vicus Iugarius. Moving between the Basilica Julia and the Temple of Divus Augustus the column looped south along the Vicus Tuscus.[19] From there the march passed around an urbanised area in the valley between the Capitoline and Palatine Hills called the Velabrum to enter the Forum Boarium, the oldest forum in Rome.[20]

All along the route, streets had been cleaned, temples were opened and their altars billowed out incense smoke, and numerous buildings and statues were adorned with garlands of flowers.[21] Next, the procession proceeded into the famous Circus Maximus to complete a full circuit around the *spina* (spine) and back out where it entered. This allowed up to 150,000 spectators to have a clear view of the procession.[22] It is possible the procession then headed south-east along the outside of the Circus Maximus and turned north to pass along the eastern side of the Palatine where it continued through the complex of Nero's abandoned Domus Aurea (Golden House). Symbolically, this route cast a Flavian shadow over the tyrant's obscene opulence.[23] The pageant subsequently turned west towards the Roman Forum, the heart of Rome, onto the Via Sacra. Here the crowds packed every space in the forum as the column passed the Regia, the Temple of Julius Caesar, the Basilica Amelia and the Senate House before arriving at the stairs of the Temple of Saturn.[24]

Titus, as *Caesar, aureus,* struck 72–73, Rome mint. Reverse, Titus on his triumphal *quadriga.* The coin commemorated the triumph he shared with his father in June 71. *Sear 1 no.2425.*

At this stage, Simon ben Giora and probably a portion of prisoners were led away for execution in the Tullianum, known today as the Mamertine Prison. John ben Levi was spared this fate and would see out the rest of his days in captivity. The most esteemed figures in the triumphal procession began their ascent up the Capitoline Hill along the Via Sacra, following time-honoured tradition. Outside the Temple of Jupiter, they paused, awaiting the announcement of ben Giora's execution.[25] When news of his death reached the crowd, applause erupted, and Vespasian and Titus dismounted from their chariots to oversee the sacrificial rites. Customarily, the victors entered the temple itself, where they placed their laurel victory wreaths and select spoils of war at the foot of the colossal statue of Jupiter as a final offering to the god of gods. However, the temple was being rebuilt following its destruction by fire at the end of the civil wars of 69. Presumably, their wreaths were nevertheless placed amidst the building works at the foot of a temporary statue of Jupiter.

Suetonius records an intriguing comment by Vespasian during his triumph that gives insight into his character and nature.

> So far was he from a desire for pomp and show, that on the day of his triumph, he did not hesitate to say: 'It serves me right for being such a fool as to want a triumph in my old age, as if it were due to my ancestors or had ever been among my own ambitions.'[26]

The evening's revelries proceeded with public banquets and private celebrations. The victorious hosts retired with friends and distinguished guests for a grand feast to complete the festivities.[27] The triumph was a success, a magnificent spectacle of Rome's might under Vespasian, and marked a turning point for the new dynasty to convey a transition towards peace and stability, the harbingers of future prosperity.

Co-ruler in All But Name

In the run up to Titus' return to Rome and within three years of his arrival, he received titles and authority that clearly maintained his designation as heir apparent and allowed him to wield enormous power. He was not a formal co-ruler of Rome, as would later occur for the first time between the co-emperors Marcus Aurelius and Lucius, but to all intents and purposes, he shared rule with his father.[28] Vespasian alone held the titles of *Augustus* (reserved exclusively for the reigning emperor), *Pater Patriae* (father of the country) and *Pontifex Maximus* (chief priest), clearly distinguishing him as the emperor with ultimate authority. Nevertheless, the following titles and authorities were bestowed on Titus:

Imperium: Power and authority – military, judicial and administrative – had been conferred on senior magistrates during the Republican era. From 23 BC, even when not holding a consulship, Augustus possessed *imperium* (and *tribunicia potestas*) granting him the authority to summon the Senate.[29] For Titus, receiving *imperium* as a proconsul solidified his status as a leader with the power to command military forces and make decisions on behalf of the Roman state. Sharing the title with Vespasian, this mandate was crucial for maintaining order within the empire, executing imperial policies and defending Rome's interests.

Tribunicia potestas: The Republican tribunes originally held rights to defend and support the plebs (common citizens). *Tribunicia potestas,* amongst other functions, significantly granted the authority to veto actions of the consuls and other magistrates. The role had held popular support but its function had long faded during the imperial period. However, the assumption of tribunician power, together with *imperium,* was the legal basis of imperial rule since Augustus had secured the annual renewal of the authority. Titus assumed the title in 71 and every year thereafter the powers were renewed (and counted). For example, Titus' ninth *Tribunicia potestas* was held in 79.[30]

Imperial salutations: Normally reserved for the emperor, Titus' receipt of salutations was a significant emblem of power. *Imperator*, commander of all Roman forces, was the salutation given on accession and subsequently repeated after victories and numbered accordingly. It is unclear what triggered the first salutation but it joined his titles in 71 and he was awarded thirteen others during Vespasian's reign, the father sharing his honours with the son and heir apparent to an unprecedented degree.[31]

Consulships: The highest magistracy had lost the vast majority of its former power to the emperor and his secretariat but the position was still the pinnacle of a senator's career and held joint presidency over the Senate. Two consuls were appointed at any one time by the emperor, who could also hold one of the offices himself. As an ex-consul, a senator could expect the best military and governorship positions and perhaps the prestigious appointment of a second consulship or even the extremely rare honour of a third. The *consul ordinarius* was the most prestigious, opening the year, and *consul suffectus* took over relinquished positions as the year proceeded. The Flavian period saw the appointment of around six to ten consuls a year.[32] Titus had been granted his first term as consul, *consul ordinarius*, along with his father *in absentia*, on 1 January 71. During his father's reign he held a further six *ordinarius* appointments alongside Vespasian. Without doubt, the holding of so many consulships by the Flavii was meant to signal their power over the state. It was not subtle and probably drew private criticism from certain senators who viewed this as open despotism. No other heir apparent had held as many consulships as Titus before he was emperor and this left no question for anyone in the Senate and beyond that Titus Caesar was next in line.[33]

Censorship: The position of censor, once highly esteemed during the Republican period, held the responsibility of conducting a census of the Roman populace. However, in the imperial era such appointments became rare occurrences, with Claudius being one of the very few emperors to hold a censorship, alongside Lucius Vitellius as his colleague. One of the crucial functions of this office was to conduct an evaluation of the Senate's composition. Vespasian and Titus chose to be censors, most probably in April 73 and held the positions for the statutory eighteen months.[34] While the emperor possessed the authority to make changes to the composition of the Senate without the need for a formal census, the censorship provided a legal cover for implementing the numerous alterations deemed necessary.[35] The aftermath of civil

war and Nero's purges of senators had left the Senate depleted. The
Flavii seized this opportunity to fill the vacancies with individuals
they trusted, reward loyal supporters and shape the socio-political
landscape according to their vision for the empire. Consequently, many
individuals were adlected into the Senate, a process through which the
Emperor could select candidates for promotion without requiring them
to hold the traditional magistracies or meet the usual prerequisites for
membership. Additionally, some were elevated to the patrician class.[36]

In summary, Titus held great responsibility and authority in Rome and across
the empire. However, there can be little doubt that Vespasian was *Augustus*
and Titus was *augusti filius*, son of the emperor. As a sign of this, Titus
assumed the administrative burden of government on behalf of Vespasian
such as imperial correspondence, drafting edicts and the rather lowly
task of reading the imperial speeches to the Senate. As Suetonius astutely
concludes, Titus 'became his father's colleague, almost his guardian'.[37]

Commander of the Praetorian Guard

The Praetorian Guard has long captivated the modern imagination with
its formidable power and intricate role in shaping the fate of emperors and
the empire itself. They were the most privileged, highest paid and shortest-
serving of all Roman soldiers. Known by the Romans as *cohortes praetoriae*,
praetorian cohorts, their soldiers could be recruited directly or promoted
from the legions.[38] Their primary duty was to serve as the personal bodyguard of the emperor and they were considered the most powerful division
of the Roman army. Thus, their station in Rome, in the imperial residences,
in the Senate and on the battlefield projected the power of the emperor and
his ability to use the strong arm of the Guard where needed. It is not possible
to ascertain the size of the Guard after Vespasian's accession, and it could
have ranged from 9,000 up to 19,000 Praetorians.[39]

One baffling question about the Praetorian Guard in this period is
why did emperors continue to maintain the unit when they had betrayed
their benefactors on so many occasions in the past? Caligula had been
assassinated by the Praetorians after they conspired with senators. Nero
had been abandoned by the corps, contributing to his suicide. Otho had
persuaded some Praetorian thugs to murder Galba in the forum. Vitellius
had disbanded the Othonian Praetorian Guard on the grounds that they had
abandoned Galba and the dismissed individuals went on to fight Vitellian

forces at the Second Battle of Bedriacum (Cremona).[40] Evidently, the idea of having Praetorian Prefects of equestrian rank to prevent mutinous acts had failed.[41] New initiatives to tackle the problem, such as Caligula's elevation of his Germanic bodyguard of elite horse guards, *corporis custos*, had failed to protect him against assassination by the Praetorians.

Consequently, Vespasian wanted to try a different tactic and appoint a single commander of the Guard, someone he could unquestionably trust: Titus. While Vespasian had been in Egypt, Mucianus had managed the appointment of Marcus Arrecinus Clemens as a prefect of the Guard, removing Arrius Varus. He was the brother of Titus' first wife, Arrecina Tertulla, whose father had also been a prefect under Caligula.[42] It is possible that Tiberius Julius Alexander was Clemens' colleague as co-prefect as a reward for his loyalty during Vespasian's accession. The job was normally a post for an equestrian, so Clemens' appointment broke with that tradition. Despite these reasonable prefects, it is thought that Titus nevertheless took over solely in 71 until his accession in 79.[43]

As sole commander of the Praetorian Guards, Titus has been condemned for his blatant persecution of mistrusted individuals. It is alleged that if Titus suspected someone of a seditious crime, he would dispatch the Guard to apprehend the accused at a public location. There, the Praetorians would announce the punishment, create an atmosphere that garner 'agreement' from those present, and then proceed with a summary execution. Even ex-consuls were not spared. Titus was 'deeply disliked at the time' for this behaviour.[44] It is problematic to reconcile this tyrannical use of the Guard when other indicators suggest that, though Titus could be ruthless, he was not a despotic executioner. Perhaps the truth lies somewhere in the middle and his role as commander did occasion merciless use of the Praetorians to tackle putatively treasonous individuals but only on rare occasions.[45]

Affairs of State

Empowered, titled, in command of Rome's elite Praetorian Guards and the heir apparent, Titus was intimately involved in his father's *consilium principis*. In matters of state the *consilium* assisted Vespasian on a range of topics. A limited number of the most dependable served as a core group of advisors and others were asked their opinion on a case-by-case basis depending on the subject. Overall, one can assume that Vespasian strove to include wise and trusted senior senators and members of the elite but he may have also selected smart equestrians and freedmen. Indeed, Vespasian's reign is recognised as one in which high-quality individuals managed the administration well. The availability and suitability of individuals serving as advisors evolved over time, so the following list of possible counsellors to Vespasian should be viewed as fluid during the early to mid-seventies, and many if not all would have had frequent interactions and correspondence with Titus who also served on his father's *consilium*.

Vespasian's *consilium principis*	
Member	*Relationship to Vespasian*
Marcus Cocceius Nerva	Descending from the newer Italian nobility, the Cocceii, and a future emperor of Rome (96–98), Nerva was awarded an extremely prestigious *ordinarius* consulship alongside Vespasian in 71. Only three other non-Flavians had this honour during Vespasian's reign. He was evidently one of the strongest supporters of the Flavii and very close to Vespasian.
Tiberius Plautius Silvanus Aelianus	Suffect consul with Titus in 74, Vespasian awarded him the triumph denied by Nero for his exemplary successes as legate of Moesia in the 60s.[46]
Domitian	In his twenties and accelerated into a *suffectus* consulship in 71, there is little doubt that Domitian was involved in certain *consilium* discussions.
L. Caesennius Paetus	*Ordinarius* consul in 61, a seasoned senator, he was married to Flavia Sabina the paternal niece of Vespasian. In 70 he was governor of Syria and probably worked closely with Traianus to oversee Vespasian's changes in the East.
Gaius Licinius Mucianus	Rewarded in 70 with a *suffectus* consulship for his crucial support of Vespasian's accession, as well as being his deputy in Rome while Vespasian remained in Egypt, he received the high honour of a third consulship in 72. After this great distinction, his influence waned.[47]
Q. Petillius Cerialis Caesius Rufus	A close family member having been married to Vespasian's only daughter, Domitilla II, now deceased.[48] *Suffectus* consulship in 70 alongside Mucianus. Was appointed governor of Britain and dealt with the Batavian revolt while on his way to his province. Awarded a second *suffectus* consulship in 74.[49]

T. Flavius Sabinus III	Vespasian's nephew was awarded a second *suffectus* consulship in 72, alongside Mucianus' third. Before this he probably served as governor of Pannonia.[50]
Titus Clodius Eprius Marcellus	Worthy and esteemed, Marcellus was a powerful senator, a survivor and Vespasian's friend.[51] Member of two respected priesthoods, the *sodales augustales* and an *augur*. In 70–73 he held the prestigious appointment of proconsul of Asia for an unusually extended three-year period and a second *suffectus* consulship in 74.[52]
Lucius Junius Quintus Vibius Crispus	Like Marcellus, a close companion of Vespasian, he was responsible for Rome's water supply before his governorship of Africa and held a second *suffectus* consulship in 74 alongside Titus' third as *ordinarius*.[53]
Marcus Ulpius Traianus	A *comes* (companion) of Vespasian and highly trusted legate during the Jewish Wars, he was rewarded with a *suffectus* consulship in 70 and then sent to govern Cappadocia during critical changes in the region. He went on to serve as governor of Syria in 73–74. His son Trajan would be a future emperor (98–117).
L. Valerius Catullus Messallinus	Granted the honoured *ordinarius* consulship in 73 alongside Domitian in an unusual year when neither Vespasian nor Titus held a consulship. Even more remarkable given his blindness.[54]
Tiberius Alexander	Born into a Jewish family in Egypt, he attained extraordinary influence and was prefect of Egypt (66–69), where he provided pivotal support for Vespasian's accession. He was subsequently Titus' second-in-command during the siege of Jerusalem. He probably served briefly as a Praetorian Guard prefect in 70–71.
C. Rantius Quirinalis Valerius Festus	In charge of a Numidian legion in 69–70, where he disposed of Piso, the governor of Africa for his allegiance to Vitellius and was rewarded with military honours and a *suffectus* consulship alongside Domitian in 71 and was governor of Pannonia in 73.[55]
Arrecinus Clemens	A Flavian loyalist and brother of Titus' first deceased wife, he was *suffectus* consul in 73 and was briefly prefect of the Praetorian Guard after Vespasian's accession.

With Titus and his advisors by his side or in close correspondence, Vespasian's greatest merit, which permeated through his actions, policies and management of imperial affairs, was his steadiness.[56] His relationship with the Senate was characterised by resolve tempered by restraint and he showed an unusual sense of humour.[57] He possessed unrivalled power through the army and swiftly acquired extensive powers through a new law known as the *lex de imperio vespasiani* in January 70, alongside the titles and authorities he gained on his accession. The eight clauses of this law delineated Vespasian's powers and drew on precedents granted to previous emperors. Tacitus later described these powers as *cuncta principibus solita*, meaning he received simply 'everything customary for emperors'.[58]

Vespasian's reign was considered by Roman historians as respectable. Notwithstanding his frugal nature, Tacitus acknowledged his amiable relations with the Senate, his virtuous modesty and diligent hard work. Suetonius too gives praise to the first of the Flavian emperors and the restoration of stability:

> The empire, which for a long time had been unsettled and, as it were, drifting, through the usurpation and violent death of three emperors, was at last taken in hand and given stability by the Flavian family. This house was, it is true, obscure and without family portraits, yet it was one of which our country had no reason whatever to be ashamed.[59]

However, there was dissent within the ranks of the Senate towards Vespasian, and by extension his heir, Titus. Helvidius Priscus, serving as praetor in 70, was an outspoken Stoic who openly rebuked Vespasian on several occasions. This opposition stemmed from a long-standing tension between the emperor and Stoicism dating back to the Julio-Claudian era. Stoicism, though not inherently anti-imperial, championed freedom of speech and governance founded on principles of self-control, integrity, justice and moral rectitude.

After Vespasian's accession and his initial absence from Rome, Helvidius made audacious attempts to empower the Senate. He advocated that the Senate lead the restoration of the Capitoline and relegate the emperor to a supporting role. The Senate should address state finances through the creation of a senatorial commission and have serving magistrates congratulate the new emperor as envoys rather than selected individuals.[60]

Despite the Senate's rejection of his proposals, Helvidius remained steadfast in his dissent. On Vespasian's return, he refused to address the emperor by his titles, referring to him by his personal name and even omitted customary honours in his official praetor's edicts. While these actions probably tested Vespasian's tolerance, they were far from treasonous. However, Helvidius' opposition to the extraordinary promotions of Vespasian's sons and his objections to Titus' conduct in Rome proved a tipping point in the first half of the seventies.[61] Compelled to act, Vespasian ordered Helvidius' arrest and the emperor left the Senate visibly distressed and prompted to declare, 'My successor shall be my son or no one at all.'[62] Helvidius faced banishment and later execution, with Vespasian purportedly regretting his decision to execute him but unable to prevent his demise in time due to communication errors. The episode underscored the delicate balance between dissent and authority in the Flavian era.[63]

The Helvidius affair was an important matter for Vespasian because it marred his relationship with senators but it did not stop his hard work reforming the organisation of the empire. As noted, he had an agenda to change the distribution of legions in the East and create a zone of influence along the Euphrates. He also reorganised two of the wealthiest provinces, Asia and Africa, installing two capable governors for the tasks: Eprius Marcellus in the former and Q. Vibius Crispus in the latter.[64] Agricola, governor in Britannia from 77, recovered losses in North Wales and subdued Anglesey. He also expanded Roman territories into Caledonia (Scotland). In terms of governorship appointments, the Flavians were reluctant to appoint patricians as governors of military provinces due to a suspicion of that class, except for those like Agricola they trusted or had adlected into the class during Vespasian's and Titus' censorships.[65]

Like his predecessors, Vespasian commissioned grand constructions in Rome and in several cases returned private areas previously owned by Nero back to the general population. Nero's sprawling Domus Aureus would be sacrificed for space and parts recycled in foundations. Three flagship projects exemplified this policy: the Flavian Amphitheatre and the Temples of Divine Claudius and Peace.

Arguably the greatest of all Roman constructions and today an icon recognisable globally, Vespasian's commission of the Amphitheatrum Flavium was his supreme contribution to the people of Rome. It replaced Nero's large artificial lake that was part of his Golden House. Better known as the Colosseum, it would hold up to 50,000 people. Construction began some time between 70 and 72 and the inauguration was held under Titus in 80.[66]

A lesser-known facet of Vespasian's building endeavours was his dedication to completing Claudius' temple and its surrounding porticoes on the Caelian Hill. While Nero showed little interest in honouring his adoptive divine father, Vespasian revitalised the cult of Claudius, recognising its potential to bolster his own eventual deification and fortify the Flavian dynasty's legacy. Of the Julio-Claudian emperors, only Augustus and Claudius had received divine status. Vespasian's personal beliefs about imperial deification may have been ambivalent, but he saw the strategic value in elevating Claudius. By doing so, he could pave the way for his own eventual deification, ensuring a smoother transition and acceptance of his dynasty among the Roman populace.[67]

One of Vespasian's notable undertakings was the construction of the Templum Pacis, dedicated to Pax, the goddess of peace and inaugurated in AD 75.[68] Situated just north of the Roman Forum, this project probably required the demolition of a western portion of Nero's Golden House to make way for the new temple. The Templum Pacis was more than just a temple, it was a grand complex. Enclosed within its sacred grounds was a diverse cultural forum that showcased arts from across the empire. Dominating the complex was a large hall featuring an apse designed to house the statue of Pax. Surrounding this were expansive marble courtyards adorned with intricate gardens, possibly complemented by water features and all bordered by elegant colonnaded porticoes. Serving as a public gallery, exquisite artworks sourced from various parts of the empire were on display. Several masterpieces were repurposed from the Golden House, while others were the precious spoils from Jerusalem. This public exhibition stood in stark contrast to Nero's private collection, emphasising the Flavians' commitment to sharing the artistic wealth of the empire. Visitors were meant to marvel at this diverse collection and recognise the Flavian vision of Roman peace, which celebrated unity by incorporating the artistic achievements of its diverse subjects.[69]

The glorious Temple of Jupiter Optimus Maximus had been destroyed by fire during the Vitellian attack against Vespasian's brother when he had sought refuge on the Capitoline Hill in 69. The emperor financed reconstruction with the *fiscus judaicus*, the tax he imposed on Jews following the revolt.[70] More than just supplying funding, he personally attended the initial works to clear the ruins, carrying away debris in a basket on his shoulders.[71] Additionally, Vespasian ordered the replacement of 3,000 bronze tablets lost with the temple that had documented senatorial decrees, alliances and other precious historical records back to the foundation of Rome.[72] The temple rebuilding was probably completed in 75.

All these public works incurred considerable expense. However, one of Vespasian's defining traits was his thrifty nature and diligent financial management, particularly in the aftermath of the devastating civil wars. While considered parsimonious in fiscal matters, he may have recognised the value of the economic stimulus that came from large construction projects. On assuming power, Vespasian acknowledged that restoring the state would require a colossal sum: 4,000 million HS – equivalent to around five years' worth of Rome's tax revenue. Fixing damages from the civil wars, recovering from Nero's extravagant spending and the upkeep of a vast army in the absence of lucrative conquests all necessitated significant expenditure. To address the financial challenges, Vespasian implemented various measures, including the recovery and exploitation of public lands, tax increases and the introduction of new levies.[73] He was even accused of having no qualms about the extraction of fees from candidates seeking public office or selling imperial pardons.[74]

A revealing anecdote survives of a conversation between Vespasian and Titus on the topic of a newly introduced tax on public urinals. The cleaning industry of Rome keenly collected urine to process it so that the urea content converted to ammonia. When trodden into dirty clothes, the ammonia-rich urine helped break down greasy strains by dissolving fats. Vespasian had seen an opportunity to raise funds by taxing the amount of urine the fullers collected. Titus expressed his indignation at the collection of such a tax and his father picked up some gold coins saying: *'pecunia non olet'* – 'money does not stink'.[75] Here we can see the pragmatism of the emperor on fiscal matters and a lesson for Titus. Overall, Vespasian understood that financial security meant political security. So, as for other state affairs, he closely oversaw the fiscal management of the empire.[76]

Family Life and Relationships

We can reliably assume that Titus was diligently involved in many affairs of state during Vespasian's reign but what do we know about the status and visibility of his family life during his years in Rome as *augusti filius*?

Titus' daughter, Julia, had probably been raised by her maternal grandmother (if she was still alive) while Titus had been away from Rome. The nurse who had helped raise Domitian, called Phyllis, also supported Julia's upbringing.[77] Wet nurses held a high status in Roman households and were often responsible for the child's care until adulthood.[78] Vespasian is thought to have proposed in the early 70s that the young Julia be betrothed to Domitian in his late teens.[79] Such a cousin marriage had been legal since the reign of Claudius and Vespasian's motive was to strengthen the Flavian dynasty further. However, Domitian persistently refused the union. He already had his eye on another, Domitia Longina, who was a more attractive option for him: she was around eighteen, belonged to the Julio-Claudian family and her father was the famed general Domitius Corbulo. Domitian appears to have got his way because Vespasian consented to the marriage after arrangements were made for Domitia Longina's divorce from her existing husband.[80] They would have a daughter in 73 and a son the year after but both children appear to have died in their childhood.[81]

Julia later married her paternal second cousin, Titus Flavius Sabinus IV, Vespasian's grand-nephew.[82]

Titus had been divorced since 65 and it is curious why he never remarried despite his eligibility. The Flavii were keen on projecting imperial stability through clearly identified heirs, but Titus had only the young Julia. With Domitian also positioned as an heir to the throne after Titus, the succession nonetheless seemed secure. At thirty-five years old in the mid-70s, Titus may have felt no immediate pressure to father a male heir. Alternatively, he might simply have lacked the inclination to enter into another marriage. The example of Emperor Tiberius, who remained unmarried for around thirty-five years, from before his accession until his death, offers an example of personal choice influencing such matters. Moreover, his own father had never remarried since the death of his mother and had resumed relations with his long-term mistress, Caenis, his wife in everything but name.[83] While she appears to have been accepted in this manner, a reflection of the respect Vespasian commanded, Domitian behaved condescendingly towards her and presumably upset her and his father. When returning from a trip, Domitian apparently held out his hand to her instead of offering the usual kiss.[84] Caenis is thought to have died at some time during the first half of the 70s and this left an enormous void in Vespasian's life.[85] He did not find another female companion but with her passing he enjoyed the company, when business was completed, of one of the numerous women he supported.[86]

In terms of associations beyond marriage, Titus had relationships both with younger males and eunuchs, as was not uncommon among Roman elites of the time.[87] However, these would have been superficial and mostly carnal. Far more controversial amongst the Roman gentry was his prolonged connection with Berenice. Their bond was significant and endured, despite many years of separation since they were last together in the East. It is possible that forces in Rome, namely Vespasian, had discouraged any further liaisons for the fear of repeating the political tensions that had resulted from Cleopatra's provocative visit to Rome in 46 BC, accompanying Julius Caesar during his triumphal procession after his victory in the Alexandrian War.[88] There had been mixed views. Some senators were outraged and despised her presence as an affront to traditional Roman values, given her status as a foreign queen and her romantic relationship with Julius Caesar; others viewed it as a political move by Caesar to solidify his power and gain support from Egypt. Rumours had abounded that Caesar would move to Alexandria and marry Cleopatra, made worse by his dedication of a gilded statue of Cleopatra in the sacred Temple of Venus. Berenice definitely fitted the profile of a second Cleopatra: the beautiful eastern royal, mysterious and powerful.

Vespasian, *aureus*, struck 71, Lugdunum (Lyon) mint.
Reverse, Titus and Domitian galloping in military attire with spears
to portray the image of virile Flavian male heirs. *Sear I no.2397.*

By the year 75, however, Vespasian's concern had waned. Presumably his Principate was sufficiently settled and his regime felt well secured, or perhaps his views had simply softened with age. Thus, Berenice travelled to Rome to unite with Titus, accompanied by her brother Agrippa. Installed in the palace and other residences with his lover, rumours swirled of their notorious passion for each other and the possibility of a marriage.[89] There was clearly real affection between them. In any event, the optics of having Berenice present in and around Rome as the de facto wife of Titus eventually took their toll on public opinion.[90] The situation had become 'an embarrassment and marriage an impossibility'.[91] Vespasian probably intervened and one can imagine a reluctant but understanding Titus asking her to leave Rome, possibly in the first half of 79.[92] Perhaps the affair had reached its natural end. In any event, Titus was able to master his feelings over her dismissal.

Conspiracy

The Roman Senate was an exclusively male organisation, riddled with corruption, increasingly redundant and a dangerous place to work. It comes as no surprise that we know of at least one serious conspiracy in 79. The nature of sedition means the details are murky but Vespasian was the target and, by extension, Titus and Domitian as his heirs.[93] One can speculate that, with Vespasian showing signs of aging – he was suffering from chronic gout – the conspirators had an eye on the implications for the succession. It was one thing for Vespasian to have rescued Rome from anarchy, another to allow a new imperial dynasty to establish itself – and one lacking the old and august lineage of the Julio-Claudians.[94] Several individuals were probably involved in the conspiracy, but only two are known: Aulus Caecina and Eprius Marcellus.

Marcellus was Vespasian's friend and a capable governor who had been given the noble task of overseeing Asia for an extended period, as well as receiving a second consulship. He was around sixty years of age in 79. Caecina was also a friend of Vespasian but is not known to have received any distinctions from the emperor. He also had a long history of abandoning emperors. At the age of thirty-six, he appears an improbable associate of Marcellus.[95] Conceivably, a more senior senator had bought them together, all united by their support for another candidate to succeed Vespasian, when their friendship towards the emperor had turned hostile. In any event, the imperial machinery uncovered the plot. A manuscript of Caecina's speech to troops that were ready to act was handed over. These troops may have amounted to a legion or two and close to Italy. If so, it was an acutely serious mutiny in the making.[96]

Vespasian endorsed the necessary action and Titus executed the order. Caecina was invited to one of the imperial residences to dine. As he rose from the meal to leave, he was cut down by Praetorian guards there and then in the dining room. Emperor and son could not risk any delay because of his potential armed support. Marcellus' status and profile as an elder statesman necessitated a different approach. He was brought to trial before the Senate and condemned. He chose to take his own life. If legionary troops had been involved then the officers concerned would have been swiftly dispatched as well and all this shattered the image of a steady Flavian dynasty. Even if the soldiery were not from among the legions, the event was almost certainly deeply embarrassing for Vespasian, Titus and Domitian, and sent shockwaves through the Senate.

Ready for the Purple

At the end of the seventies, Titus had been in Rome and Italy nearly the whole decade and secured unprecedented powers as the heir to the emperor.[97] He held the powers of *imperium* and *tribunicia potestas*, had held the *ordinarius* consulship seven times and had accumulated fourteen salutations as *imperator* that Vespasian had shared with him. As censor, with his father as a partner, they had adlected numerous supporters and loyalists into the Senate and patrician class, strengthening their regime in Rome and across the empire. He had shared a triumph through the streets of Rome with the emperor, arguably the pinnacle of Roman military prowess. As commander of the Praetorian Guard, he also had the coercive arm of the Roman army's most powerful division under his control in the vicinity of Rome. Not afraid to use the Guard when needed to oppress any opposition, Titus had drawn public criticism for his ruthlessness.

As a core member of Vespasian's inner circle, his *consilium*, Titus learned much about the machinations of state and imperial power and played an influential role in the policies and decisions that emerged. His exceptional memory served him well in this period when a plethora of different state matters would be in play at any one time and he had taken on a lot of the administrative burden fróm his father.[98] Titus also played an important part in the Flavian efforts to appease the Senate and in the implementation of the necessary fiscal measures that typified Vespasian's reign. Together, Vespasian and Titus navigated the complexities of Roman politics and administration, implementing policies aimed at consolidating power, ensuring stability and promoting prosperity throughout the empire. Yet at least one serious conspiracy was uncovered, exposing the fragility of the supposedly stable Flavian dynasty. He had also shown the ability to forgo his personal interests, exemplified by his reluctant dismissal of Berenice from Rome. In totality, his contributions during his father's reign were laying the foundation for his own rule as emperor, demonstrating his capability as a leader and statesman in his own right. He was the unquestionable heir to the Principate and a faithful son to his father.

CHAPTER 9

ACCESSION AND REIGN

Not all Roman emperors met their end in dramatic or suspicious circumstances. Vespasian was visiting Campania when he developed a fever. His illness was enough for him to hasten to Rome and on to his beloved summer retreat near Reate, the rural area of his birth. He sought treatment at the nearby Aquae Cutiliae, where the baths were supplied by hot mineral springs and also invigoratingly cold ones. The latter were renowned for their healing properties and praised for their effectiveness in curing stomach disorders. After supposedly over-indulging in the cold waters, Vespasian's condition deteriorated with gastrointestinal symptoms. Determined and hardworking to the end, he still held meetings in a country villa from his bedside until severe diarrhoea caused him to almost faint.[1] Knowing the end was near, he quipped, 'Oh! I think I'm becoming a god!', doubtless reflecting a dry scepticism for the deification of his predecessors. In a final act of defiance of his failing health, Vespasian attempted to rise from his bed muttering, 'An emperor ought to die on his feet.' But he collapsed into the arms of his attendants and expired. He passed away on 23 June 79, in the tenth year of his reign, aged sixty-nine.[2]

It seems that Vespasian's passing was the result of a suspected gastrointestinal infection exacerbated by his frequent cold baths and advanced age.[3] We do not know if Titus rushed to his father's side before he passed away. If he was in Rome he would have received the news late on the same day or early the next morning. One can envisage a moment of shock and sorrow, coupled with the weight of suddenly inheriting the responsibilities of the most powerful man in the world as he knew it at the age of forty. It appears that Titus had always held a deep affection for his father and he mourned the news of his passing while the word spread and those around him declared him emperor.[4] While it is not documented, it is reasonable to assume that the Senate convened on 24 June formally to proclaim Titus emperor and bestow on him the titles of *Augustus, Pontifex Maximus*, and *Pater Patriae*. He was also named *Imperator* as a first title.[5] Of all these new glorious new titles, *Augustus* was the most important as it symbolised Titus' virtues as more than human, blessed and revered. Awarded to Octavian as the first emperor of Rome, it bestowed a sacred nature on Titus because the Romans viewed all precious and sacred entities as august.[6]

Subsequent confirmations would have taken the form of acclamations or a variety of oath-taking ceremonies in which senators and other officials pledged allegiances. The hand-over of power was smooth and without incident. As the long-anticipated successor to Vespasian, a transition anticipated for over a decade, the challenge of Titus not belonging to the Julio-Claudian line was history, although the Marcellus and Caecina conspiracy was a recent reminder that sedition was ever present. Titus was the first biological son to take over from a father as emperor. Unlike his predecessors, he did not claim an *imperator* salutation to mark his accession; he had fourteen salutations already and accepting one for his accession would have undermined his image of already being a co-ruler alongside his father.[7]

Titus' initial acts are not well recorded but we can reliably assume that news management was paramount during his first days as emperor. Numerous scribes were tasked to write messages to be sent across the empire to governors, military commanders, senior magistrates and allies. He would have wanted to convey a successful and legitimate succession with reassurances that he would ensure stability and the prosperity of Rome, Italy and the provinces. Attending the Senate and addressing urgent matters of state, to avoid any impression of a lack of continuity in the imperial oversight of affairs, was also crucial for Titus and his administration. Security would have been paramount and one can assume he promptly relinquished his immediate command of the Praetorian Guard and presumably appointed two prefects he thoroughly trusted. Essential to Titus' power, the legions swore allegiance to their new emperor as news reached their postings and their legates solicited the legionaries' oaths. This amounted to over 300,000 troops swearing their loyalty and obedience to Titus, promising to follow any order he issued as their supreme military head.[8]

Amidst the flurry of activities following Vespasian's passing, the management of his body, the organisation of his funeral and the consideration of his deification were paramount. Titus took personal charge, commencing with the reading of Vespasian's will as his body, ritually cleansed, was brought back to Rome. Skilled craftsmen produced *imagines*, lifelike wax masks capturing the features of the deceased. Full-body wax figures of Vespasian were crafted in addition.[9] Vespasian's body first lay in state in an imperial property for intimate funeral rites attended by family and close associates, but preparations for the public commemoration were under way.

In line with the customs of imperial funerals, a wax effigy of Vespasian reclining on a funeral couch (*lectus funebris*) was prominently displayed atop the main bier, and the body placed in a coffin beneath. Titus led the procession through the streets of Rome, culminating in a sacred location where the effigy lay in state, affording dignitaries and others an opportunity to pay their respects. On the day of the cremation of his body and the effigy, Titus delivered the eulogy and ignited the elaborate multi-tiered funeral pyre, symbolising the passage of his father's spirit.[10]

The formal ceremonial consecration – or deification – of Vespasian did not take place until early 80, six months after his death. While this might appear delayed, Titus needed time to prepare Vespasian's imperial cult. He could not simply extend the existing illustrious cult of the Julio-Claudians, and various administrative and political matters needed to be addressed that naturally took time. Furthermore, at least the start of construction of a temple for the *divus* Vespasian was expected. A site was identified, squeezed into a space on the western side of the Roman forum at the foot of the Tabularium.

Although the ceremonial aspects of Vespasian's veneration were delayed, the decision on his deification was made soon after his death, and a foregone conclusion before his death. Moreover, Titus would not have missed the opportunity during the lighting of his father's funeral pyre to release an eagle from a hidden cage. This symbolic act represented Vespasian's ascent to the pantheon of gods. The actual administration and logistics for the complete consecration could follow later, allowing Titus to ensure that all necessary arrangements were in place for the formal deification process.[11]

At this time, early vows and decrees were also important first acts to set the tone of Titus' Principate. These immediate proclamations or decrees outlining his policies, intentions and vision for his reign would have covered various aspects of governance and reforms. After drawing sharp criticism for his heavy handedness as commander of the Praetorian Guard, the one characteristic that Titus wanted to project was *clementia*, clemency.[12]

Promptly assuming the position of Pontifex Maximus, responsible for overseeing the Roman religious institutions and rituals, Titus claimed this sacred role would safeguard him against committing any crimes, and he appears to have kept his word.

> [Titus] was never directly or indirectly responsible for a murder; and, although often given abundant excuse for revenge, swore that he would rather die than take a life.
>
> *Suetonius*[13]

The minting and distribution of coins hailing the new emperor and embodying the virtues he wanted to define his reign were crucial immediate tasks following his ascension. Fortunately, the artists responsible for crafting the dies already had access to his portrait, which had been used on coins during his time as *Caesar* and could now be adapted for his portrayal as *Augustus*.[14] Among his first coins, one early issue replicated a reverse design from the coinage of Octavian. This design featured a radiant figure atop a column adorned with the prows of enemy ships.[15] The Octavian column had been erected by the Senate in honour of his triumph over Antony and Cleopatra at Actium. Titus' decision to restore this image symbolised a desire to be connected to the esteemed first emperor. Despite lacking prominent hereditary ties, Titus sought to align himself with the legacy of Augustus, and the column served as a potent symbol for the end of civil strife, a theme central to the Flavian dynasty. By incorporating imagery associated with Augustus, Titus aimed to underscore continuity with Rome's illustrious past while also signalling his commitment to peace and stability.

Titus, *denarius* (equivalent to the *aureus* described above), Struck mid–late 79, Rome mint. Reverse, statue of radiate male figure facing on rostral column, with spear and dagger. Part of a restoration of an Octavian coinage. *Sear I no.2509.*

Another set of *aurei* from Titus' early coinage copied a design from Octavian's time. This particular coin featured a depiction of the semi-nude

Venus wielding a spear and donning a helmet.[16] Venus, goddess of love and beauty, also held symbolic significance as a representative of imperial power and she was a greatly favoured Roman icon. By featuring Venus on his coins, Titus conveyed the message that his imperial authority was sanctioned by the divine and aligned with the esteemed traditions of his predecessors Julius Caesar and Augustus.

Titus, *aureus*, struck after 1 July 79, Rome mint. Reverse, Venus.
Part of a restoration of an Octavian coinage. *Sear I no.2489*.

On the two reverses of two other early *aurei*, one depicts Ceres the goddess of agriculture, suggesting Titus' role in maintaining plentiful food supplies, and the other a triumphal four-horse chariot (*quadriga*) carrying what look like ears of corn that had also been used on coins when Titus was *Caesar*.[17] The imagery of the chariot pulled by four horses is often associated with triumphal processions through the streets of Rome. The addition of corn ears on the *quadriga* possibly symbolises abundance and prosperity, as corn was the staple food of the capital. In essence, Titus was trying to convey a visual representation of military victory, prosperity and the glory of the Roman state all as one entity – thanks to the Flavians.

Titus continued the minting of the significant *Iudaea Capta* (Judea Captured), commemorative coin series, which his father had initiated as early as December 69. These coins were issued in all denominations, with reverse designs featuring powerful imagery. A common motif depicted a personified Judea as a mourning woman, either seated or reclining beneath a Roman standard, or overshadowed by the advancing figure of Victory, the Roman goddess of triumph. This imagery conveyed a clear message of Rome's military dominance and the subjugation of the Jewish people. Vespasian had previously issued a dramatic coin in this series that depicted Titus, as *Caesar*, on horseback charging over a fallen Jewish warrior, spear in hand.[18] Such vivid depictions underscored the reality of the Roman campaign while glorifying the role of the Flavian dynasty in quelling the revolt. These coins served as quintessential propaganda tools, reinforcing

Rome's supremacy and legitimising the Flavian claim to power. However, their messaging was fundamentally misleading. Unlike Claudius' conquest of Britannia, Judea had not been captured but rather recovered after a bloody and protracted rebellion. The truth is reflected in a far rarer coin bearing the inscription *Iudaea Recepta* (Judea Recaptured), which accurately conveys the situation.[19]

Titus, as *Caesar*, sestertius, Struck 72, Rome mint.
Reverse, Titus on horseback spearing a fallen enemy. *Sear I no. 2462.*

During the early period after Titus' accession, his brother Domitian would have been prominent in many affairs. The later damnation of Domitian by the elite after his reign means that mostly hostile accounts have come down to us today about his relationship with Titus.[20] However, the reality was probably different. From the first day of Titus' reign, Domitian was his 'partner and chosen successor'.[21] That may not have been Titus' long-term view, as he presumably could have still fathered his own child or Julia could have borne him a grandson, but in June 79 Domitian was the available heir within the Flavii. He remained *Caesar* and *Princeps Iuuentutis*; the latter title meant 'leader of the youth' and signalled that he was being groomed for higher leadership and the succession.

Titus would also appoint Domitian as his colleague in the *ordinarius* consulships on 1 January 80. A *sestertius* of the same year showed Titus and Domitian with hands clasped in union.[22] Previously, after Vespasian's accession, the new emperor had received word from Rome that Domitian was behaving badly and it was Titus who persuaded his father to be understanding and forgiving, citing their strong ties of blood.[23] These were all hardly the acts of bitter rivals and estranged siblings.

This situation may not have been enough for Domitian if he expected to be given the power that Titus held under Vespasian: namely *imperium* and *tribunicia potestas*. However, the situation was entirely different compared to the early years after the civil war, when Vespasian needed a rock-solid and empowered heir. Besides, Domitian was twelve years younger and lacked experience. Thus, there may have been some animosity towards Titus from Domitian in his desire for more power and titles. This was probably confounded by the fact that they grew up very differently in terms of education and the status of the family. Titus had benefited from an imperial court education and grew up in the 40s, during which time the family excelled. Domitian's education would have been high-quality but still inferior to that of Titus, the years of his childhood being a more static period for the family. Moreover, Titus' absence during Domitian's formative years meant they were unlikely to be close as brothers. Overall, they needed each other and were bonded by a desire to see the Flavian dynasty flourish and prosper but there was probably tension between them that stemmed both from their character differences and Domitian's desire for more power and the chance to prove himself.[24]

Rebranding

By the end of the summer, Titus' accession had been sealed. Many of his legions had sworn allegiance to their new emperor, except for the more distant postings yet to receive the news. Immediate matters of state were also in hand.

At this stage of his life, aged forty, what did the Emperor Titus look like? His demeanour was described as being dignified and commanding.[25] If his depiction on coins is accurate, his features were typical of Roman aristocracy: a prominent nose, deep-set eyes and a pointed dimpled chin. Considered handsome and muscular he did have some paunchiness and a plumpness that gave him a round face, double chin and heavy neck. His hair was typically styled in the fashion of the time: short, curled and neatly trimmed. He was clean-shaven, as was the custom for Roman men of his status in this period. Overall, he presented as a dignified and imposing figure, with a manner that commanded respect and admiration, befitting his position as the new emperor of Rome.

With a firm grip on power following his accession, Titus embarked on a reign that echoed many of the trends established by his father, such as financial prudence, the execution of public works projects and the meticulous management of the empire's provinces. Yet, amidst his visions for the empire, Titus would have to face the daunting task of managing a series of serious disasters. As we delve into the intricacies of his administration, we will encounter a narrative steeped in timeless themes of power, ambition and the complexities of leadership.

For many Romans, Titus' rise to power ushered in a period of uncertainty and apprehension. Entering his Principate, Titus found himself confronted with a strongly unfavourable public image, stemming from his perceived authoritarian use of the Praetorian Guard to safeguard the Flavian dynasty. His brutality may have been exaggerated but nevertheless resulted in widespread resentment and a blackened reputation.

> Although by such conduct [Titus] provided for his safety in the future, he incurred such odium at the time that hardly anyone ever came to the throne with so evil a reputation or so much against the desires of all.
>
> *Suetonius*[26]

Additionally, rumours circulated about Titus' personal conduct, including allegations of riotous living, late-night revelry and unchaste behaviour involving his retinue of male courtesans and eunuchs.[27] There could well be elements of truth here. It was not unusual for wealthy members of the Roman elite to indulged in nocturnal carnal pleasures. Indeed, a tombstone found in Rome dedicated to a Tiberius Claudius Secundus, humorously captures an attitude towards self-indulgence:

> Bathing, wine and sex ruin our bodies, but only bathing, wine and sex make life worth living.[28]

Titus' desire for Queen Berenice and his decision to invite her for a second visit, despite the public outcry during her first stay in Rome, further fuelled apprehensions. It is possible that Titus was besotted with Berenice.[29] This raised eyebrows because the Romans viewed love for one's partner as effeminate and unbecoming for an upstanding citizen. Furthermore, public displays of fondness were scowled on. Lastly in the list of disreputable behaviours, Titus had a reputation for taking bribes to influence cases brought before his father during his reign. This was hardly unusual in the world of Roman politics but, in totality, many do seem to have feared he would become a second Nero.[30]

Aware of the prevailing perception, Titus swiftly endeavoured to shape his public image as a just and benevolent ruler known for his generosity and his ability to bring stability to a tumultuous world. This undertaking involved a significant rebranding effort, beginning with his personal life. Berenice was sent away once more after a brief return to Rome.[31] This decisive action, rejecting his beloved for a second time, served as a clear signal that there were no plans for them to have a child who might vie for the succession. There would be no second Caesarion, the son of Julius Caesar and Cleopatra, who stirred political turmoil as an infant when his mother claimed he was the only true heir of Caesar after his death.

Titus also took steps to distance himself from the extravagant lifestyle often associated with emperors, particularly in the shadow of Nero's excesses. He dismissed his cherished concubines, some of whom went on to be renowned stage dancers, and he refrained from attending their performances. He appears to have stopped, or at least been far more discreet with raucous night parties, and instead held banquets that were 'pleasant rather than extravagant'.[32]

In a deliberate effort to distance himself from any comparisons to Nero and to honour the memory of his dear friend Britannicus, poisoned by the tyrant, Titus commissioned an exquisite gold statue of Britannicus. Produced at enormous cost, the effigy was displayed in the imperial palace as an arresting reminder for all who visited. Additionally, Titus organised processions featuring an ivory equestrian statue of Britannicus during public games, sending a message that he revered Nero's victim and the people of Rome would not see similar murders during his reign.

Also to restore his reputation, Titus issued a single edict that validated all favours and gifts granted by previous emperors.[33] This was particularly important due to the inconsistent record-keeping practices of the time. Promises made by his father or predecessors often lacked clear evidence, potentially leading to protracted disputes. By endorsing these prior commitments with a single decree, Titus streamlined the process, sparing himself from the burden of adjudicating numerous petitions and pleasing those who sought the endorsement.

Furthermore, Titus displayed a commitment to addressing the needs of those who sought his assistance. He took proactive measures to accommodate petitioners, going to great lengths to ensure that no one left his presence feeling neglected or dismissed. His conscientious approach even prompted concerns from his secretariat that he might be making promises that were beyond his capacity to fulfil. His underlying principle was to avoid disappointing anyone who sought an audience with the emperor. In a rare insight into Titus's mindset, a surviving quotation reveals his sense of responsibility towards his subjects. During a dinner conversation, he expressed regret at having been unable to assist anyone throughout the day, lamenting, 'Friends, I have lost a day!'[34]

Conscious of the importance of winning favour from the equestrian and patrician classes, Titus pledged to not commit any crime, especially murder. Taking conclusive action, he abolished the notorious charge of *maiestas* (high treason) across all jurisdictions. This reform marked a departure from the practices of some of his predecessors, notably Tiberius, whose oppressive reign had been characterised by repeated use of treason charges. The core issue was the abuse of the charge by a class of men called *delatores* (informers) who made a living from the process, accusing people of likely non-existent crimes and being rewarded with a proportion of the accused's property, if they secured a conviction. The legacy of fear was perpetuated by the pervasive presence of these informants in Rome and beyond. In another rare statement that sheds light on Titus' approach to defamation and offence, he articulated his commitment to maintaining his integrity and remaining impervious to denigration:

> It is impossible for me to be insulted or abused in any way. For I do naught that deserves censure, and I care not for what is reported falsely. As for the emperors who are dead and gone, they will avenge themselves in case anyone does them a wrong, if in very truth they are demigods and possess any power.

Titus[35]

The remark also bears the repeated undertone of scepticism that Titus and his father appear to have had regarding the deification of emperors. To solidify his position on *maiestas* charges, Titus banished informers from Rome.[36] This was a significant action because it meant rounding up by force probably a large number of individuals, parading them in his new amphitheatre and subsequently selling them into slavery or banishing them from the city.

Titus' commitment to his pledge was put to the test when two unnamed patricians were deemed guilty of harbouring ambitions to seize the throne, an unmistakable act of treason under Roman law. On being informed of the situation, the emperor chose to respond with restraint, opting to issue a warning rather than resorting to execution. He emphasised to the accused that imperial power was bestowed by fate and not to be unlawfully seized. In a gesture of goodwill, he even sent a messenger to one of their mothers that no harm would come to her son to relieve her anxiety. Moreover, Titus extended invitations to both accused patricians, inviting them to dine with him among his close friends. The following day, he afforded them the rare privilege of joining him at the gladiatorial games, even allowing them to inspect the contestants' swords alongside him.[37] This peculiar turn of events appears to have been a carefully orchestrated public relations stunt. It could not have been a serious attempt on his throne because they would have been banished at least – and so his pledge remained intact. Ominously, Titus is said to have discovered that their horoscopes predicted future danger to them from another. The prediction apparently came true; perhaps Domitian later had no hesitation in finishing the punishment.

Continuing his efforts to present a righteous public image, Titus recalled Musonius Rufus from exile. This was Musonius' second exile: the first was under Nero; the second during Vespasian's reign for his philosophical opposition to the actions of the Principate. The recall was an olive branch to the philosopher community that the Flavii had railed against during Vespasian's time.[38]

Titus' Key Officials

The consulships and proconsul governorships were the most important positions for an emperor to oversee and Titus wasted no time in reviewing these. The Praetorian Guard prefects were also extremely important appointments but we do not know Titus' choices during his reign. For the following year, 80, Vespasian had already designated the consuls in advance, meaning Titus only had to replace his father with his brother as *consul ordinarius*. Thus, on 1 January he and Domitian assumed the consulships, their eighth and seventh respectively. For 82, Titus designated himself and his brother again for the *ordinarius* consulships. Evidently Titus was following in his father's footsteps so that the Flavii would hold a monopoly over the prestigious consulships that opened each new year.[39] However, confident in his regime, Titus did allow two non-Flavians to hold the *ordinarius* consulships of 81, namely, Lucius Flavius Silva Nonius Bassus and Asinius Pollio Verrucosus. Silva was a seasoned general who had commanded X *Fretensis* and laid siege to the near-unassailable mountain-top fortress of Masada that was finally captured in 73. This was the last point of Jewish resistance to fall, formally marking an end to the uprising. Favoured by Vespasian and Titus he was adlected into the patrician class during the census and subsequently appointed *legatus Augusti pro praetore* of Judea for an extended period. Little is known about Verrucosus other than that he was descended from the Asinii.[40] Both men were clearly highly respected and trusted by Titus and may have been distantly related to the imperial family.

Titus appears to have continued with his father's efforts to supervise the provinces carefully and meticulously appoint capable governors with solid reputations. Maintaining his father's existing appointments, Titus hand-picked the following individuals to represent him for immediate or near-term vacancies:

Q. Corellius Rufus	governor, Germania Superior, from Sept. 82
L. Funisulanus Vettonianus	governor, Dalmatia, from 81 or 82
C. Vettulenus Civica Cerialis	governor, Moesia, from 81 or 82
A. Caesennius Gallus	governor, Cappadocia-Galatia, from 80 or 81[41]

Probably initiated by his father, Titus continued a significant change in provincial policy that assigned senators of eastern Greek origin as judicial officials, *iuridici*, to assist proconsul governors or military commanders in the East. Titus even selected a senator of the same origin, C. Caristanius Fronto, to govern the imperial praetorian province of Lycia-Pamphylia.[42] The change was innovative and broke from tradition. It was a smart move because such individuals had a deeper understanding of the local customs, languages, and political dynamics in the eastern provinces. This could facilitate better governance and management of these regions, improving communication and cooperation between the Roman authorities and the local populations. By appointing senators with ties to the eastern provinces, Titus aimed to improve diplomatic relations and foster goodwill among the local elites and communities. These senators could provide valuable insights and advice, enabling more effective governance and military operations in the region. The symbolism was also important as the appointment of senators from varied backgrounds to these roles suggests a trend to increase diversity in the Roman administration. It sent a message of inspiration for different cultures and ethnicities within the empire, potentially enhancing loyalty and cooperation among the range of populations under Roman rule. Titus had spent many years in the East and was an astute diplomat; he keenly understood the advantages of these changes.

Three other notable appointments set a precedent under Titus' reign. All three stemmed from the exercise of *suffragium*, patronage and political influence, which had enormous sway over an individual's career. At the centre of this influence was a remarkable figure and Flavian careerist called Tiberius Julius. He was a freedman of an emperor, an *Augusti libertus* (abbreviated to *Aug. lib.* after his name). It appears he had been manumitted, given senior administrative tasks and married into an equestrian family during the reign of Claudius. Tiberius Julius was an extremely talented individual known for financial expertise. Continuing to excel during Nero's reign, he was posted to the East where he met Vespasian, who had a keen eye for fiscal diligence. Vespasian appointed him *praepositus a rationibus*, a high-ranking financial official who was responsible for managing the emperor's finances and overseeing the imperial treasury. This was a position of substantial authority, working closely with the emperor and his administration to ensure the financial stability of the empire. Vespasian showered him with rewards. He and his sons were elevated into the equestrian class. Well known and trusted by Titus, he continued as his chief financial accountant. Having served four emperors over several decades, Tiberius Julius was arguably one of the best-informed and most influential financial gurus of the imperial age.[43]

The lengthy introduction to the gifted Tiberius Julius explains why he was able to exert extraordinary influence over Vespasian and subsequently Titus. Amongst other achievements based on his counsel, he almost certainly played a part in persuading Titus to appoint three of his relatives as governors. Tettius Julianus, his brother-in-law, was rescued from political exile to command the Numidian military district with III *Augusta* under Titus in 81.[44] The equestrian C. Tettius Africanus Cassianus Priscus was assigned the prefecture of Egypt in 80. The third relative, L. Funisulanus Vettonianus, as already noted, was assigned the governorship of Dalmatia, probably around 81. This province was far less important than the other two but nevertheless a province of Rome. In effect, Titus had awarded two Tettii unprecedented potential power. The forces in Numidia could easily take over the province of Africa and the two united Tettii could therefore gain control over a large proportion of the grain supply to Rome.[45] Titus clearly had significant trust in Tiberius Julius' advice and the relatives he appointed.

Consilium

Just like his father and other predecessors, Titus' consilium was an essential means of seeking counsel from trusted individuals and friends. As before, involvement was fluid, depending on the matter at hand and the added value anyone could offer. Some might be away from Rome and provide advice through correspondence. The table overleaf details Titus' advisors, many of them retained from his father's pool of counsellors.

Titus' consilium principis	
T. Flavius Sabinus III	Vespasian's advisor, Titus' cousin and suffect consul in 72, alongside Mucianus. He was Titus' curator of sacred buildings, public works and public spaces.[46]
Marcus Arrecinus Clemens	Vespasian's advisor, the brother of Titus' first deceased wife, served as governor of Hispania Tarraconensis under Titus.[47]
M. Pompeius Silvanus Staberius Flavinus	Suffect consulship II, probably in 76. Was Curator Aquarum in 71. One of the elder statesmen advising Titus.[48]
Marcus Cocceius Nerva	It is hard to imagine that Nerva was not retained after serving as an important advisor to Vespasian – but he received no known roles under Titus.
Aelius Lamia Plautius Aelianus	Suffect consul in 80 and friend and confidant of Titus.[49] His father had probably been on Vespasian's *consilium*.
Aulus Didius Gallus Fabricius Veiento	Consul under Vespasian in an unknown year and suffect consul in January 80. A priest of the new Vespasian cult.[50]
L. Valerius Catullus Messallinus	Granted the honoured *ordinarius* consulship in 73 and Vespasian's advisor. Close friend of Nerva and Veiento.[51]
Domitian	Brother and shared the *ordinarius* consulship with Titus in 80 and designated for the same in 82.
L. Junius Q. Vibius Crispus	Second suffect consulship in 74 alongside Titus' third as *ordinarius*.[52] Also served as Vespasian's advisor.
Praetorian Guard Prefects	Essential core members of Titus' *consilium* but their names are not known for his reign.

Sextus Julius Frontinus	As urban praetor he had summoned the Senate to confirm the historic *ordinarius* consulships of Vespasian and Titus on 1 January 70. Governor of Britannia from 74.[53]
L. Plotius Pegasus	One the greatest legal experts of the imperial age, he was head of the renowned Proculian School of Law: his colleagues nicknamed him 'The Book' for his extensive knowledge. An ex-consul and governor of Dalmatia under Vespasian.[54] The unusually named Pegasus was Titus' encyclopaedia for all legal matters.
M. Hirrius Fronto Neratius Pansa	Consulship held in the 70s and adlected by Vespasian and Titus into the patrician class in 73/74, he went on to govern Cappadocia and Galatia in around 77–79. If still alive during Titus' reign he almost certainly served on his *consilium*.[55]
Marcus Ulpius Traianus	A fellow legion commander from the Jewish War and a hardcore Flavian loyalist. At the zenith of his career, he was proconsul of Asia in 79.
M. Acilius Aviola	Consul *ordinarius* in 54 and governor of Asia in 65/66, he served all the Flavii as Curator Aquarum, 74–97.[56]
Tiberius Julius, Aug. lib.	A highly gifted financial advisor who had served Claudius, Nero, Vespasian and now Titus.
Tiberius Claudius, Aug. lib. Classicus[57]	An imperial freedman given significant dual responsibilities under Titus: firstly, *procurator castrensis*, the official responsible for managing the imperial residences and its surrounding areas; secondly, *a cubiculo*, the chamberlain who served in the emperor's private apartments, known as the 'cubicle'. He was responsible for Titus' personal needs within his private quarters, such as organising his personal servants and ensuring his comfort and security in the intimate confines of his living space.

Public Works

Titus and his father may not have comprehended that the Flavian Amphitheatre they commissioned, better known today as the Colosseum, would become the most iconic, notorious and yet endearing symbol of the Roman Empire. Funded with spoils from the Jewish War, Vespasian started the works in the early 70s; the first stage required parts of Nero's Domus Aureus to be demolished and his ornamental lake drained. Marvels of engineering delivered colossal foundations, over 3,000 metres of water drainage systems and the towering superstructure of arches on which the seating was laid. Vespasian completed the first two storeys and Titus added two more for its inauguration in 80. With an overall surface area of 23,500 square metres and fifty metres high, it had eighty entrances at ground level and required over a thousand men to lower and raise the gigantic canvas roof awnings that offered shade to spectators. It was then, as it remains today, a sight to behold.[58] Despite earthquakes, fires, lightning and looting, the Colosseum survived and is the fourth-most-visited monument in the world, receiving over seven million visitors a year.[59]

On the south-eastern corner of the Oppian Hill, Titus hastily constructed a bath complex that was dedicated in 80.[60] Entered from the plaza of the Colosseum up gracious stairways, patrons were welcomed by a large *palaestra*, wrestling school or gymnasium, then an open courtyard for physical exercise before entering into the central bathing areas, each side a symmetrical mirror of the other. Vast vaulted ceilings provided a sense of grand space for the visitors as they enjoyed the cleansing and the relaxations of the waters.[61] To show his accessibility, Titus sometimes bathed in the complex with the general public, doubtless with some bodyguards nearby.[62]

To establish the imperial cult for his father's deification, Titus had selected one of the few spaces left in the Roman Forum, at the foot of the Tabularium, for the Temple of Vespasian. Titus probably completed the foundations and beginnings of the podium that was finished by Domitian in the early years of his reign. On completion, the temple would house a colossal statue of *divus* Vespasian that is possibly the bust on display today in the National Museum in Naples. Although it was somewhat screened by the Temple of Saturn, it was partially visible to senators coming and going from the Senate house and so in a strategically well-chosen location. At considerable expense, Titus also continued the restoration of the Temple of Jupiter on the Capitoline Hill.

More mundane, but important for the average Roman, Titus repaired two aqueducts, the Marcia and the Claudia, that supplied Rome. Across the empire, numerous projects were supported by Titus, either continuing his father's work or starting his own: amphitheatres, stadiums, canals, water diversion systems and repairs of edifices. He provided funds for the completion and reconstruction of roads in Italy and across the empire. In particular, he appears to have given attention and resources to strengthening the new consular complex of Cappadocia-Galatia and its associated eastern frontiers. After appointing Caesennius Gallus governor in 80/81, a network of military roads and *limites* (border demarcations, observation posts and paths) was constructed.[63]

Administration and Policies

The brevity of Titus' reign makes it challenging to discern the long-term policies he envisioned for Rome and the empire. However, as part of his efforts to cultivate a favourable image for his Principate, he prioritised a policy of imperial generosity. While this magnanimity may have appeared lavish on the surface, it was something of a mirage; he was an astute financier like his father. His acts of generosity were not driven by decadence but rather had pragmatic limitations aimed at maintaining fiscal responsibility and achieving specific objectives. Titus would project his munificence but there would be common sense behind his actions.[64]

A prime example of this approach was the tried and tested method of offering public games to the people of Rome. Hosting lavish spectacles, including gladiatorial tournaments, was a way for Roman emperors to boost their popularity and prestige among the populace. Such events served as extravagant displays of wealth and power, showcasing the emperor's ability to provide entertainment and leisure activities for the people. The festivities would also serve as a distraction from the catastrophic Vesuvius eruption and other disastrous events discussed further in Chapter 10. In 80, Titus took this tradition to new heights during the inauguration of the Colosseum and the dedication of his new baths, organising an extravagant run of spectacles with the magnificent amphitheatre as the focal point.[65] During the celebrations, enormous numbers of animals were pitched against each other or slain. Specially trained fighters staged hunts of both tame and wild animals collected from across the empire such as elephants, big cats, bears, wolves, crocodiles and even cranes. Nine thousand animals were sacrificed for the bloodthirsty crowds. Even women took part in the slaughter.[66]

Countless gladiatorial shows topped the bill of festivities. Contrary to popular belief, defeated gladiators were frequently spared because they were extremely valuable to their owners.[67] Elaborate infantry battle scenes within the arena were held between groups of fighters. For one of the highlights of the entertainments, Titus approved the flooding of the Colosseum's arena. Animals adapted to water were brought in and presumably hunted in the aquatic environment. Next up, to the amazement of the crowds, warships were launched, complete with warriors impersonating the Corinthians and Corcyraeans at the Battle of Sybota, fought in 443 BC. During these events, Titus on occasion threw wooden balls into the crowds inscribed with prizes that could be redeemed: food, clothing, silver or gold vessels, horses, pack-animals, cattle or slaves.[68]

Titus, *sestertius*, struck 80, Rome mint. Obverse, view of the Colosseum from the south-east, seen from above to reveal the dotted crowds and the imperial box, the two-storey *porticus* of the Baths of Titus to left, and the Meta Sudans obelisk to right. Reverse, Titus seated, left arm across his lap, holding a branch in his outstretched right hand; around his feet, helmets, shields and a cuirass. An extremely rare coin sold for $67,500. *Sear I no.2536.*

Elsewhere at the Naumachia Augusti, built by Augustus, Titus used the artificial lake to host a concurrent set of tournaments. On the first day, gladiatorial fights and wild-beast hunts were staged on wooden platforms constructed over the basin. A staggering 5,000 animals were killed in one day. On the second day there were horse races and on the third day was the finale: a naval battle between 3,000 men in dozens of ships. The troops represented the Athenians defeating the Syracusans after storming the central island, where they attacked a wall constructed for the spectacle, representing Ortygia at Syracuse.[69] The scale and lavishness of these entertainments would have cost Titus several million HS.[70]

Another critical policy decision for Titus, driven by his desire to project generosity, involved issuing cash gifts to the people and the armies, known respectively as *congiaria* and *donativa*, to mark his accession. New emperors customarily followed this practice, and Titus seems to have adhered to this tradition. This substantial infusion of money additionally served to stimulate the economy. It was also essential to strategise when future distributions could be expected. Titus inherited a healthy financial position from his father, enabling him to allocate a *congiarium* of 300 HS to each citizen in Rome who already benefited from the corn dole, a *donativum* of 400 HS to each legionary and 2,000 HS to every member of the Praetorian Guard. This totalled approximately 138 million HS, equivalent to around 17 per cent of the empire's entire annual tax revenue. Tiberius Julius, Titus' financial advisor, would have presented various financial scenarios for the emperor's consideration when determining these distributions.[71]

As we have seen, many of Titus' programmes involved the distribution of funds for public works, celebrations and handouts. Complementing this munificence, he instigated policies that offered fiscal relief. Gifts were offered frequently to emperors as a means to gain favour, reinforce social hierarchies and express symbolic and material support for imperial rule. However, it was a burden on those bestowing the offerings so Titus issued an edict that he would not accept such largesse from any citizen, city or king.[72] It is also thought that Titus had a respect for private property and would abstain from the practice of some of his predecessors who had confiscated private estates for imperial gain.[73]

In the provinces there were examples of generosity that were not quite what they seemed, one hand giving and the other taking away. Titus pronounced that Rhodes and Cos would receive back their special free and immune status, including tax exemptions. Caesarea, a city Titus knew well from his time in the East, was given a lenient interpretation of special rights, *ius Italicum*, exemption from land tax. The capital city of Helvetia, Aventicum (Avenches), was probably granted tax concessions. However, while in isolation these substantial tax reductions could be perceived as part of Titus' liberality, taxation in Egypt was significantly increased. In the end, Titus wanted a healthy treasury and Tiberius Julius was his master accountant to maintain balanced financial ledgers.[74]

Turning to legislative administration and policy the brevity of Titus' reign again makes it difficult to detect general themes and objectives except for popular social reforms, particularly for the army. A handful of military diplomas survive from 79–81 during his reign. These bronze records of citizenship and the right to marriage were issued not only to men already discharged from auxiliary service but also, in some cases, to serving soldiers. The coexistence of these practices in Titus' reign appears to mark an administrative transition, later standardized into the more regular veteran-only grants of the second century.[75] There were also civil reforms related to testamentary freedoms. Titus reduced the number of *praetores fideicommissarii*, judicial officials responsible for overseeing inheritances and ensuring the faithful execution of the testators' wishes regarding the management and distribution of bequests. By Titus' reign, that area of law had been regularized by successive measures, which clarified heirs' and trustees' obligations and cut down on litigation. With the workload lighter and the rules clearer, Titus could reduce the number of special praetors. He further imposed a requirement of twenty years' delay before a claimant could take ownership of a property of someone who had died intestate. This requirement served various purposes, including providing a clear time-frame for resolving disputes over intestate deaths, protecting the rights of potential heirs and ensuring the stability of property ownership within Roman society.[76]

In terms of provincial security, it is notable that Titus approved the creation of a permanent fort for a detachment of III *Augusta* at Lambaesis in Numidia. The location served as one of the most important military bases in Roman North Africa. Here, the legion could play a significant role in maintaining Roman control over the region, participating in various military operations and ensuring stability along the frontiers of the Empire. The legion played a crucial role in maintaining Roman authority and security in the province, ensuring the prosperity of the region under Roman rule. As we have seen, Titus continued in earnest the implementation of his father's vision for an improved zone of influence in the East, along parts of the Euphrates and by strengthening the province of Cappadocia-Galatia. Likewise in the northern provinces, Titus continued his father's attempts to close the gap in military infrastructure between the Rhine and Danube legions with the installation of fortifications, roads and *limites*. In correspondence with his governor-general in Britannia, Agricola, he approved plans in 80/81 for the consolidation of gains in Scotland before further conquests beyond the River Forth.[77]

Finally, studying Titus' coins allows one to tease out administrative and policy goals to some extent. In 80, Titus issued an entire range of restoration coinage of Julio-Claudian *aes* (bronze) types: *divus* Augustus, Livia, Agrippa, Tiberius, Drusus, Nero Claudius Drusus, Germanicus, Agrippina Senior, Claudius and, surprisingly, Galba. This was a concerted effort to present the Flavian administration in continuity with the prestigious families of the past. Galba's inclusion was a clever way of saying that emperors did not need to come from the Julio-Claudian lines.

A False Nero and Parthian Disturbance.

During Titus' reign, only one disturbance is recorded and it emerged from a peculiar case of false identity. Although Nero's death was certain, the circumstances surrounding it were somewhat shrouded in mystery, as it occurred in a secluded location outside Rome with few witnesses. The news of his demise was particularly lamented by certain segments of the lower classes in Rome and by groups in the Eastern provinces. Consequently, it is not entirely unexpected that impostors sought to capitalise on the situation. In the year 80 or 81, a man named Terentius Maximus appeared in Asia, who bore a striking physical resemblance to Nero. Not only did he look like Nero, but his voice and musical talents, particularly his skill with the lyre, were reminiscent of the late emperor. Maximus managed to gather followers around him, presumably by promising them rewards for their loyalty once he regained the throne in Rome. He claimed to have narrowly escaped his would-be executioners, fleeing into exile for his own safety, and now asserted his readiness to resume his authority. As the false Nero journeyed through the eastern provinces, his following grew steadily, attracting ever larger numbers of gullible supporters who were swayed by his convincing impersonation and promises of a return to power.

When he reached the Euphrates, or the vicinity of that region, it appears that some Roman intervention occurred, forcing the bogus Nero to flee over the river to the Parthians. Craftily, he was able to draw attention to the real Nero's agreement to the Treaty of Rhandeia that provided a settlement between Rome and Parthia over Armenia.[78] His case was well received by Artabanus IV, who was grappling for the Parthian throne and despised Titus for not supporting his claim. Artabanus threatened to restore the false Nero to his rightful place and march on Rome. It was clearly a foolish threat and possibly a limited Parthian splinter uprising was easily quashed by eastern Roman forces. Maximus was exposed and killed. The enigmatic case was never a real risk to Titus but it was a reminder that Parthian interference was an ever-present possibility.[79]

Family Affairs

As emperor, Titus inherited several imperial properties in and outside of Rome, as well as his father's private estates, all available to him as residences. However, like his father he opted to avoid the decadence and opulence of the upgraded Neronian palace on the Palatine Hill (interconnected as it was with other nearby residences). However, an enigmatic trail of clues suggests that Titus had a lavish house, Domus Titi, north-east of the Colosseum on the Oppian Hill. One important clue comes from the site of the rediscovered sublime statue *Laocoön and His Sons*, also called the *Laocoön Group*, which depicts Laocoön, a priest of Poseidon, and his sons being attacked by sea serpents. Pliny the Elder described it as one of finest works of art in the ancient world when he saw it in the Domus Titi. Three Rhodians reportedly created the masterpiece from a single block of marble. It was excavated in 1506 in the grounds of Maecenas' residence that was bequeathed to Augustus and had become an imperial property. Thus, it is quite possible that Titus occupied this domus, delighted amongst other features by the *Laocoön Group* on display, and at times occupied other imperial residences.[80] Vespasian had spent most of his time in the Gardens of Sallust.[81] A group of exquisitely maintained gardens, pavilions and villas, the property originally belonged to Julius Caesar. It eventually ended up in the hands of Claudius as an imperial estate. Vespasian's preference for a rural and more frugal setting than the lavishness of the Palatine explains his selection of the grounds as a home. Moreover, it was important for the Flavian image that they divorce themselves from Nero's monumental complexes that the elite had so despised.[82]

When her father ascended to the throne, Julia was approximately fifteen years old. Domitian had declined the opportunity for a betrothal to Julia during her childhood and now in her early teens she was the most eligible young woman in Rome. After careful consideration, Titus decided to arrange Julia's marriage to her second paternal cousin, Titus Flavius Sabinus IV, who was Vespasian's grand-nephew. This union probably took place towards the end of the 70s or shortly after Titus' accession, and Sabinus IV must have made a very favourable impression on his new father-in-law.

Married and the daughter of the emperor, Julia held a highly respected position within the Flavian family.[83] In appearance she supposedly had youthful beauty, with a full and rounded face, well-proportioned features, alluring if slightly protruding eyes and plump lips. Her hair was styled in fashionable arrangements, often adorned with a wreath of tight curls from ear to ear, braided at the back and secured in a bun. Alternatively, she would wear a small set of curls at the front, allowing the braids to flow into a ponytail. Julia seemed the epitome of Flavian imperial beauty and innocence, serving as a symbol of the dynasty's prestige and refinement.[84]

Titus held his daughter in the highest regard and sought to elevate her status within Roman society. In addition to carefully selecting Julia's husband, he bestowed on her the title and honours of *Augusta* soon after his accession, symbolising her as one of the most prominent women in Rome.[85] The title *Augusta*, derived from *Augustus*, was traditionally used to link its holders to the esteemed first emperor. It was a highly prestigious recognition of Julia's exemplary virtues, her esteemed position within the Flavian dynasty and a title rarely granted in the past. Augusta was initially a posthumous honour bestowed on Augustus' wife, Livia, and subsequently only four others had received this distinction. This conferred on Julia a considerable influence and significant de facto power, arguably a match for even a distinguished Roman senator. The title signified Titus' aspiration that his daughter have a more active role in public affairs and it provided strong links with prior *augustae* from among the Julio-Claudians. To commemorate this significant occasion, Julia became the first *augusta* to be honoured with a range of coins in precious metals as well as bronze, exclusively bearing her name and image. This marked not only her elevated status but also her significant contribution to the Flavian dynasty and Roman society at large.[86] Effectively, she was an empress and, given that Titus lacked a wife, her position was even more significant.

Domitian and Domitia Longina suffered the loss of their two children, presumably to childhood illness.[87] These deaths would have been felt deeply within the Flavian family and it meant that there were no more potential heirs to the dynasty. Domitia probably shared a bond with Julia and together they were the most senior women amongst the Flavian family. Regarding other women in the family, it is probable that Domitilla II, Titus' sister, had married Quintus Petillius Cerialis Caesius Rufus back in 68. She was wed at around fifteen years of age and had a daughter in 69. She died soon after, before her father Vespasian became emperor. Her daughter, Flavia Domitilla III, the granddaughter of Vespasian and niece of Titus and Domitian, therefore lost her mother at a very tender age. She was raised by her father, Cerialis, and probably in the care of other family members. Cerialis was appointed suffect consul for a second time in 74. Domitilla III was approximately eleven or twelve years old during Titus' reign and her family probably anticipated her marriage in the next three to four years. Overall, the Flavian family remained relatively small and Titus found himself without an immediate biological heir. Thus, Domitian continued to hold the position of heir apparent, ensuring succession within the dynasty.

CHAPTER 10

CONSECUTIVE DISASTERS

Titus returned to Rome in early September 79, faced with the daunting duty of managing resources in the wake of the Vesuvius disaster described in the Prologue of this biography. Eager to project an image of benevolence and effective governance, he took decisive action by appointing a special commission, led by two ex-consuls, to oversee rebuilding and the restoration of the region. Doubtless seeking advice from his trusted financial advisor Tiberius Julius, he grappled with the urgent need to secure substantial funds for the enormous task at hand. Although Titus had issued a decree stipulating that estates left without heirs as a result of the disaster would contribute to the rebuilding efforts, it was clear that a far greater financial commitment would be required.[1]

Vigilant in overseeing the aftermath of the disaster in Campania, Titus returned to the region in the spring of the following year to inspect progress and ascertain the need for further financial support. However, during his visit alarming news reached him from Rome: a massive fire was sweeping through the city and escalating into a major incident.[2] Over the course of three days and three nights the inferno raged unabated, transforming into a disaster of significant proportions, second only in magnitude to the infamous fire during Nero's reign in 64.[3]

The blaze appears to have originated in the Campus Martius and spread east and south-east on the prevailing winds.[4] Several buildings in that region were destroyed: the Pantheon, the Temple of Isis, the Saepta, the Diribitorium, the Temple of Neptune, the Baths of Agrippa, the Theatre of Balbus, parts of Pompey's Theatre and an invaluable library built during the Octavian period. Moving east, it destroyed the Temple of Serapis in the Quirinal region and south-easterly winds then drove the flames up onto the Capitoline where the inferno consumed the Temple of Jupiter and its surrounding temples. This destroyed all the efforts made by Vespasian and Titus to rebuild the Temple of Jupiter after its destruction at the end of the civil wars. Furthermore, the destruction of the prized mint located on the Capitoline Hill dealt a severe blow to coin production. Although the mint was eventually relocated to the Caelian Hill, east of the Colosseum, it meant an end to the minting of precious metal coins during Titus' reign.[5] The blaze may have also consumed parts of the Velabrum south of the Capitoline. Many other buildings, especially densely packed residential blocks, were destroyed in all these areas. The Roman Forum seems to have been spared.[6]

The immediate response in Rome came from the *vigiles*, the fire brigade. Instituted by Augustus in AD 6, the *vigiles* comprised seven cohorts, with eighty men per century, seven centuries per cohort, a theoretical full strength of 3,920 men. Each cohort was responsible for covering two regions of Rome. In this period, the corps had fourteen watch-houses, one in each region, as a location to report to, an equipment store and a place for shelter. This was a high concentration of manpower; hypothetically, each fireman covered an area about the size of half a football pitch.[7] The reason for this concentration was the limited effectiveness of their tools to tackle major fires. Their firefighting equipment essentially comprised buckets, blankets and axes. Damp blankets could beat back fires and be draped over buildings to shield them. In dire situations, pickaxes could be employed to demolish buildings and prevent fires from spreading further. Access to water for their buckets depended on the nearest source and in rare cases water pumps may have been used. Overall, one can assume that the scale of any significant fire rendered the *vigiles'* efforts inadequate and that results were greatly influenced by the strength and direction of the winds.[8]

The exact cause of the fire is unknown, yet it was a disaster waiting to happen. Firstly, Rome's people used countless open flames, from hearths and oil lamps to various heating systems and workshops. Moreover, the city was full of highly flammable materials such as stored grains, olive oil, fabrics and wood, found in granaries, warehouses and shops scattered throughout the Campus Martius and beyond. Compounding the risk, densely packed residential areas were dominated by wooden structures clustered closely together along narrow streets; the need to accommodate the crowded population had led to the construction of high-rise tenement blocks with timber frames, balconies and roofs. This volatile combination posed a significant threat, especially during the drier spring and summer months.

Efforts were made to mitigate the risk of such outbreaks. Today, remnants of these efforts can be seen on Via Tor de' Conti in the form of tall stone firewalls, designed to shield the *fora* from the densely populated ancient Suburra area that was particularly prone to fires. Following the devastating inferno during Nero's reign, sensible regulations were enacted to prevent future catastrophes, including the requirement for additional open spaces, enhanced protection of water sources, requirements for broader streets and height restrictions on buildings.[9] However, the implementation and enforcement of Nero's measures would require decades and appears to have had little impact on the fire of 80.

The toll of the fire remains unknown but it is reasonable to estimate that hundreds perished in the flames and suffocating smoke, while thousands were left homeless in the fire's wake. The blaze wreaked havoc on essential public infrastructure, disrupting grain distribution, water supplies from cisterns, sewage systems, public baths and other services. Heightening the disorder, Rome's population was swollen due to the influx of individuals displaced by the Vesuvius eruption, further straining these overburdened services. In the aftermath, widespread looting probably ensued as many found themselves plunged into poverty amidst the devastation.

On his prompt return to Rome from Campania, Titus almost certainly further mobilised the urban cohorts and Praetorian Guards to quell any looting, maintain order and bolster relief efforts.[10] Reflecting on the magnitude of the disaster and its financial impact, Titus lamented, 'This has ruined me!' With plans already in place to allocate resources to Campania, Titus now faced the challenge of finding additional funds for the reconstruction of damaged areas. Displaying self-sacrifice, he decided to strip imperial residences of their precious artworks, distributing them among buildings and temples in an effort to rejuvenate the city and replace lost masterpieces. Furthermore, he convened a council comprising individuals of equestrian rank to ensure the swift implementation of his directives in response to the catastrophe.[11]

In all humanitarian disasters, rampant infectious disease can be a grim consequence of reduced living conditions, degraded sanitation and displaced populations. Consequently, the third disaster of Titus' reign struck after the great fire in the form of an epidemic caused by a pathogen not seen frequently before.[12] The population of Rome at this time was approximately 750,000.[13] As many as 10,000 people a day may have died at the peak of the fatality rates.[14] This equated to around one per cent of Rome's population succumbing to the disease daily. Often ignored in the history of epidemics, this was possibly one of the most significant outbreaks between the better documented plague in Athens in 434–430 BC and the Antonine Plague of AD 165–180.[15]

To determine the causative agent behind the epidemic, we must consider three key epidemiological factors: time, population and place. Regarding time, the epidemic emerged suddenly and persisted for months, not years.[16] The seasonality, peak period and duration of infectivity are unknown. Concerning the population, Rome was a densely populated metropolis with a typical age distribution for the era, including around thirty per cent children.[17] There was no general concept of isolating symptomatic individuals or adequate sanitation to prevent transmission, facilitating person-to-person spread. It is reasonable to assume that the very young, elderly and individuals with pre-existing conditions were most susceptible to severe illness, resulting in higher mortality rates within these sub-populations. Such high mortality rates suggest that the epidemic was caused by a pathogen circulating in a population lacking natural immunity, rendering the majority highly susceptible to severe disease. As for the place, the central and suburban areas of Rome were probably the epicentre of the outbreak, with other nearby urban centres in Latium possibly affected. The extent of the epidemic across Italy is unknown. Living conditions for the majority of people in Rome, especially those in poverty, were poor in terms of hygiene and sanitation, exacerbated by the recent great fire that displaced thousands and reduced access to clean water, latrines and baths. Even under normal circumstances, poorer residents disposed of raw sewage in the streets, further contributing to unsanitary conditions.[18] Following the Vesuvius eruption, the influx of displaced individuals fleeing the disaster zone into Rome would have played a role in the described epidemic.[19]

Modern science, including developments made in the response to COVID-19, suggests three possible pathogens infectious enough and lethal enough to have been the cause of the epidemic: the ancestors of the smallpox and the measles viruses or bacterial plague.[20] The precise characteristics of the variants of these that might have been in circulation in Titus' Rome are unknown but their effects in an immunologically naïve population could have been dreadful.

Regardless of which pathogen caused the outbreak, there were limited effective measures Titus could implement. He approached the crisis with utmost seriousness, exhausting 'every imaginable means' to combat it.[21]

In line with the prevailing belief that plagues were the result of divine discontent, religious rituals and sacrifices were conducted, probably involving consultations with famous oracles. Titus may have authorised specific religious events such as a *lectisternium*, a sacrificial feast for the gods, a practice employed during the Republican period in response to disease outbreaks. The benefit of these approaches was to rally the community together and mitigate panic by emphasising the belief that the gods would eventually intervene and end the epidemic.[22] Titus also encouraged access to the available remedies. Preparations were derived from botanical, animal and mineral sources yet, without effective antivirals and antibiotics, their impact on the epidemic was non-existent. Medical practitioners of the time varied from quacks to a few learned individuals practising elements of Greek medicine as philosopher-doctors. Practically, Titus had to manage the large number of fatalities, presumably organising mass burials. Ultimately, the rising level of natural immunity in the surviving population would have curbed the outbreak.

Despite the enormous challenges posed by these disasters, Titus demonstrated astute fiscal management, leveraging the inherent wealth of the Roman Empire to navigate these crises. His prudent handling of the treasury ensured that he would later pass on a healthy financial legacy to his brother and successor, Domitian. His proactive approach and genuine concern for prompt responses are evident in his appointments of commissioners and boards to oversee the response efforts. In the face of the Vesuvius eruption, the fire in Rome and the epidemic, Titus remained resolute, ensuring that resources were deployed to provide relief and support to the affected regions. His careful planning and decisive actions probably mitigated the immediate and longer-term impact of these disasters and set the stage for recovery and rebuilding efforts.

CHAPTER 11

DEATH AND LEGACY

A defining feature of Titus' reign was its brevity. Just as he had managed to turn around his image and rebrand himself as a benevolent ruler and bring the three disasters under active management 'death intervened'.[1] At the end of the summer of 81, Titus attended the closure of games held in Rome. Apparently, he wept publicly in front of the crowds, presumably an exaggerated expression of his grief for all the calamities endured by his people. Adding to his melancholic mood, as he was about to offer a sacrifice to the gods his intended victim escaped, an ill omen made worse by the sound of distant thunder despite clear skies. Under these auspices, Titus left Rome on a planned trip to the Sabine region where his father had always enjoyed summer retreats.

En route along the Via Salaria, Titus reached a posting station outside Rome where he collapsed with a fever. These stations were strategically roadside buildings or inns where travellers, messengers and officials could stop to rest, change horses or obtain provisions during their journeys. Titus was clearly suffering from a significant ailment to have collapsed. A litter was organised for him to continue his journey reclined within the comfort of the compartment. Perhaps partially delirious from the fever, it is said that he pulled back the curtain of his litter and lamented that his life was being 'undeservedly' taken from him and only one sin rested on his conscience.[2] Conceivably, Titus sensed the seriousness of his illness or he had been warned in the past of a terminal condition. We will never know. Nor will we know the reason for his guilt.[3]

Reaching his father's beloved summer retreat above the sacred Lake of Cutilia (Lago di Paterno near Rieti), the region of his ancestors, he may have sought the water treatments at the nearby Aquae Cutiliae, just as his father had done when he was taken ill before his death. Domitian and probably

Julia with other close family and friends were present, called urgently from Rome.[4] With Titus unable to care for himself, his brother took charge of his treatment including using snow to try to lower his fever, a potentially counter-productive method that is still applied by some today using cold baths and other means to cool a patient.[5] His condition deteriorated and he passed away in the same country property where his father had died. It was 13 September 81. He was aged forty-one and had ruled for only 807 days.[6]

The rapid onset of Titus' illness, the presence of a debilitating high fever and his quick demise, all suggest an acute malarial infection. Rich or poor, emperor or slave, mosquitoes carrying malaria were impossible to avoid entirely even with bed screens. The Romans were aware of the association between swamp waters and disease – which motivated the draining of marshes around Rome not only to claim land but for health reasons, though this was only completed in the twentieth century.[7]

It seems that Domitian decided to leave his brother's deathbed before he passed away. He may have wanted to be in Rome to prepare the Senate and the Praetorian Guard in person for his accession, rather than send news by courier from the Sabine region. It seems callous, but Titus' imminent death was probably obvious to those present and a peaceful succession was more important than a bedside vigil.[8] When the news reached Rome there was an outpouring of grief for the loss of their emperor.

> When the news spread, the entire population went into mourning as though they had suffered a personal loss. Senators hurried to the House (Senate Curia) without waiting for an official summons, and before the doors had been opened, and then when they were open, began speaking of him [Titus], now that he was dead, with greater thankfulness and praise than they had ever used while he was alive and among them.
>
> *Suetonius*[9]

This passage ends Suetonius' portrayal of the life of Titus in his ancient biography, a poignant way to close his account of an emperor he generally admired.

Domitian's accession and the transfer of power was smooth. He made a bee-line to the Praetorian camp where he promised the Guard their expected financial reward and was hailed as emperor. Presumably Domitian was not so stupid as to take the oath until he actually received word that Titus was dead but he was certainly ready for the news. When the dispatches arrived, the senators assembled to honour Titus, though not to ratify Domitian's accession immediately. He had to wait for the following day, 14 September, to be hailed formally as emperor by the Senate, a delay that set a tone of animosity between Domitian and his senators.[10]

Domitian organised an elaborate funeral for his brother with all the formalities that his father had received. The new emperor delivered the eulogy and, over tears, called for his brother to be deified.[11] Whether the tears were staged or not, Titus was duly deified by his brother some time after 1 October.[12] It was of course highly beneficial for Domitian to have a divine father and brother to solidify his position. Contrary to what some of the ancient sources would have one believe, Domitian made considerable efforts to venerate his deceased brother. He completed the Flavian Temple in the Roman forum dedicated to Vespasian and Titus. A priesthood for Titus was created to accompany that of Vespasian's cult. On the site of the Villa Publica, destroyed by the great fire of 80, a building that had played an important role in Vespasian and Titus' triumph, he constructed a Temple Divorum that included two temples for *divus* Vespasian and *divus* Titus. Gold aurei were issued with a bold portrait of the divine Titus on the obverse and a portrait of Julia on the reverse.[13] Brass sestertii depicted Titus enthroned holding a branch and sceptre with an altar at his feet.[14] Last but not least, Domitian constructed the magnificent triumphal arch, still standing today on the edge of the forum over the Via Sacra, dedicated to Titus' victories and his apotheosis: the transformation from mortal to divine. Walking under the arch today, one can look up into the vault to see a fine relief panel of Titus riding a majestic eagle to the heavens.[15] Lesser known today but even more spectacular at the time, Domitian also built a second triumphal arch at the entrance to the Circus Maximus and dedicated it to his brother.

Julia's life after Titus' death remains clouded in controversy, especially given the contentious verdict on Domitian's rule from the Senate after his death that would call for his memory to be condemned. Julia remained an empress, *Augusta*, although Domitia Longina would also be awarded the same title within weeks of Domitian's accession, a title she would hold for a remarkable forty-five years. Rumours abounded about alleged sexual depravities involving Domitian, his wife and niece, with hearsays ranging from Julia's supposed pregnancy by Domitian to accusations of adultery levelled against Domitia as grounds for divorce. However, a more plausible explanation was Domitia's failure to produce an heir, making the younger Julia a more desirable prospect for securing a successor. Despite Domitian pushing for divorce, strong support for Domitia managed to avert such an outcome and the couple continued to live together until Domitian's later demise. Julia probably passed away from natural causes in late 89 and was subsequently deified by Domitian in the following year.[16] So ended the last direct blood line of the divine Titus Flavius Vespasianus.

Titus' brief yet impactful reign and life left an indelible mark on Roman history. Born into the echelons of elite Roman society, though initially acquainted with familial financial struggles, the eventual family rise to wealth and privilege granted him a unique vantage point in Rome's socio-political sphere. Educated alongside Britannicus, the ill-fated son of Emperor Claudius, and later invited to join Nero's tour of Greece, Titus was exposed to the inner workings of the imperial court from an early age. These formative experiences provided him with invaluable insight into the complexities of Roman imperial power, laying the groundwork for his future influence. We can detect a major shift in the family's fortunes during Nero's Greek tour when Vespasian was appointed supreme commander of the Roman forces in the Jewish War, while Titus himself received the rare and accelerated appointment to command XV *Apollinaris* under his father's authority. Titus' rapid rise was a testament to the confidence placed in his abilities, as well as the prominence of the Flavian family during a time of escalating unrest in Judea. Titus' military leadership during the Jewish War bolstered his reputation as a capable commander – he clearly played a key role in suppressing the rebellion in Galilee. Together, father and son made a formidable partnership, operating as general and legate in one of the most significant military endeavours of the time.

Often under-appreciated in historical accounts, Titus may have been one of the first to recognise his father's potential to seize power during the tumultuous civil wars of 69. Through his diplomatic finesse, Titus secured the crucial support of Mucianus, governor of Syria, for Vespasian's imperial ambitions. His covert negotiations with Mucianus marked a pivotal moment in Roman history, as the backing of the Syrian governor and his legions tipped the delicate balance of power in the empire in favour of Vespasian, who could then rally all the eastern legions to his cause. Titus' influence in this period extended to his participation in his father's *consilium* meetings and the historic gathering on Mount Carmel, all of which contributed to Vespasian's eventual decision to pursue the Principate.

As the young *Caesar* and heir apparent to the new Emperor Vespasian, Titus' most prominent legacy from the Roman perspective remains his triumphant siege and capture of Jerusalem, which effectively ended the rebellion. His military campaigns and the complete destruction of the Jewish capital affirm his reputation in history. The restoration of order to the province allowed Rome to move past the embarrassment of losing control over an entire territory. His decisive punitive actions also served as a stark warning to any potential rebel forces across the empire that might contemplate rebellion. His victories were worthy of a spectacular triumph in Rome and the spoils of war filled the imperial coffers.

The legacy of the Jewish War and its place in the Flavian propaganda story evolved over time. Following Vespasian's accession, the Flavians appear to have framed the victory as part of a larger narrative portraying the new emperor as the restorer of peace to a fractured Roman world. This claim held some truth, as Vespasian's reign brought an end to the brutal civil war that had ravaged the empire – the likes of which had not been seen since the Republic's transformation into imperial rule. Judea was just one of several regions where peace had been restored, and the war there was a recovery of Roman control, not a new conquest. Tellingly, neither Vespasian nor Titus adopted the honorific title *Judaicus*, Conqueror of Judea, to make that distinction.

However, over time, the narrative of the Jewish War was reimagined and elevated. The conflict became a cornerstone of Flavian propaganda, used to legitimise their dynasty and consolidate their authority as bringers of stability. This shift is evident in the '*Iudaea Capta*' coinage series, the extensive building projects funded by the spoils of the war, and the historical accounts that glorified their achievements. Domitian's commissioning of the Arch of Titus is a prime example of this branding. Titus is portrayed in a triumphal chariot crowned by Victory, symbolising imperial power and divine favour. The arch celebrates Rome's dominance, Titus' divinity, and the subjugation of Judea. All these were statements clearly designed to exalt Flavian superiority. The Jewish War thus became more than a military campaign to quell a rebellion; it was a symbol of Flavian triumph, carefully crafted to solidify the dynasty's place in Roman history.[17]

Beyond the Flavian propaganda, the ruthless suppression of the Jewish population and the utter destruction of Jerusalem set off a chain of events that reshaped the Jewish identity and had profound implications for the region. The forced diaspora spread large numbers of Jewish communities far beyond their ancestral homeland, fostering a deep longing for a return to Zion that has been central to Jewish religious and cultural identity for millennia. These historical events laid the groundwork for complex historical, political and cultural dynamics that still resonate in the region today.

The modern situation in the Middle East, particularly the Israeli–Palestinian conflict, is partially rooted in the historical displacement and subsequent return of Jewish communities to their ancestral homeland, fuelled by the ideals of Zionism in the late nineteenth and early twentieth centuries. The Roman-era diaspora served as the foundation for a Jewish global identity, which was central to the establishment of the State of Israel in 1948, and has become a focal point of tension with the Arab population of Palestine. Competing narratives of ancestral claims, dispossession and rights to the land stem from the disruptions initiated by Roman imperial rule. The ripple effects of these events manifest in the modern Middle East as a clash of identities, histories and territorial claims. They underscore how ancient history continues to shape contemporary political realities, influencing debates over legitimacy, historical grievances and the pursuit of peace. Titus' destruction of Jerusalem was not just a military act, it was a transformative moment that fundamentally altered the region's cultural and demographic fabric, with consequences that still reverberate today.

Vespasian, *denarius*, Struck 69–70, Rome Mint. Reverse, personification of *Judea* in mourning. This was one of the earliest types struck after Vespasian became emperor and developed into a series commemorating 'Judaea Capta'.
RIC 11, 2

For the Jewish survivors, Titus is remembered as a cruel tyrant who oversaw the death and enslavement of countless men, women and children. The magnificent civilisation of Jerusalem was vanquished and the entire city razed to the ground. Titus did not spare even the Second Temple, the centre of Jewish religion and worship. The sacred treasures of the Jewish people were looted and taken to Rome. Titus became infamous in Jewish lore as *Titus Ha-Rasha*, or Titus the Evil, for his role in the destruction and desecration of the Second Temple. It was believed by some Jews that the disasters endured during his reign were retribution from God. The Babylonian Talmud – a collection of Jewish texts compiled around AD 450–550 – provides one damning view of Titus' actions during the destruction of the Second Temple:

> What did [Titus] do? He took a prostitute by the hand and entered the Holy of Holies and spread out a scroll of the Law and committed a sin on it [i.e. sexual intercourse]. He then took a sword and slashed the curtain. Miraculously blood spurted out, and he thought that he had slain himself.[18]

The phrase 'he thought that he had slain himself' is meant to suggest that Titus ignorantly believed he had harmed or killed a representation of God. The miracle of blood spurting out from the curtain can be seen as a divine response, indicating that Titus's actions were not just a desecration of a physical space but an affront to the divine. Therefore, the 'himself' is a euphemism for God. Titus thinks he has killed God but in truth he is condemning himself – his soul and his fate – by his actions. Here we don't see the darling of Rome, conqueror and hero, but rather a depraved commander in the midst of battle, enthralled in a fantasy that he was killing God. The account goes on to accuse Titus of using the same curtains to carry away a bundle of sacred Temple treasures.

In the wake of the Jewish rebellion, while Vespasian worked to solidify his rule and authority, Titus' diplomatic efforts in the region had a lasting impact, paving the way for significant changes aimed at enhancing security and stability along Rome's eastern frontiers. Titus' ambassadorial mission to the Parthians was to convey Rome's commitment to peace and regional consolidation under Vespasian's leadership, reassuring envoys from King Vologeses. Escorted by two legions, Titus demonstrated Rome's military might during his diplomatic endeavours, earning recognition from the Parthians in the form of a crown for his victories. As a result of Titus' successes, Vespasian was able to implement strategic reforms in the East. This included a more efficient distribution of Roman legions across the region and the amalgamation of Cappadocia and Galatia into a single consular charge that later incorporated Lesser Armenia. Additionally, the kingdom of Commagene was annexed and integrated into the province of Syria. These actions, facilitated by Titus' interactions with Parthia, led to the establishment of a new military zone along the Upper Euphrates, bolstering Roman presence and influence in the area. Overall, Titus owed much to the

Orient. It was the inherent power of the eastern empire that had created the new Flavian dynasty.

Throughout Vespasian's reign, Titus wielded significant influence over his father, effectively serving as a co-ruler in all but name, and he supported the responsibilities of imperial power and administration. In his role as commander of the Praetorian Guard and designated heir, Titus played a pivotal part in ensuring stability within Vespasian's administration, laying the groundwork for the establishment of the Flavian dynasty. Furthermore, their joint tenure as censors allowed Titus and Vespasian to shape the composition of the Senate and alter the social fabric of Rome for years to come. Through the adlection of new senators and the elevation of individuals into the patrician class, they left a lasting mark on the Senate's membership and the broader societal structure of Rome, influencing generations yet to be born.

Titus' ascent to the throne marked a significant turning point in Roman history. He became the first biological son to succeed his father as emperor, solidifying the acceptance of the Flavian dynasty and paving the way for his brother's seamless accession. Demonstrating his reverence for his father, Titus dutifully deified Vespasian after his death, establishing the Flavian imperial cult. Although Titus's reign was short, its impact reverberated across several provinces. Continuing his father's legacy, he carefully managed the empire by appointing capable governors to ensure stability and prosperity in various regions. He also introduced a notable change by allowing senators of Greek descent to serve as judicial assistants to proconsular governors or assume military commands in the East, thereby diversifying Roman administration. In all these aspects, his legacy remained intricately intertwined with that of Vespasian through the continuity of many policies, and infrastructure projects initiated by his father. Moreover, Titus relied heavily on loyalists from his father's reign and had a diverse collective of trusted individuals to help him manage the affairs of the Roman Empire.

At the start of his reign, Titus took personal and public measures to rebrand his image and during his short reign the effort was remarkably successful, suggesting the negative aspects were probably more a matter of anecdotal exaggeration than deeply ingrained despotism. Suetonius provides a favourable verdict on Titus' rebranding:

> But this reputation [poor prior to his accession] turned out to his
> advantage and gave place to the highest praise, when no fault was
> discovered in him, but on the contrary the highest virtues.[19]

Titus had been in the honeymoon period of his reign and clearly that gave him a chance to turn opinion around. We can never know if he would have maintained this benevolence because his reign was so short.

Ever-prominent in the modern landscape of Rome today, Titus' completion of his father's work on the Colosseum is by far their greatest legacy in terms of iconic Roman images. More important practically to the average Roman or provincial subject, however, were works under Titus to maintain various aqueducts and roads. Titus also implemented social reforms for the army during his reign that impacted the lives of many serving soldiers and veterans.

Titus' reign was marked by a series of calamities occurring in rapid succession. Despite grappling with these formidable challenges – the eruption of Vesuvius, the great fire in Rome and a devastating epidemic – he demonstrated effective crisis management, fiscal prudence and genuine concern for his people. His adept and prudent monetary control ensured the empire's financial stability, enabling swift responses to crises. Demonstrating foresight, Titus appointed competent commissioners and boards to oversee relief efforts, underscoring his commitment to addressing his subjects' needs. He implemented measures to alleviate the impact of disasters, including resource distribution, relief organisations and support for affected populations. His reign appears to epitomise effective imperial governance, crisis-management and compassion for his people.

Titus' legacy has endured through the ages, particularly through artistic representations of the war in Judea, which has inspired dramatic scenes of conflict, especially in the nineteenth century. One remarkable example is Francesco Hayez's *Destruction of the Temple of Jerusalem*, an oil painting completed in 1867. The chaos of battle is vividly depicted with the Holy of Holies engulfed in dark smoke and the great altar in the Priests' Court the scene of a mêlée between Roman soldiers who have breached the Temple and Jewish fighters. At the bottom of the altar, Titus, easily identifiable by his red cloak, stands surrounded by his guards observing the destruction. Elsewhere, scenes of carnage unfold with many Jews depicted pleading for mercy amidst the chaos. Meanwhile, Roman soldiers are depicted carrying away the golden menorah. The sense of realism in Hayez's work sets it apart from other portrayals of the destruction by artists such as Wilhelm von Kaulbach (1846) and Nicolas Poussin (1626).

Another poignant depiction of the events is seen in the painting *Siege and Destruction of Jerusalem by the Romans Under the Command of Titus* by the Scottish artist David Roberts dated to 1850. This sweeping composition offers an aerial view of Jerusalem from the Mount of Olives where Roman troops are depicted in the foreground poised for battle. Below, in the Valley of Kidron, columns of Roman soldiers can be seen advancing towards the city. While the urban structure and buildings of Jerusalem are stylised, Roberts skilfully captures the topography and the prominence of city monuments, although the depiction of the Holy of Holies erroneously resembles a Roman temple. The focal point of the composition is the conflict unfolding at the Third Wall, where billowing smoke rises into the atmosphere tinted orange from the glow of fires. Amidst this disorder, a sharp orange and yellow light pierces through the smoke, creating a sense of divine intensity.

One of the most renowned paintings capturing the Flavians is Lawrence Alma-Tadema's *Triumph of Titus*, dated 1885, which subtly references rumours surrounding Titus and his family. In the covered stairway of a temple complex, Vespasian, portrayed as Pontifex Maximus, is escorted by his lictors at the forefront of his family. With his head covered by his toga, the elderly emperor exudes dignity and statesmanship. Following closely behind Vespasian is Domitian, adorned in an ornate bronze military breastplate, delicately holding the hand of his recent bride, Domitia Longina. Domitian's gaze is resolute and forward-looking while Domitia casts a longing glance over her left shoulder towards Titus, who is also clad in religious regalia. Titus gazes back at his sister-in-law. In the background, triumphant sacrifices have taken place and the golden menorah serves as a reminder that the composition is part of Vespasian's and Titus' Jewish triumph. Alma-Tadema's masterful painting subtly alludes to the probably unfounded rumours of an affair between Titus and Domitia that circulated during their time.

Seventeenth century French and English playwrights were particularly inspired by the affair between Titus and Berenice. Jean Racine's *Bérénice*, Pierre Corneille's *Tite et Bérénice* and Thomas Otway's *Titus and Berenice*, all cover the story of Titus reluctantly choosing his duty as emperor over his love for Berenice, sending her away from Rome. The great Mozart wrote an opera, *La Clemenza di Tito* (*The Clemency of Titus*) that premiered on 6 September 1791 in Prague to honour the coronation of King Leopold II, the forty-fourth Holy Roman Emperor. The opera follows Vitellia, daughter of the late emperor Vitellius, who seeks revenge on Titus. The plot unfolds with themes of jealousy, guilt and assassination attempts, concluding with Titus' clemency as he pardons the condemned.

Titus' benevolence shines through in Mozart's opera and speaks to the tradition of Roman emperors being divided between those that were moral and good and those who were immoral and wicked. Titus has always been assigned into the former category by both ancient and modern historians, even though he failed to live long enough as emperor fully to justify his favourable ranking. Suetonius opens his account of Titus in his book *The Twelve Caesars*, dedicated thirty-eight years after Titus' death to his friend Gaius Septicius Clarus, with resounding praise:

> Titus, of the same surname as his father, was the delight and darling of the human race; such surpassing ability had he, by nature, art, or good fortune, to win the affections of all men, and that, too, which is no easy task, while he was emperor.[20]

Dio Cassius, writing over 130 years after Titus' death is more suspicious in his interpretation of Titus' legacy given the short time he was tested as emperor:

> [Titus] is regarded as having equalled the long reign of Augustus, since it is maintained that Augustus would never have been loved had he lived a shorter time, nor Titus had he lived longer. For Augustus, though at the outset he showed himself rather harsh because of the wars and the factional strife, was later able, in the course of time, to achieve a brilliant reputation for his kindly deeds; Titus, on the other hand, ruled with mildness and died at the height of his glory, whereas, if he had lived a long time, it might have been shown that he owes his present fame more to good fortune than to merit.[21]

Without doubt, Titus will be remembered most for the capture and destruction of Jerusalem over 1,950 years ago. Thus, it is apt to leave the final word to Rabbi Judah Leib Fishman Maimon, who visited the Arch of Titus in Rome in 1926 and sent a postcard to his father back in Tel Aviv. Over time, the arch had become a symbol for Jewish resilience and his message defies the defeat depicted in the scenes on the arch.

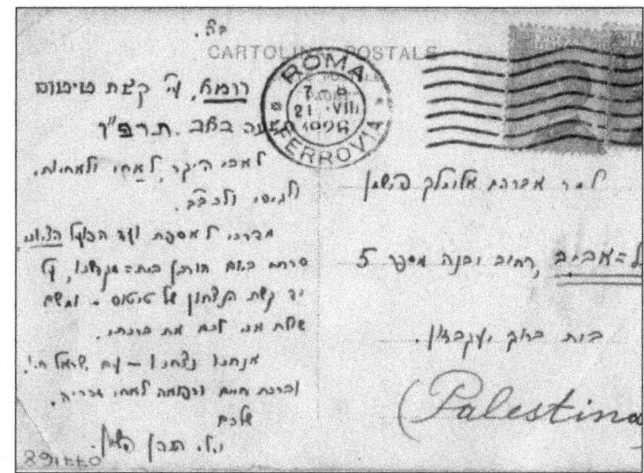

Rome, near the Arch of Titus,
20 July 1926

On my journey to the congress of the Zionist General Council on the day of the destruction of our holy Temple, I went to the Victory Arch of Titus – and I send my greetings to you from there. We won! The People of Israel live!

Rabbi Fishman Maimon[22]

NOTES

Preface

1. The Flavian Dynasty were the three members of the Flavian family, Vespasian, Titus and Domitian who held the imperial throne 69–96.
2. Power, T., 'Suetonius' Tacitus'. It is thought that the *Twelve Caesars* was published between 119 and 122.
3. Birley, A. R., 'The Life and Death of Cornelius Tacitus'. Birley provides estimates for the years of Tacitus birth, attainment of senatorial status and quaestorship.
4. Abdy, R., *Legion, Life in the Roman Army*, 'Enlisting'.
5. Duncan-Jones, R., *Money and Government in the Roman Empire*, 'The Imperial Budget'. Jones's lower limit estimate for around. 150 is 643 m. *sestertii*.

Prologue

1. This places it at about VEI 5 on the Volcanic Explosivity Index.
2. Based on corpses found in Pompeii's excavated areas and estimates for unexcavated areas, around 2,000 perished in the town out of a population of around 20,000 residents. Strabo, *Geography*, 5.4 describes the coastal region as a densely populated continuous suburb. I therefore estimate another 20,000 lived in Herculaneum (*ca.* 5,000), Stabiae (*ca.* 5,000) and numerous other towns, hamlets, farms, estates and villas in the vicinity of the eruption. Although around only 10 per cent were found dead in Pompeii, one should not assume that those who fled the town easily survived. Victims have been recovered outside the city walls. Even surviving the eruption could have meant death from starvation, exposure and disease for many. For ejected mass see Cioni, R., et al., 'Assessing pyroclastic fall hazard through field data and numerical simulations: Example from Vesuvius'.
3. Doronzo, D. M., et al. 'The 79 CE Eruption of Vesuvius: A Lesson from the Past and the Need of a Multidisciplinary Approach for Developments in Vulcanology'. See Figure 9.
4. Forsyth, P. Y., 'In the Wake of Etna, 44 B.C.' An event but vaguely described.

5. Foss, P. W., *Pliny and the Eruption of Vesuvius*, 'Two Days'. Foss has extensively evaluated the totality of evidence that supports the start of the eruption on 24 August. The oldest copies of Pliny's letters state 24 August and I view it as inconceivable that Pliny, as an eye-witness to the momentous event that killed thousands, including his uncle, would have got the date wrong. No coinage disputes the 24 August date. Moreover, Foss dismisses theories based on seasonal wind directions, braziers, carpets, clothing and archaeobotanical evidences that have been used to argue a later date. Importantly, he provides arguments that the graffiti discovered in October 2018 in the Casa del Giardino could have been made on any number of October 17ths prior to the eruption.

6. Doronzo, et al. 'The 79 CE Eruption of Vesuvius …' Stratigraphic layer EU1. I argue that this event occurred earlier than Doronzo believes in order to match Pliny's account. Foss, *Pliny and the Eruption of Vesuvius*, 'Two Days', places the first eruption in the morning and reaching a height of around 15km.

7. Dio Cassius, 66.21–2. Describes the yearly tremors and vent smoke.

8. Strabo 5.4.8. He describes the lush lower slopes of Vesuvius and the barren, flattened summit and fires that forged blackened rocks, making reference to Mount Etna's eruptions in Sicily. Virgil's Aeneid 8.407–53 describes his mythical interpretation of Mount Etna.

9. Giacomelli, L., et al. 'The eruption of Vesuvius of 79 AD and its impact on human environment in Pompeii'.

10. There is no evidence of how the courier travelled but the timing of delivery suggests on horseback. The plea for rescue is curious given that the courier was able to leave.

11. Travelling at 150–200 km/hr.

12. Thomas, C., 'Claudius and the Roman Army Reforms'. Starr, C. G., *Coastal Defense in the Roman World*.

13. Pliny, *Letters*, 6.16.

14. It is probable that many perished near the town, having failed to travel to a sufficiently safe distance.

15. Carlos, G., et al., 'Volcanic Eruptions and Threats to Respiratory Health'.

16. Assumes an average adult can normally walk 5 km in an hour. Under the fallout, within 3 hours over half a metre of pumice and ash would have fallen in open areas reducing movement to a crawling pace. Moving directly away from the fallout zone would have eventually allowed a regular pace. Estimates are based on a varying range of conditions underfoot.

17. Foss, P. W., *Pliny and the Eruption of Vesuvius*, 'Two Days'.

18. The fact that excavations have found that all the boathouses were empty by the time they were covered by the eruption suggests that a wave of boats did at least make it out into the bay, probably heavily laden with people. Roads west would also have aided escape.

19. Speed equivalent to 9–11 km/hr.

20. Sigurdsson, H., et al. 'The Eruption of Vesuvius in A.D. 79: Reconstruction from Historical and Volcanological Evidence'. 0.6–1.0g/cm³.

21. Sigurdsson, H., et al. 'The Eruption of Vesuvius…'. 2–3g/cm³ and 9–11cm in diameter. Sigurdsson also provides the estimate of the height of the column.

22. Doronzo, 'The 79 CE eruption of Vesuvius'. Stratigraphic layer EU3f.

23. Sigurdsson,. 'The Eruption of. Vesuvius'.

24. Giacomelli, L., et al. 'The Eruption of Vesuvius'. Of the 394 corpses found in the pumice fall, 88 per cent were inside buildings of whom a proportion may have been injured or even killed by collapsing structures.

25. Foss, *Pliny and the Eruption of Vesuvius*, 'Epistulae 6.16, The Elder's Story'.

26. Pliny, *Letters*, 6.16.

27. Howe, T., *The Social Status of the Villas of Stabiae*.

28. Sigurdsson. 'The Eruption of Vesuvius.'

29. Pliny, *Letters*, 6.16.

30. Foss, *Pliny and the Eruption of Vesuvius*, 'Two Days'. The timing of 7–8 p.m.

31. Ibid., Figure 3.4(a).

32. Mastrolorenzo, G., et al., 'Herculaneum Victims of Vesuvius in AD 79'.

33. Petrone, P., et al., 'A hypothesis of sudden body fluid vaporization in the 79 AD victims of Vesuvius'.

34. Giuffuida, A., 'Sensational: skeleton buried in Vesuvius eruption found at Herculaneum'. Capasso, L., 'Herculaneum victims of the volcanic eruptions of Vesuvius in 79 AD'.

35. Foss, *Pliny and the Eruption of Vesuvius*, 'Two Days'. Figure 3.6 for distribution of the pyroclastic flow.

36. Petrone, P., et al. 'Heat-Induced Brain Vitrification from the Vesuvius Eruption in C.E. 79'.

37. Foss, *Pliny and the Eruption of Vesuvius*, 'Two Days'. Figure 3.4(a).

38. Sigurdsson, 'The Eruption of Vesuvius in A.D. 79'. Foss, *Pliny and the Eruption of Vesuvius*, 'Two Days'. Stratigraphic layer EU3pf1.

39. Foss, *Pliny and the Eruption of Vesuvius*, 'Two Days'.

40. Cioni, R., et al., 'Temperatures of the A.D. 79 pyroclastic density current [PDC] deposits (Vesuvius, Italy)'. Cioni extensively describes PDC temperature ranges of 180–380°C with most samples showing temperatures of 240–340°C. Temperatures drop significantly as the PDCs extend over kilometres. The average temperature of EUpf3 at various locations was around 300°C.

41. Foss, *Pliny and the Eruption of Vesuvius*, 'Two Days'. Stratigraphic layer EU3pf2.

42. Pliny, *Letters*, 6.16.

43. Doronzo, D. M., et al. 'The 79 CE eruption of Vesuvius: A lesson from the past and the need of a multidisciplinary approach for developments in volcanology'. Foss, *Pliny and the Eruption of Vesuvius*, 'Two Days'. Stratigraphic layer EU3pf3.

44. Sigurdsson, 'The Eruption of Vesuvius in A.D. 79'. Surge S3, p.379.

45. Foss, *Pliny and the Eruption of Vesuvius*, 'Two Days'.

46. Pliny, *Letters*, 6.20, 6.20.8.

47. Foss, *Pliny and the Eruption of Vesuvius*, 'Two Days'. A complex pyroclastic occurrence with a first dilute current, a short fallout interval and then the last part of the current, simplified here into one event. Stratigraphic layer EU3pf tot I, II, III.

48. Doronzo, 'The 79 CE eruption of Vesuvius …'. Figure 7, EU3pftot.

49. Scorrano, G., et al., 'Bioarchaeological and palaeogenomic portrait of two Pompeians that died during the eruption of Vesuvius in 79 AD'. Victims' location Regio I, Insula 10, civic 7, room 9. Luongo, G., et al., 'Impact of the AD 79 explosive eruption on Pompeii, II. Causes of death of the inhabitants inferred by stratigraphic analysis and areal distribution of the human casualties'. Luongo points out that 'the data from ancient excavations are not sufficiently detailed to report the exact position of the corpses with respect to the stratigraphic reports'. In 'The Eruption of Vesuvius in A.D. 79', Sigurdsson cites human remains found in S4 (EU3pf tot I) and S5 (EU3pf tot III) that were buried by S6 (EU4 pf). I assume that the couple found in Casa del Fabbro and subsequent examples of victims due to this event were killed along with the majority who had survived up until that point; stratigraphic layers EU3pf tot I & III.

50. Pompeii location: Region IX, Insula 4, 5.

51. Finding reported in *The Local*, Italy, 26 April 2018.

52. Pompeii location: Region VI, Insula 17, 42.

53. Archaeological Park of Pompeii, Press Release, 'The DNA of the inhabitants of Pompeii Moving towards a complete genetic mapping of the population', 30 May 2022.

54. 610 grams of gold is equivalent to 84 *aurei*.

55. Abdy, R., 'The Last Coin in Pompeii: A Re-Evaluation of the Coin Hoard from the House of the Golden Bracelet'.

56. Pompeii location: Region II, Insula 7.

57. Luongo, 'Impact of the AD 79 explosive eruption on Pompeii, II. Causes of death ..

58. Ibid.

59. https://research.ncl.ac.uk/expandedinteriors/projectinformation/ houseofthecryptoporticuspompeii/

60. Technically termed the caldera-forming phase.

61. Stratigraphic layer EU4pf up to 5 metres deep.

62. Luongo, 'Impact of the AD 79 explosive eruption on Pompeii, II. Causes of death …' Luongo states that he and his colleagues established without doubt that groups of victims lie several centimetres above the base of stratigraphic level E (S6, EU4pf).

63. Dellino, P., et al., 'The Impact of pyroclastic density currents duration on humans: the case of the AD 79 eruption of Vesuvius'. Dellino contradicts Cioni, 'Temperatures of the A.D. 79 pyroclastic density current deposits (Vesuvius, Italy)', who estimated temperatures of 280–300 °C in Pompeii for EU4 (Table 2). Dellino also seems to report the physical strength of EU4 erroneously in terms of structural damage.

64. Pliny, *Letters*, 6.16. The time of his death is not known, but assumed to be at around this time of the morning.

65. Foss, *Pliny and the Eruption of Vesuvius*, 'Two Days'.

66. Pliny, *Letters*, 6.20.

67. Doronzo, 'The 79 CE eruption of Vesuvius: A lesson from the past…' Stratigraphic layers EU5, EU6, EU7 and EU8.

68. Pliny, *Letters*, 6.16.

69. Pliny, *Letters*, 6.20.

70. Radice, B., *The Letters of the Younger Pliny*, 'Introduction'.

71. Cioni, R., et al., 'Assessing pyroclastic fall hazard through field data and numerical simulations: Example from Vesuvius'. Cioni estimates a Volcanic Explosivity Index rating of 6 for Vesuvius. The Mount St Helens eruption of 1980 is rated 5 and has been estimated as around 24 megatonnes. Vesuvius thus surpassed this power.

72. If they left Pompeii around 1 p.m. on 24 August and walked for 8–10 hours per day, they could have arrived in Rome between 28 and 30 August.

73. Jones, B., *The Emperor Titus*, 'Reign of Titus'. Jones cites two visits, one immediate and one the following year (the latter referenced by Dio 66.24)

74. Dio Cassius, 66.24. Suetonius, *Titus*, 4.8.

75. The 12 January 2020, Taal Volcano eruption in the Philippines experienced the ash turning first into a mud-like texture, due to rainfall, that hardened after a few months. See Scandone, 'Death, Survival and Damage…' for details of dangerous mud and pumice landslides.

76. A hypothesis suggested by Professor Steven Tuck, Miami University, from a lecture sponsored by the Herculaneum Society, March 2021.

77. Tuck lecture, March 2021.

78. Inscription presently at the National Archeological Museum of Naples.

79. Tuck lecture, March 2021..

80. Delile, H., et al., 'A lead isotope perspective on urban development in ancient Naples'.

81. Tuck lecture, March 2021.

82. Tuck lecture, March 2021.

83. Turner, B., 'War losses and worldview: Reviewing the Roman funerary altar at Adamclisi".

84. Personal communication, Professor Steven Tuck, Miami University.

85. Tuck lecture, March 2021. See CIL X 1784.

86. Tuck lecture, March 2021.

87. 'Discovery at Pompeii', *Scientific American*, 35(14), 216 (1876).

Chapter 1: *Humble Beginnings*

1. Galba had illustrious ancestors, Otho had noble Etruscan origins, Vitellius' background was questionable according to Suetonius' assessment and Vespasian only an equestrian.

2. Bowman, Garnsey, Rathbone, *The Cambridge Ancient History XI*, 'The Flavians'. For details on his equestrian status 'at most', see Griffin, *Nero*.

3. The *Optimates*, a faction that represented the aristocratic wing of the Roman Senate, viewed Caesar as a dangerous demagogue who threatened their power and the traditions of the Republic. They supported Pompey as their military leader to uphold the authority of the Senate and curb Caesar's growing influence. The *Populares*, a political faction that sought to represent the interests of the common people against the established elite, sought to continue Caesar's reforms and expand his power, portraying themselves as defenders of the people against a corrupt and oligarchic Senate. This meant Titus' paternal great-grandfather was on the side of the *Optimates*, although in reality as a centurion he was drawn onto a side because of his legion's allegiance.

4. Suetonius, *Vespasian*, 1.

5. Jones, B., *The Emperor Titus*, 'Early Career'. Nicols, J., *Vespasian and the Partes Flavianae*, 'Vespasian in Julio-Claudian Politics'.

6. Suetonius, *Vespasian*, 1 & 2. Levick, B., *Vespasian*, 'Stemma I: The Flavians'.

7. Suetonius, *Vespasian*, 2. Coarelli, F., Stephen, K., & Patterson, H., *'Investigations at Falacrinae, the Birthplace of Vespasian'*. It is thought that Falacrinae was in the vicinity of Lago di Paterno (Lake Cutilia).

8. Stephen Kay, British School of Rome, personal communication. Between 2008 and 2012 field excavations under his direction at the site of San Lorenzo, a 4-km drive south of Cittareale, revealed a high status early imperial residence with no evidence of association to the Flavian family. Dr Kay suggests that 'Villa di Tito' above Lago di Paterno (Lake of Cutilia) is a more likely candidate for the place referred to in the sources as Vespasian's summer villa. Situated off the Via Salaria (modern day SS4) the Villa di Tito is 1.7 km north-east of the Laghetto Sulfureo di Cotilia thermal springs. The villa is often confused with the bath and sanctuary complex, Aquae Cutiliae, 3 km south-west.

9. The birth date of Sabinus II is unknown.

10. Suetonius, *Vespasian*, 2.

11. For his accent, see Levick, B., *Vespasian*, 'A New Man in Politics'.

12. Suetonius, *Vespasian*, 3. La Monaca, V., 'Flavia Domitilla as "delicata": a new interpretation of Suetonius, Vesp. 3'. Wardle, D., 'Suetonius on Vespasian's rise to power under the Julio-Claudians'. Barrett, A., 'Vespasian's Wife'. See La Monaca for newer insights into the understanding of *delicata*, which I have adopted as the leading hypothesis. See Barrett for an alternative view in which Flavia Domitilla was born free as a Roman citizen, reduced to a servile status and raised as a slave by Statilius, granted informal freedom and then legally restored to citizenship. See Barrett for arguments that the marriage to Vespasian probably occurred when he was unsure about a political career and the 'unsuitable match' with Flavia Domitilla was therefore acceptable.

13. Jones, B., *The Emperor Titus*, 'Early Career'.

14. Suetonius, *Vespasian*, 2.

15. Jones, 'Early Career'. Three-year period, see Levick, B., *Vespasian*, 'A New Man in Politics'.

16. Suetonius, *Vespasian*, 2.

17. Talbert, R., *The Senate of Imperial Rome*, 'The Senate'.

18. Suetonius, *Vespasian*, 2. Nicols, *Vespasian and the Partes Flavianae*, 'Cursus Vespasiani'. For theories to explain his failure, see Levick, 'A New Man in Politics'. I favour the hypothesis that he was simply a 'new man' lacking sufficient patronage. Levick & Nicols date the aedileship to 38 AD.

19. Suetonius, *Vespasian*, 5.

20. Personal communication, Philip Matyszak: Gaetulicus was an associate of Sejanus. When Tiberius summoned him to Rome he apparently responded that he would come, along with his army. Tiberius didn't challenge the popular commander's implied threat and G. remained in Germany until Caligula caught him unawares with a sudden unannounced visit and executed him.

21. Suetonius, *Caligula*, 24. Stewart, Z., 'Sejanus, Gaetulicus, and Seneca'. Jones, B. W., 'Agrippina and Vespasian'.

22. Suetonius, *Vespasian*, 3. Although Suetonius say that Vespasian stopped the relationship during his marriage, I consider this highly unlikely given the later influence she had on him and the probable benefits he had from the relationship through the reigns of Caligula and Claudius.

23. Suetonius, *Vespasian*, 3.

24. Suetonius, *Vespasian*, 2. Jones, 'Early Career'. Levick,, 'A New Man in Politics'.

25. Nicols, J., *Vespasian and the Partes Flavianae*, 'Cursus Vespasiani'.

26. Suetonius, *Titus*, 1. Note that Suetonius erroneously gives his year of birth as 41 and then later contradicts this. Perhaps Suetonius confused the year with that of Britannicus' birth.

27. Storey, G., 'The "Skyscrapers" of the Ancient Roman World'.

28. Suetonius, *Titus*, 1.

29. Suetonius, *Titus*, 2.

30. Jones, 'Early Career'.

31. Garcia y Garcia, L., *Pupils, Teachers and Schools in Pompeii*, Morford, M., 'The Training of Three Roman Emperors'. There is no evidence that Titus was exposed to court life but it is assumed given his close friendship with Britannicus and who *was* being prepared for power.

32. Quintilian, *Institutio Oratoria*, 2.15.33

33. McNally, J. R., 'Toward a Definition of Rhetoric'.

34. Jones, 'Early Career'. Crispinus 43–51, Geta 44–51 & Burrus 51–62.

35. Kleijwegt, M., '"Iuvenes" and Roman Imperial Society'.

36. Suetonius, *Titus*, 3.

Chapter 2: *The Rise of the Flavii*

1. Brunt, P. A., 'Nobilitas and Novitas'.

2. Jones, 'Early Career'. Nicols, *Vespasian and the Partes Flavianae*, 'Vespasian in Julio-Claudian Politics'. Jones and Nicols both provide comprehensive evaluations of patrons and associates. *CIL* 6.12037, funerary inscription for Antonia Caenis.

3. Nicols, 'Vespasian in Julio-Claudian Politics'.

4. Suetonius, *Caligula*, 46. Campbell, D. B., 'Did Emperor Caligula plan to invade Britain? Caligula's capers on the North Sea Coast'. Filtering the typical negative narrative against Caligula, he may well have made preparations for operations that Claudius was able to later adopt such as establishing supply lines and docking platforms for boats.

5. Claudius had been denied a normal senatorial career by Tiberius, despite appeals.

6. Manley, J., *AD 43 The Roman Invasion of Britain: a Reassessment*. See Manley for a comprehensive argument that south-east Britain was already extensively Romanised.

7. McPake, R., 'A Note on the Cognomina of Legio XX'. There was no honorific title for Legio XX until after AD 61.

8. Fields, N., *Britannia AD 43, The Claudian Invasion*, 'Opposing Forces'.

9. Dio 60.19.2

10. Manley, J., AD 43, 'Why was Richborough eventually chosen by modern historians?'

11. Burn, A. R., 'The Battle of the Medway, AD 43'. Burn suggests the Romans arrived between Aylesford and Cuxton, where the river cuts through the down.

12. Elliot, S., *Great Battles of Early Imperial Rome*, 'The Battle of Medway'.

13. Hassall, M, 'Batavians and the Roman Conquest of Britain'.

14. Kaye, S., 'The Roman invasion of Britain, 43 AD: riverine, wading and tidal studies as a means of limiting the possible locations of the invasion-ground and the two-day river battle'.

15. Burn, 'The Battle of the Medway, AD 43'.

16. Dio 60.20.6

17. Dio 60.21.1. Fields, *Britannia AD 43*, 'The Campaign'.

18. Dio 60.22.1–2. Levick, *Vespasian*, 'The Command in Britain'.

19. Levick, 'The Command in Britain'.

20. Suetonius, *Vespasian*, 4.1

21. Nicols, *Vespasian and the Partes Flavianae*, 'Cursus Vespasiani'.

22. Levick, *Vespasian*, 'A New Man in Politics'.

23. Suetonius, *Vespasian*, 4.1

24. Dio 61.31.1–6.

25. Dio 61.31.6, describes her beauty and manipulation of Claudius.

26. Dio 61.31.8.

27. Dio 61.32.2.

28. Dio 61.32.1. 'complete control over Claudius'.

29. Dio 61.31.8.

30. Rogers, R. S., 'Heirs and Rivals to Nero'.

31. Hiesinger, U., 'The Portraits of Nero'.

32. Examples include RIC I 79 & RIC I 83.

33. Dio 61.32.6

34. Dio 61.32.5–6

35. Suetonius, *Vespasian*, 4.

36. Jones, B., *The Emperor Titus*, 'Early Career'. Jones suggests that the birth of Domitilla II was soon after Domitian but it is not attested. I assume she was born in early 53, possibly the same year for the births of Domitia Longina and Sabinus IV.

37. Suetonius, *Claudius*, 45.

38. Suetonius, *Nero*, 8.

39. Cordes, L, 'Iuvenis Infandi Ingeni Scelerum Capaxque: Flavian Responses to Nero's Youth'

40. Born 12 February 41.

41. Rogers, R. S., 'Heirs and Rivals to Nero'.

42. Rogers, R. S., 'Heirs and Rivals to Nero'. Rogers argues that these behaviours were in character.

43. Tacitus, *Annals*, 13.14.

44. Suetonius, *Nero*, 33. Tacitus, *Annals*, 13.15–16. Dio, 61.7.4. Suetonius' account describes a failed initial attempt before the fateful dinner with Titus also inadvertently poisoned. Tacitus also describes an initial attempt and provides the details of the drink as the source. Dio's account suggests poison and the additional detail that Nero used gypsum to disguise Britannicus' discoloured skin.

45. Suetonius, *Nero*, 34.

46. Dio 62.12.2–3; 62.13.1–5.

47. Levick, B., *Vespasian*, 'The Command in Britain'.

48. Jones, B., *The Emperor Titus*, 'Early Career'. Jones describes numerous advances following the death of Agrippina.

49. Jones, B., *The Emperor Titus*, 'Early Career'. Jones dates the vigintivirate to 60.

50. McAlindon, D., 'Entry to the Senate in the Early Empire'.

51. Jones, J. R., 'Mint magistrates in the early Roman Empire'. Jones, B., *The Emperor Titus*, 'Early Career'.

52. Nicols, J., *Vespasian and the Partes Flavianae*, 'The Flavian group in AD 67'.

53. Jones, 'Early Career'. I have adopted Jones' analysis that a *montales* role was possible.

54. Suetonius, *Titus*, 4. Jones, 'Early Career'. See Jones for dating to 61.

55. Suetonius, *Titus*, 4.

56. Goldsworthy, A. K., *The Roman Army at War, 100BC–AD200*, 'The Generals' Battle'.

57. A Roman fort dated to 63 has been discovered at Fenchurch Street.

58. Jackson, N., *Trajan: Rome's Last Conqueror*, 'The Making of a Military Officer'.

59. Suetonius, *Titus*, 4. Jones, 'Early Career'.

60. Suetonius 4.3. Its not clear why Vespasian was still in financial difficulties but his credit was exhausted and after he returned from Africa he mortgaged all his estates to his brother.

61. Suetonius, *Titus*, 4. Jones, 'Early Career'. PIR2 A 1073. Jones provides two possible dates for the marriage to Arrecina Tertulla: in 63 or 64. I favour the first half of 63

after Titus' return from Britannia as this would align with the birth of their daughter in 64 and Titus probably married his second wife in 65. PIR for Clemens the elder.

62. Talbert, R. A., *The Senate of Imperial Rome*, 'The Senate'. Aged 22 was young for the quaestorship; typically held around 24–25 years of age.

63. Talbert, R. A., *The Senate of Imperial Rome*, 'The Senate'.

64. Jones, 'Early Career'. Talbert, 'The Senate' & 'Attendance'. See Jones for the date of the quaestorship and gap period until his 28th year (minus one from the 29th requirement because of his daughter Julia) and see Talbert for quaestorship numbers and function.

65. Jones, B., *The Emperor Titus*, 'Early Career'. Kohn, T. D., 'The Enigma of Julia Augusta Titi'. The mother of Julia has been a source of considerable debate. Kohn argues that Suetonius is clear that the mother was Marcia Furnilla and Philostratus of Athens, who states that Titus had two daughters cannot be trusted. Jones leans towards Arrecina Tertulla, given that Suetonius provides no name for the daughter. Philostratus cites two daughters and importantly Arrecina Tertulla's family had a Julia in the family line that could explain Titus' daughter bearing that name. In conclusion, I assume Arrecina Tertulla was the mother, with the additional postulation that her early death after marriage might have been from complications during Julia's birth.

66. Suetonius, *Titus*, 4. The marriage is not mentioned by Suetonius but is thought to have occurred in 64.

67. Jones, 'Early Career'.

68. Jones, 'Early Career'.

69. Bunson, M., *Encyclopedia of the Roman Empire*, entry for the Pisonian Conspiracy.

70. Suetonius, *Nero*, 36.

71. Titus' wife had a cousin, Servilla, married to Annius Pollio who was exiled in connection with the Piso plot.

72. Thrasea Paetus and Helvidius Priscus: the dates when Vespasian broke off connections are not known but probably in this period, 65/66.

73. We can never know definitively if Nero did poison Britannicus, but it seems highly probable given his strong claim to the Principate as the biological son of Claudius and the nature of his death, which was documented by several Roman sources.

74. Suetonius, *Titus*, 2. I assume the 'Circus' refers to the Colosseum.

Chapter 3: *The Path to Power and War*

1. Bradley, K. R., 'The Chronology of Nero's Visit to Greece A.D. 66/67'. The exact date is not known but it is thought he left Rome at some time between mid-June and mid-September. Mouratidis, J., 'Nero: The Artist, The Athlete and His Downfall'.

2. Suetonius, *Nero*, 40.

3. Gisela, R., 'The Pheidian Zeus at Olympia'.

4. Dio Cassius, LXII, 11.

5. Dio Cassius, LXII, 14.1. Suetonius, *Nero*, 24.

6. The contemporary sources are silent on this point. It is likely they wanted to whitewash Vespasian's connections with public enemy, Nero.

7. Suetonius, *Vespasian*, 4.

8. Bradley, K, R., 'Nero's Retinue in Greece, A.D. 66/67'.

9. Josephus, 3.8

10. Suetonius, Vespasian, 4.

11. Its important to note that Josephus' dates are not definitive, so particular calendar estimates should be considered within a range of variability.

12. Josephus, 1.414

13. Foerster, G., 'The Early History of Caesarea'.

14. Nero's initial reaction to the first outbreaks is not known, but he was likely informed and his procurators and governors in the region charged with its resolution.

15. Rome temporarily lost control over parts of its Illyrian provinces (modern-day Balkans, specifically in areas like Illyricum and Pannonia). The revolts were significant enough to challenge Roman authority in the region, though they did not result in a permanent loss of the provinces.

16. The republican Crassus later robbed the Temple to help fund his campaign against the Parthians in 54 BC.

17. Zeichmann, C. B., *The Roman Army and the New Testament*, 'Who were the soldiers in early Roman Palestine ?'

18. Josephus, 2.184–203.

19. Josephus, 2.272. Albinus served as the Roman *procurator* of Judea in 62–64 a period that saw growing tensions between the population and the Roman authorities.

20. Josephus, 2.264–5.

21. Udoh, F., 'Taxation of Judea under the Governors'. Tacitus, *Ann.* 2.42, also mentions heavy taxation in Syria and Judea.

22. Josephus, 2.284–92.

23. Zeichmann, 'Who were the soldiers in early Roman Palestine?'

24. Josephus, 2.293–332.

25. Josephus, 2.333–5.

26. Josephus, 2.408.

27. Josephus, 2.409. Eleazar was Captain of the Temple (2.410).

28. Josephus, 2.457–458. There is no specific mention of Florus approving the massacre but there can be little doubt he was involved in the decision to allow it to happen in the Roman capital of the province. Florus was notoriously corrupt and extorted money from the Jewish population, treating them with open contempt. Florus was seen as favouring the Greeks of Caesarea. He may have calculated that a full-scale rebellion would justify harsher Roman crackdowns and possibly enrich him further through looting and military actions.

29. Josephus, 2.17.9.

30. Nicols, *Vespasian and the Pates Flavianae*, 'The Chronology of Events, AD 67–70'. Nicols provides a description of imperial post operations and average delivery times.

31. This is postulated on the basis that Cestius' experience as a statesman would incline him to take the initiative.

32. Levick, *Vespasian*, 'From Nero's Court to the Walls of Jerusalem' Dando-Collins, S., *Conquering Jerusalem*, 'The Impending Storm'.

33. Dando-Collins, *Conquering Jerusalem*, 'The Impending Storm'.

34. Josephus, 2.509.

35. Josephus, 2.528. October 66.

36. Josephus, 2.535–541.

37. Josephus, 2.545. 'Baggage' is specifically mentioned, which could mean individual legionaries' marching packs or the mule baggage train.

38. Josephus, 2.544.

39. Josephus, 2.546.

40. An actual ambush is not attested and Josephus (2.547) states that the Jews moved in 'once they [the Romans] were confined in the narrow pass' but anticipating the Romans' best route would better explain the Jewish ability to be so well placed around the pass and also ahead of the Romans.

41. The precise location of the narrow pass where the Romans were attacked is not known but this was clearly not a simple route through a two-sided valley because Josephus (2.547–9) describes heights above the Romans as well as treacherous 'cliffs and ravines' that one could fall into. Studying historical pictures and the topography of the area confirms this notion.

42. Josephus, 2.546–50.

43. The remains of Antipatris are known today as Tel Afek.

44. Many authors claim that the eagle of the XII Legion was also lost but I have found no references to support this.

45. Dando-Collins, *Conquering Jerusalem*, 'A Roman Disaster'.

46. Josephus, 2.562–3 for appointment of co-leaders. Tal, I., & Price, J., 'Seven Onomastic Problems in Josephus' Bellum Judaicum'.

47. Josephus, 2.564–5.

48. Josephus, 2.566–84.

49. Josephus, 3.1–3.

50. Suetonius, *Vespasian*, 4.

51. Levick, B., *Vespasian*, 'From Nero's Court to the Walls of Jerusalem'. Levick describes this crucial notion that Vespasian's 'rise to a position of eminence was due to the death of [Corbulo]'.

52. Levick, B., *Vespasian*, 'From Nero's Court to the Walls of Jerusalem'. Jones, B., *The Emperor Titus*, 'Judea'. Nicols, *Vespasian and the Partes Flavianae*, 'The Chronology of Events, AD 67–70'. All authors thoroughly examine the details of Vespasian's appointment.

53. Josephus, 3.8.

54. Suetonius, *Titus*, 4.

55. Jones, *The Emperor Titus*, 'Judea'.

56. Josephus, 3.6.

57. Jones, 'Judea'. Jones notes this as further evidence of Nero's view that the Flavii posed no threat to his authority.

Chapter 4: *The Jewish War, Campaign of 67*

1. Josephus, 3.8.

2. Nicols, 'The Chronology of Events, AD, 67–70'. Nicols argues that February was the most likely month.

3. Josephus, 3.31. Gallus is attested to have negotiated peace terms with the authorities of Sepphoris, probably towards the end of 66, but then in 67 returned to Rome and was not part of Vespasian's officer group.

4. Josephus does not mention the involvement of the XII Legion in Vespasian's campaign of 67. Professor Mordechai Aviam, Kinneret Institute for Galilean Archaeology, personal communication, has not found archaeological evidence for the name or symbol of any legion later during the siege of Jotapata. A coin commemorating the establishment of the *colonia Ptolemais* minted under Nero shows on the reverse four legionary standard plaques bearing the numbers of four Roman legions, III, VI, X, and XII, apparently based in Judaea. This suggests the involvement of Legio XII but it appears erroneous to reference Legio VI which remained in Syria during the rebellion. Dando-Collins, S., *personal communication*, concludes that two depleted cohorts of XII *Fulminata* left there by Governor Cestius during his retreat went on to serve under Vespasian during the war and eight cohorts of XII *Fulminata* retired to Laodicea in Syria to discharge and re-enlist legionaries later in 67.

5. Josephus, 3.8 for XV *Apollinaris*. Dando-Collins, *Conquering Jerusalem*, 'Enter Vespasian and Titus' regarding V *Macedonica* in Egypt. I calculate approximately two weeks for Titus to reach Alexander from Achaia, Greece. There are numerous later examples of Titus taking great personal risk during the Jewish Wars. Egyptian governors were only allowed from the equestrian order and so a senatorial legate was not appropriate to command a legion, hence a tribune was in command of V *Macedonica*.

6. Josephus 3 is clear that XV *Apollinaris* and V *Macedonica* were in Egypt. In 66 they had been in the north-east of the Empire under Corbulo for the Armenian campaign and had been sent to Egypt for Nero's planned campaign in Ethiopia. This contradicts Tacitus, *Histories*, 1.31 that mentions the 'German' legions back from Alexandria and favourable to Galba.

7. Wheeler, E. L., 'Legio XV *Apollinaris*: From Carnuntum to Satala – and beyond', in Y. Le Bohec & C. Wolff, (eds), *Les Légions de Rome sous le Haut-Empire*.

8. Scene 10, Trajan's column, Rome, for example, shows the typical attire of a legate in the imperial period.

9. Dando-Collins, *Conquering Jerusalem*, 'Fire and Blood in Galilee'.

10. Ibid.

11. The brief marriage between Titus and Marcia Furnilla, the sister of Traianus' wife.
12. Dando-Collins, *Conquering Jerusalem*, 'The Impending Storm'.
13. Josephus, 3.12.
14. Josephus, 3.325.
15. Josephus, 3.326.
16. Josephus, 3.344. Dando-Collins, *Conquering Jerusalem*, 'The Siege of Jotapata'.
17. Josephus, 3.344. Dando-Collins, 'The Siege of Jotapata'.
18. Dando-Collins, 'Fire and Blood in Galilee'. Nicanor joined Titus' staff.
19. Josephus, 4.48.7
20. Josephus, 3.449.
21. Tal, I., & Price, J., 'Seven Onomastic Problems in Josephus' Bellum Judaicum'. These authors discuss onomastic complexity and here I assume Gurion ben Joseph is an error by Josephus and the same man as Joseph ben Gurion. It is odd that Josephus introduces such an important person, 2.563, never to mention him again. He may have had a ceremonial role and therefore faded into the background. The fate of Gurion may refer to a Gurion (no patronymic given) who was murdered by the Zealots, 4.358.
22. Josephus, 2.563
23. Josephus 2.564–5. Tal & Price, 'Seven Onomastic Problems'. Tal & Price argue that he must have come to prominence before the Battle of Beth Horon and that is assumed here.
24. Josephus 2.409–10 and the Eleazar mentioned 2.424, 2.443 and 2.453.
25. Josephus, 2.566. The Eleazar named here is probably ben Neus.
26. Josephus, 2.566.
27. Josephus, 2.566
28. Josephus, 3.11.
29. Josephus, 4.235.
30. Josephus, 4.235.
31. Josephus, 4.235.
32. Josephus, 4.235.
33. Josephus, 2.567
34. Josephus, 2.567
35. Josephus, 2.567
36. Josephus, 3.12
37. Josephus, 2.568.
38. Josephus, 2.568
39. Josephus, 2.585–9 & 4.85.
40. Josephus, 3.11
41. Tal & Price, 'Seven Onomastic Problems'.
42. Josephus, 3.450, erroneously called ben Saphias instead of Sapphias in 2.599.
43. Tal & Price, 'Seven Onomastic Problems'. Josephus, 4.159
44. Josephus, 4.18.

45. Josephus, 3.66–90 provides a seemingly accurate list of units.

46. I assume 10 per cent attrition for X/V/XV (15,400 total), and 30 per cent for the two cohorts of XII *Fulminata* (670) because of heavy losses at the Battle of Beth Horon.

47. Josephus, 3.67. Imperiumromanum.pl, an *ala*, meaning 'wing', was a division of Roman cavalry; there were two types of *ala*. An *ala milliaria* consisted of about a thousand riders divided into 24 *turmae* of 42 riders, and an *ala quinquenaria* with approximately 500 riders divided into 16 *turmae* of 30 riders. The size is not mentioned so I assume they were *alae milliariae* but after 10 per cent attrition. Dando-Collins, *Conquering Jerusalem*, 'Fire and Blood in Galilee', for *ala* Gaetulorum Veterana.

48. Dando-Collins, 'Fire and Blood in Galilee'. Governor Cestius had left Tribune Placidus in charge of two depleted cohorts from XII *Fulminata* and a cavalry wing at Ptolemais in 66.

49. Double-strength 800, total 7,200 accounting for 10 per cent attrition and regular strength 480, 5,600 accounting for 10 per cent attrition. I assume Josephus (3.68) refers to a detachment of 120 cavalrymen for each of the twenty-three cohorts he cites, 2,480 accounting for 10 per cent attrition. Stephen Dando-Collins, personal communication, for helping to understand the complex availability of these troops. Although auxiliaries were normally attached to a given legion, I propose that X *Fretensis* from Syria left their auxiliary companions behind to garrison the Syrian base, with the roles of light infantry and cavalry for the operation being filled by the units provided by the allied kings of the region.

50. Josephus, 3.66, and Dando-Collins, 'Fire and Blood in Galilee'. Five at full strength of 480 with 10 per cent attrition totals around 2,100.

51. No attrition is assumed for the allied numbers because they were probably committed regardless of their own attrition levels.

52. I assume X *Fretensis*, V *Macedonica*, XV *Apollinaris* with 180 scorpions and 30 *ballistae* in total. XII lost all its artillery in 66.

53. Sheppard, S. I., *The Jewish Revolt* AD *66–74*, 'Opposing Armies'. Sheppard provides a detailed summary of logistics.

54. Goldsworthy, *The Roman Army at War*, Appendix: Logistics.

55. Trajan's Column, casts 123–4.

56. Goldsworthy, *The Roman Army at War*, Logistics. Goldsworthy concludes around 1,000 animals for a legion. I assume a comparable amount for auxiliary cohorts and *alae*.

57. Sheppard, 'Opposing Armies'.

58. Goldsworthy, Logistics. Davies, R. W., 'The Roman Military Diet'.

59. Trajan's Column depicts Roman soldiers foraging in the summer months.

60. Egypt is a strong assumption given its sizable grain production and close proximity.

61. Vegetius, *De re militari*, Book III

62. Josephus, *Life*, 199–207. An example of the Jerusalem leadership sending Jonathan with armed forces, paid in advance, to Galilee.

63. Gross estimate based on Josephus, *Life*, 199–207.
64. Josephus, 2.576 & 2.583, gives implausible numbers of 100,000 assembled Galilean men of whom 60,000 were trained. I assume this is an order of magnitude too high and more realistically there might have been around 6,000 trained. Thus approximately 36,000 in total raised by the regional generals. Josephus also records the recruitment of 350 cavalry and 600 elite troops as a bodyguard, which appears to be a more realistic number. I have multiplied this by five as a rough scale for all the regional generals.
65. Josephus 2.583 notes 4,500 in Galilee. I have rounded this up to 10,000 as a crude estimate for other areas.
66. Sheppard, 'Opposing Armies'.
67. Josephus 4.234–5. Described as rising up against Jerusalem on behalf of the Zealots.
68. This is an order of magnitude estimate of local militia raised *ad hoc* during the rebellion and independent of the junta and regional Jewish generals. John ben Levi is one example of such an independent commander, Josephus 2.585.
69. Examples of relentless Roman atrocities during war are numerous, such as the war against Mithridates (88–63 BC) and against Vercingetorix (52 BC).
70. Josephus, 4.82, for an example of Roman soldiers throwing children to their deaths into a ravine after the capture of Gamla.
71. Josephus, 4.320–1.
72. Josephus, 3.35–43.
73. Except when the Romans brutally attacked the Samaritans in 67, but the region remained under imperial control.
74. Also called Perea.
75. The time Vespasian spent in Antioch is not known but I assume he required several weeks. Predefined centres may have included Ptolemais and Caesarea Maritima.
76. There is no period attested but I assume that the size of the force and Vespasian's diligence would not have rushed these preparatory tasks. Besides, the ideal spring campaign conditions were in March and April.
77. Trajan's Column, casts 272–3, depicts Emperor Trajan performing the ceremony.
78. Josephus, 3.30. Nicols, *Vespasian and the Partes Flavianae*, 'The Bellum Judaicum and the bellum Neronis'.
79. Josephus, 2. 652.
80. Josephus, 3.10, describes a 'constant feud'.
81. Josephus, 3.25.
82. Josephus does not detail the number that returned. This is assumed based on his stated death tolls.
83. At a distance of around 700 kilometres and a pace of approximately 28 km per day, given the reasonable roads and trails along the route, marching every day.
84. Josephus, 3.59–61, 3.110. This was a large force to hand over to a tribune early in the campaign, so presumably he was highly regarded by Vespasian.
85. Josephus, 3.110.

86. Josephus, 3.111.

87. Josephus, 3.113

88. No evidence of a report has been found but it seems highly likely given Vespasian's subsequent engagement of his whole army.

89. Josephus, 3.115–26

90. Josephus, 3.126. Josephus' description 'mercenaries' appears erroneous. This was more likely the place for auxiliaries and allied troops.

91. Josephus 3.132. The location of Gabara is debated and may have been at the modern site of Arraba. I assume that Vespasian had left the border location of his first camp and was now in the interior of Galilee.

92. Josephus, 3.132–4. He describes an easy direct assault for the Romans because of an insufficient defensive force. The method of the assault I describe is a typical approach for the Romans.

93. Josephus, 3.133, says that all were killed whatever their ages. Rape and pillage were certain during such bloodshed.

94. Josephus, 3.130.

95. Josephus, 3.138–40.

96. Josephus mentions no reply, suggesting he received none.

97. Josephus, 3.141. Nicols, 'The Bellum Judaicum and the bellum Neronis', gives May as the date.

98. Josephus, 3.158–60.

99. Mordechai Aviam: 'Yodfat (Jotapata): The Life and Death of a Jewish Galilean Town', The David A. Kipper Ancient Israel Lecture Series, Oriental Institute, 2018. Archaeological evidence supports Josephus' account although there is no definitive dating to 66.

100. Professor Mordechai Aviam, personal communication. Estimates based on town buildings and the number of human bones found in the houses and in the cisterns. Josephus' number was clearly exaggerated for his own reasons as there was physically no room for such numbers in the town

101. Josephus, 3.144. Goodman notes in the translation that Aebutius was enrolled in King Agrippa's army.

102. Professor Aviam, personal communication. Aviam has found no evidence of Roman field camps to date. Josephus, 3.146–7, describes 'a camp' close to Jotapata for the purposes of intimidation. I speculate that one large temporary camp was constructed, not unlike the vast Roman temporary camp of the early third century AD at Ardoch in Scotland that covered around 525,000 square metres. Using Alan Richardson's formula in the *Oxford Journal of Archaeology*, Vespasian would have needed around 315,000 square metres for his army.

103. Josephus, 3.155–7.

104. Aviam, personal communication. Aviam has found archaeological evidence for the ramp and estimates the height of Jotapata's northern wall at around 5–6 metres.

105. The details of the ramp design are not known but were typically dictated by the immediate topography leading up to a wall and the nature of the fortifications. Josephus, 3.171, says that the objective was to reach the battlements – as opposed to just reaching the base of the wall to permit a battering ram to begin its pounding. Professor Aviam emphasises the height of the Roman assault towers, tall structures that could facilitate breaching the upper part of the wall. For example, if the excavations of Gamla are correct in their location of the breach, it was not at the base of the wall.

106. Josephus, 3.161–9.

107. Josephus, 3.169–71.

108. Josephus, 3.172–5.

109. Josephus, 3.178.

110. Josephus, 3.186–7.

111. Josephus, 3.187–8.

112. Josephus, 3.190–2.

113. Josephus, 3.204–6.

114. Josephus, 3.207–12. The number of missiles per day is not described. Based on the massive quantity of missiles found at other siege sites such as Gamla and the vast number of engines deployed, it is likely that thousands per day were fired.

115. Korfmann, M., 'The Sling as a Weapon'. A comprehensive review of the sling.

116. Josephus. 3.226. The important later detail that the ram was causing the 'fresh masonry of the wall' to give way indicates that the Romans had successfully raised the ramp up to the level of the new section described in 3.174.

117. Josephus, 3.213–31.

118. Josephus, 3.229–32. Weight is an assumption.

119. Josephus, 3.235–6. I speculate on the boot as there is no mention by Josephus.

120. Josephus, 3.237–40.

121. Josephus, 3.243–9. The distance the unborn child was thrown seems exaggerated at 100 metres.

122. Josephus, 3.250–2. Large numbers of casualties are described but no specifics are given.

123. Josephus, 3.260–1.

124. Josephus, 3.265.

125. Josephus, 3.270. Presumably the second line, because the front line held long lances.

126. Josephus, 3.271–5. The description suggests oil was thrown against one *testudo* but it is not clear if this was successful against any others or whether any additional tortoises were formed.

127. Josephus, 3.277.

128. Josephus, 3.283–8.

129. Josephus, 3.323–8. Nicols, J., *Vespasian and the Partes Flavianae*, 'The Bellum Judaicum and the bellum Neronis'. Nicols gives the date.

130. Josephus, 3.336–9.
131. Aviam: 'The Life and Death of a Jewish Galilean Town'. Human remains have been excavated in every house.
132. Josephus, 3.340–91.
133. Josephus, 3.400–2.
134. Josephus, 3.403–4.
135. Josephus, 399–408.
136. Josephus, 3.289–97.
137. Josephus, 3.299.
138. Josephus, 3.302–6.
139. Josephus, 3.307–15.
140. Nicols, 'The Bellum Judaicum and the bellum Neronis'. Table 2.
141. Jones, B. W., *The Emperor Titus*, 'Judaea'.
142. Josephus, 3.412–13.
143. Dando-Collins, *Conquering Jerusalem*, 'Take Tiberias and Tarichea'.
144. Josephus, 419–27.
145. Josephus, 3.443.
146. Jones, 'Judaea'. Jones analyses Berenice's political and economic influence.
147. Crook, J. A., 'Titus and Berenice'. Macurdy, G. H., 'Julia Berenice'. There is no direct evidence for Berenice's presence at the palace but it is highly probable she was there given her involvement in the uprising and the strength of her alliance with Rome.
148. Anagnostou-Laoutides, E., & M. B. Charles, 'Titus and Berenice: The Elegiac aura of an Historical Affair'.
149. Josephus, 3.443–5. Tarichea is associated with the ancient town of Magdala, believed to be the home of Mary Magdalene.
150. Josephus, 3.447.
151. Josephus, 3.450–2. Erroneously called ben Saphias, and is the previously mentioned ben Sapphias (2.599).
152. Josephus, 3.453–8. It appears surprising that Vespasian would be concerned with the loss of a dozen horses but, like the battle of the breach at Jotapata, the general was clearly sensitive even to minor losses, a trait that exemplifies his extraordinary regard for the welfare of his forces.
153. Josephus, 3.462–91.
154. Levick, *Vespasian*, 'From Nero's Court to the Walls of Jerusalem'. Appendix of dates.
155. Josephus, 3.497–504.
156. An ancient Galilean fishing boat was found in 1986 with these dimensions.
157. Josephus, 3.522–31.
158. Nicols, 'The Bellum Judaicum and the bellum Neronis'.
159. Josephus, 3.532–42. Agrippa was offered his people but he in turn sold them.
160. Syon, D., Yavor Z., Getzov, N., 'Gamla, 1997–2000'.

161. Israel Antiquities Authorities, Archaeology map of the eastern quarter, Yavor, 2010. Examples are the 'study room' next to the synagogue hall and rooms L1052 & L1053.

162. Dr D. Syon, Research Associate, The Institute for Galilean Archaeology, Kinneret Academic College, personal communication, Dr Syon has found no fortifications along the ridge. There are some cliffs and rocks, but no traces of man-made fortifications. The archaeologists even searched on the steep slope for collapsed blocks, but none were found.

163. Josephus, 4.10.

164. Josephus, 4.14–16.

165. Josephus, 4.17, gives the impression that works were completed quickly.

166. Dr Syon, personal communication. Josephus, 4.20, describes three breaches. However, there is only clear evidence for one breach, in the wall room L1072. Syon suspects the Romans were told of the weak spot or, because it had no roof at the time, it may have been possible to see the narrow wall section from the cliffs.

167. There is no evidence for this but it is plausible given the 'coincidence' of the breach being attempted at the weakest point.

168. Danny Syon, 'The Breaches', Israel Antiquities Authorities.

169. Josephus, 4.20–30.

170. Josephus, 4.39–40.

171. Gamla archaeology site.

172. Josephus, 4.69–70. It is not explicit that the pause was to wait for Titus but I assume it was related.

173. I assume it was a pre-dawn raid, like the one Titus led in Jotapata. Josephus, 4.70 mentions 'cavalry' which I assume meant dismounted troopers because the town was not suitable for horses.

174. Josephus, 4.80, gives an impossibly high number of deaths: 4,000 slaughtered and 5,000 killed falling down the slopes. Probably only a few hundred at most remained and there was no 'cliff' that would have killed so many. It seems more likely that he saw people scrambling their way down rather than suicidal acts.

175. Josephus 4.82

176. Levick, *Vespasian*, 'From Nero's Court to the Walls of Jerusalem', Appendix of dates.

177. Josephus, 4. 54–61.

178. Josephus, 4.32–3

179. Levick, 'From Nero's Court to the Walls of Jerusalem'.

180. De Kleijn, G., 'C. Licinius Mucianus, Leader in Time of Crisis'.

181. Suetonius, *Vespasian*, 6.

182. Levick, 'The Bid for Empire'. Suetonius, *Vespasian*, 13.

183. Tacitus, 2.5. For Titus' role in smoothing relations between Vespasian and Mucianus.

184. Caldwell, T., *The Career of Licinius Mucianus*, 'Vespasian's 'Secret Hopes'' and 'The Relationship Between Titus and Mucianus'.
185. Josephus, 4.9.2
186. Josephus, 4.115–20.

Chapter 5: *Bellum Judaicum: the Jewish War– Campaign of 68–69*

1. Josephus, 4.121–365.
2. Josephus, 4.366–76.
3. Josephus, 4.413.
4. Levick, 'From Nero's Court to the Walls of Jerusalem', Appendix of dates.
5. Nicols, 'The Bellum Judaicum and the bellum Neronis'. Nero would have received the news about Vindex between 19 and 23 March, and important news like this would have reached Caesarea about three weeks later.
6. Josephus, 4.443–4.
7. In 2019 archaeologists claimed they had finally identified Kiriath Yearim as Emmaus.
8. Josephus, 4.445.
9. Josephus, 4.449. The location of Coreae is not known but is possibly near modern-day Nablus.
10. Josephus, 4.451.
11. Josephus, 4.486.
12. Nicols, 'The Bellum Judaicum and the bellum Neronis'.
13. Brunt, P. A., 'The Revolt of Vindex and the Fall of Nero.' Griffin, M., *Nero, the End of a Dynasty*, '"What an artist dies with me!"'
14. Griffin, *Nero, the End of a Dynasty*, 'Why did it happen?'
15. Suetonius, *Nero*, 49.
16. There is no specific evidence that Vespasian needed approval from Galba but he had been appointed by Nero and re-endorsement would secure his position.
17. Levick, *Vespasian*, 'The Bid for Empire'. Talbert, *The Senate of Imperial Rome*, 'The Senate'. The praetorship could in effect be held at 29.
18. Suetonius, *Otho*, 7–8. Dio Cassius, LXIV, 8.
19. Suetonius, *Titus*, 3. Suetonius says Titus had 'a natural aptitude alike for almost all the arts of war and peace'.
20. Judea: V *Macedonica*, X *Fretensis*, XV *Apollinaris*; Egypt: III *Cyrenaica*, Legio XVIII; Syria: XII *Fulminata*, IV *Scythica*, VI *Ferrata*.
21. Suetonius, *Otho*, 3. *Vitellius*, 4 & 13. Dio, LXIV, 8. Tacitus, *Histories*, 2.76.
22. XI *Claudia* in Dalmatia, X and XIII *Gemina* in Pannonia, III *Gallica*, VII *Claudia* and VIII *Augusta* in Moesia.
23. Levick, 'The Bid for Empire'.
24. Nicols, *Vespasian and the Partes Flavianae*, 'From the Death of Nero to Bedriacum (June 68–April 69).
25. Levick, 'The Bid for Empire'.
26. Levick, 'The Bid for Empire'. I support Levick's notion that Titus' role was important.

27. Jones, 'Judaea'. Jones makes the important point that despite all the negotiations Vespasian remained very much in charge.

28. Tacitus, *Histories*, 2.73–4.

29. Antiochus was the last king of Commagene, reigning from 38 to 72.

30. Simon Elliot, personal communication.

31. Tacitus, *Histories*, 2.74.

32. No emperor had yet been succeeded by a natural son. Being part of the Julio-Claudian dynasty, adopted or not, with the support of the Praetorian Guards had been sufficient.

33. Josephus, 4.511.

34. Josephus, 4.550–5.

35. Levick, B., *Vespasian*, 'The Bid for Empire'.

36. Dio Cassius, LXIV, 10. Forty thousand on both sides is clearly an inflated number.

37. Tacitus, *Histories*, 2.70.

38. Nicols, *Vespasian and the Partes Flavianae*, 'From Bedriacum to Cremona (April–October 69)'. Nicols makes a case that Vitellius had started off well at least.

39. Tacitus, *Histories*, 2.76. Josephus, 4.592.

40. I have assumed that such a meeting occurred in Caesarea before the Mount Carmel summit because it seems highly improbable that the fundamental decision to revolt was not made before.

41. De Kleijn, G., 'C. Licinius Mucianus, Leader in Time of Crisis.' It is possible that Carmel was not the location.

42. Tacitus, *Histories*, 2.78.

43. It is not clear exactly who attended but it seems reasonable to assume that all the key players were present, including Tiberius Alexander, who could have returned to Alexandria well in time for the oath to Vespasian on 1 July because it is around 370 nautical miles between Alexandria and the Mount Carmel area; 2.5 days sailing in a small vessel at an average speed of 6 knots if no stops were made.

44. Tacitus, *Histories*, 2.76–7.

45. Tacitus, *Histories*, 2.5.

46. Tacitus, *Histories*, 2.5.

47. Tacitus, *Histories*, 2.79.

48. Tacitus, *Histories*, 2.80. Nicols, 'From Bedriacum to Cremona (April–October 69)'.

49. Jones, *The Emperor Titus*, 'Judaea'.

50. Tacitus, *Histories*, 2.81. Josephus, 4.620–1.

51. Tacitus, *Histories*, 2.82.

52. Levick, 'The Bid for Empire'. Levick makes the comparison to the Emperor Tiberius wanting to be the last resort. I further assume Vespasian wanted to avoid the disgrace of being involved in a civil war.

53. Tacitus, *Histories*, 2.82.

54. Tacitus, *Histories*, 2.85–6.

55. Waters, K. H., 'The Character of Domitian'.

56. Dando-Collins, S., *Conquering Jerusalem*, 'Nero's fate changes everything'.
57. Tacitus, *Histories*, 2.83. Nicols, *Vespasian and the Partes Flavianae*, 'From Bedriacum to Cremona (April–October 69).'.
58. Tacitus, *Histories*, 2.99.
59. Nicols, 'From Bedriacum to Cremona (April–October 69)', provides an analysis of dates.
60. Tacitus, *Histories*, 3.14.
61. Tacitus, *Histories*, 3.15.
62. Tacitus, *Histories*, 3.33.
63. Tacitus, *Histories*, 3.54–5.
64. The fleet at Misenum revolted on 1 December.
65. Tacitus, *Histories*, 3.65–6.
66. Tacitus, *Histories*, 3.69–74. Suetonius, *Vitellius*, 15.
67. Tacitus, *Histories*, 3.84.
68. Tacitus, *Histories*, 3.84–5. Suetonius, *Vitellius*, 17.
69. Tacitus, *Histories*, 3.86. Suetonius, *Domitian*, 1.
70. De la Bédoyère, G., *Praetorian*, 'To the Victor, the Spoils'.
71. Tacitus, *Histories*, 4.3
72. Dio Cassius, *Histories*, 65.2. Suetonius, *Domitian*, 1.
73. It is very unlikely all these appointments were made independently without Vespasian's specific direction.
74. De la Bédoyère, 'To the Victor, the Spoils'. De la Bédoyère concludes that a manageable number of cohorts was consolidated but the total of guards per cohort and of the cohorts themselves is uncertain. I use his estimate, however, and I have assumed that Mucianus also dealt with the Othonian Praetorians at the same time as he dealt with the other claimants.
75. Nicols, 'From Bedriacum to Cremona (April–October 69)'.
76. Tacitus, *Histories*, 4.52.
77. Another extreme example was Pompey the Great's appointment as consul when he had never even been a senator.
78. Examples issued January–June 70, BMC 7. BN 1. Cohen 5. RIC 16.

Chapter 6: *The Siege and Destruction of Jerusalem*

1. Jones, 'Judaea'.
2. Jackson, N., *Trajan: Rome's Last Conqueror*, 'Impressionable Years'. Traianus would go on to receive a suffect consulship in late 70, and later became governor of Cappadocia and finally proconsul of Asia. He was the first of his family to be adlected into the patriciate.
3. Josephus, 4.659–63.
4. His force is typically presented as only four legions, but he had large detachments from three others.
5. Jones, 'Judaea'. Josephus, 5.45–6.

6. Isaac, B. H., and Roll, I., 'A Milestone of A.D. 69 from Judaea: The Elder Trajan and Vespasian'. The milestone proves the presence of Traianus in Judaea after 1 July 69.

7. Baldwin Bowsky, M., 'A. Larcius Lepidus Sulpicianus and a Newly Identified Proconsul of Crete and Cyrenaica'. Josephus, 6.237.

8. Isaac & Roll, 'A Milestone of A.D. 69'.

9. PIR, T, 208. Josephus, 6.237, refers to him as Titus Phrygius.

10. Frugi did not receive his consulship until 80 when Titus was emperor.

11. Dando-Collins, 'Target Jerusalem'.

12. PIR, L, 287. Josephus, 6.238.

13. Dando-Collins, 'Target Jerusalem'.

14. PIR, J, 260.

15. Dando-Collins, 'Target Jerusalem'.

16. Josephus, 5.261.

17. Josephus, 5.340.

18. Jones, *The Emperor Titus*. Josephus, 6.238. Julianus replaced Florus.

19. Josephus, 5.21–6.

20. Josephus, 2.564–5.

21. Tal & Price, 'Seven Onomastic Problems in Josephus' Bellum Judaicum'. The authors argue that he must have risen to prominence before the Battle of Beth Horon and that is assumed here.

22. Josephus, 5.7–8.

23. Josephus, 2.585–9 & 4.85.

24. Josephus, 5.9, 5.254.

25. Josephus, 5.11, 5.252–4.

26. Josephus, 5.249, 6.381.

27. Josephus, 5.249

28. I assume 10 per cent attrition for X/V/XV, 15,400 total, at the start of the war, another 5 per cent depletion from the campaigns of 67–8 and all minus 2,000 for detachments to Mucianus. Total: 8,630.

29. Jackson, *Trajan*, 'Trajan's First Dacian War': 5,700 men for the full theoretical strength of a legion. Legio XII was probably recuperated through new recruits so is listed at full strength.

30. Josephus, 5.44. Millar, F., *The Roman Near East, 31 BC–AD 337*, 'The Jewish War and its aftermath'. Dando-Collins, S., *Legions of Rome*, 'The Legions'. Aylward, W., (ed.), 'Excavations at Zeugma. Conducted by Oxford Archaeology'; Elton, H., 'Zeugma's Military History in Light of the Rescue Excavations'. Millar and Elton describe evidence for IV *Scythica* regarding the 3,000-man detachments from the Euphrates cited by Josephus. It is thought that IV *Scythica* replaced X *Fretensis* at Zeugma when the latter was dispatched to Judaea in 66. However, although there is some evidence that IV *Scythica* was posted at Zeugma, there is no evidence for the date of arrival. Dando-Collins argues that Titus chose not to select the legion because of prior defeats. However, on balance, I assume Titus would have needed the numbers and

therefore it is reasonable to postulate that the detachments cited by Josephus were legionaries from IV *Scythica*, presumably under the command of a tribune.

31. Josephus 5.42–4. Levick, *Vespasian*, 'Stabilization: The Winning of Peace'.

32. Josephus 5.42.

33. Taking the numbers from the prior campaigns, accounting for some attrition as a result of those campaigns and the additional Syrian contingents, I arrive at a gross estimate.

34. Josephus 5.42. and Tacitus, *Histories*, 5.1 provide no scale for the increases so I assume an additional 10,000 on top of the 15,000 provided in the 67–8 campaigns. Attrition is factored against this increase.

35. I assume in proportion to the strength of the legion or the size of the detachment.

36. Josephus, 4.128–134 & 161. Horsley, R., 'The Zealots. Their Origin, Relationships and Importance in the Jewish Revolt'. Horsley describes Zealots as radicalised individuals 'primed' for war. It is important to note that Josephus makes specific reference to Zealots only when Roman forces advanced in the autumn of 67. Horsley provides a thorough assessment and concludes that the Zealots were not a religious sect advocating violent resistance against the Romans but in fact villagers fleeing for their lives and forced to live in the countryside, eventually forming up in Jerusalem. They did challenge the high priestly government that held control of Jerusalem.

37. Sheppard, S. I., *The Jewish Revolt* AD 66–74, 'Jerusalem: Investiture'.

38. Josephus frequently cites Titus' concern for the preservation of the Temple but Titus had absolutely no intention of sparing any part of the city. His goal was the destruction and capture of the capital. Josephus was expressing Flavian propaganda to give the impression that Titus was all benevolent.

39. Josephus, 5.136–246 provides an extensive description of Jerusalem and its defences. It should be noted that the description does not always match up with the archaeological evidence.

40. Josephus, 2.530.

41. Long debated, the Israel Antiquities Authority ('New Studies in the archaeology of Jerusalem and its Region Conference, 27 October 2016') located remains of the Third Wall and a tower base with more than seventy Roman *ballistae* bolts and sling stones nearby in the historic district known as the Russian Compound. One stone weighing 24 kg surely required a large onager.

42. Arbiv, K., 'Evidence of the Roman Attack on the Third Wall of Jerusalem at the End of the Second Temple Period.'

43. Josephus, 5.146. There is no definite evidence for the location of the Gennath Gate but it is generally thought to have stood in the northern line of the old First Wall.

44. Josephus, 5.144

45. Herod's construction was designed to protect the holy centre and its priceless contents.

46. Matthew 21:12.

47. Josephus, 5.242, contrary to modern depictions of a classic fort with towers in each corner, Josephus rather describes a tower structure.

48. Josephus, 2.330–1, 2.403–5, 5.238–45, 6.165, 7.376–7. Sams, M., 'Antonia: The Fort Jerusalem Forgot'. Martin, E., *The Temples That Jerusalem Forgot*. Gordon, R. J., 'Fort of Antonia or Temple Mount?' Murphy-O'Connor, J., 'Where was the Antonia Fort?' There is significant controversy surrounding the location of Antonia and its connection with the Temple, as well as the size and design of the fortress. The debate has drawn into question whether the current Temple Dome is on the site of the Temple of Antonia. There are two schools of thought: Antonia was located immediately next to the Temple; or alternatively it was more distant from the Temple and connected by two aerial walkways. Unfortunately, several of Josephus' descriptions are vague and open to different interpretation. Sams, Martin, Gordon and Murphy-O'Connor provide varying views. I favour the evidence suggesting that the current Temple Mount is in fact on the site of the Antonia Fort and therefore the fort was much larger than typically depicted and was separated from the northern vicinity of the Temple by a plaza (not embedded in the perimeter) and connected by walkways and stairwells between the north section of the Temple colonnade structures and the elevated floor level of the Antonia. Intriguingly, the 1584 map of Christiaan van Adrichem clearly shows a larger physical distance between the Temple and Antonia with elevated walkways between them. If one concludes that the Western Wall of the Temple Mount is actually the Herodian foundations of the Antonia, it is worth noting that the largest Herodian foundation stone has colossal proportions: 12.8 metres in length, 3.4 metres high and 4.3 metres deep, weighing about 660 tonnes.

49. Ben-Ami, D. & Y. Tchekhanovets, 'The Lower City of Jerusalem on the Eve of Its Destruction, 70 C.E.: A View From Hanyon Givati'.

50. Thornton, S., 'Water Works'.

51. Its also worth noting that the Antonia was Roman property and there was honour to be regained by its recapture at the earliest time.

52. Josephus, 5.42.

53. Josephus, 5.51.

54. Josephus, 5.52–8.

55. Josephus, 5.59–66.

56. Josephus, 5.67–8.

57. Josephus, 5.71–4.

58. Red Heifer Bridge

59. Josephus, 5.75–80, describes a scene in which the Romans were surprised and routed. This is inconceivable, knowing Roman defensive tactics when preparing a field camp. Thus, I assume it was sheer numbers rather than surprise that caused the Romans to pull back. Besides, the Jews would have been exhausted as they reached the Mount of Olives site and therefore outnumbering the Romans would have been the only way to force their retreat.

60. Josephus, 5.82, refers to elite troops. However, such soldiers would probably not have abandoned their general later, see 5.86.
61. Josephus, 5.87–90. Clearly exaggerating, Josephus gives the impression that Titus and a small group of men were able to hold back the Jewish charge. It is far more likely that Titus was able to rally the Roman line successfully.
62. Levick, 'From Nero's Court to the Walls of Jerusalem', Appendix: Josephus' dates for the Jewish War.
63. Its hard otherwise to explain why over 2,000 Zealots went over to John's side.
64. Josephus, 5.98–105.
65. Josephus, 5.261. It appears the survey was conducted during the levelling project.
66. Josephus, 5.114.
67. Josephus, 5.121–7.
68. Josephus, 5.114. The negotiation happened the day before the trap, 5.109–120.
69. Assuming two metres gap between each man, over a distance of 2 km.
70. Josephus, 5.133.
71. Josephus, 5.133–5.
72. Josephus, 5.262–4.
73. Arbiv, 'Evidence of the Roman Attack'.
74. Josephus, 5.270. Arbiv, 'Evidence of the Roman Attack'. Josephus describes the impact. Arbiv notes the small area of clustering.
75. Josephus, 5.271–4.
76. Josephus, 5.281.
77. Josephus, 5.284–9.
78. Josephus, 5.291–8.
79. Josephus, 5.302. Dating is challenging and the Jewish month of Artemisius corresponds roughly to parts of April and May in the Julian calendar. I assume the breach occurred on or around 7 May, with the start of the siege works on or around 22 April.
80. Josephus, 5.302–3.
81. Josephus, 5.304. The description is not clear for Simon, so I assume he and his men essentially defended the Second Wall along all its sections.
82. Josephus, 5.306–7. The means of the assault are not specified but all manners of fighting are suggested. However, it is clear that a ramp and earthworks were not needed for the Second Wall.
83. Josephus 5.331–41. The description begins a repeating theme that Titus wanted to spare the New Town and offered safe passage and peace terms to fighters and citizens. I dismiss this as Flavian propaganda. It is far more likely that the Romans were simply ambushed in the more densely urbanised area and they made a mistake to not widen the breach first thereby hindering their ability to pull back quickly.
84. Josephus, 5.339–40.
85. Josephus, 5.346

86. Josephus, 5.348–356. The event is portrayed as if Titus cared about the deliberations of the Jews and thus allowed them time to consider their position. I assume it is much more likely as a case of psychological warfare.

87. Josephus, 5.356 appears erroneously to reference the start of earthworks after the ceremonial event. Whereas 5.466–7 describes the completion on 29 May only seventeen days after the start. Levick, 'From Nero's Court to the Walls of Jerusalem', Appendix of dates, has different ideas. I follow Levick for the construction dates, 12–29 May. Titus had ample reserves to direct simultaneous works during assaults on the walls.

88. Josephus, 5.356–357 & 5.467–468. The precise locations are not known. For Antonia, Josephus cites a location near the Struthion Pool, identified today against the north-western perimeter of the Temple Mount. The Amygdalon Pool is identified today as the Pool of Hezekiah.

89. Josephus, 5.359.

90. Josephus, 5.361.

91. Tacitus, *Histories*, 5.13.3.

92. Josephus, 5.435.

93. Josephus, 5.429–31. Presumably this view was derived from deserters.

94. Josephus, 5.422. It is hard to reconcile this clemency against the crucifixion of those caught foraging beyond the city walls, 5.449–50. Thus, I assume that it was not a majority spared and probably a minority.

95. Josephus, 5.451.

96. Josephus, 5.463.

97. Josephus, 5.464–5.

98. Josephus, 5.469–72.

99. Josephus, 5.481 mentions camps in the plural but does not specify their location. The X *Fretensis* camp was some distance away on the Mount of Olives and XV *Apollinaris* was based within the New Town.

100. Josephus, 5.481.

101. Josephus, 5.489–490. It is not clear how so many fighters could pull back so quickly and why the Romans did not chase them down. Presumably the Jews flooded back through heavily fortified gates or up retractable ropes and ladders.

102. Josephus, 5.491

103. Josephus, 5.495–501.

104. Josephus, 5.523.

105. Josephus, 5.502–507. It is claimed that the build was completed in 3 days (5.509), which appears an impossibility. I assume it was rather 2–3 weeks' work.

106. Assumes length 6.8km, height 3m and width 0.35m. Rounded to 20,000 for the towers and other accessories.

107. Precise estimates are not possible, so I have made a gross estimate.

108. Josephus, 5.518–19.

109. Josephus, 5.519.

110. Josephus, 5.527–533 & 5.562–6.
111. Josephus, 5.550–2.
112. Josephus, 6.5–28.
113. Josephus, 5.31 & 5.67. I assume the incident of Sabinus was on the same day that the back-up wall was revealed.
114. Josephus, 6.54–7.
115. Josephus, 6.70–1. It is not explicitly mentioned but almost certainly Titus and his officers would have approved the daring action.
116. Josephus, 6.74–6.
117. The uncertainty here relates to the ability of Julianus to have advanced so quickly into the Temple. As previously assumed, the connecting walkways between Antonia and the Temple were a possible route.
118. Josephus, 6.81–91.
119. Josephus, 6.93–4, to 'create an easy way up for the whole of his army'.
120. Josephus, 6.94–5
121. Josephus, 6.131.
122. I assume XII had 60 centuries, V/X/XV 35 each, III/XVIII 12 each and IV 38. A total of 227 centuries contributing each 30 legionaries.
123. Josephus, 6.94. I assume 17 May refers to the opening of the works to demolish Antonia. 6.149, meanwhile the rest of the Roman army demolished Antonia suggests Cerialis' attack was during the demolition.
124. It is not clear how the attack was made except that space was still too limited for entire legions to form up.
125. Josephus, 6.131–48.
126. Josephus, 6.150–1. A confused description of four ramps is given. I assume that one bridged the gap between the floor level of Antonia to the ramparts of the Temple on the northern side and another on the western side.
127. Josephus, 6.180. A clear indication that access was possible by climbing up.
128. Josephus, 6.153–5 & 177.
129. Josephus, 6.157.
130. Josephus, 6.165–6.
131. Josephus, 6.166. It is very difficult to explain the destruction of these sections without these postulations.
132. Josephus, 6.181–2
133. Josephus, 6.220–1. It is clearly stated that other rams were brought up after the first attempts failed, so I assume even bigger versions were tested. The second attempt also failed, 'defeated, as the others were too'.
134. Josephus, 6.222.
135. Its particularly odd that after the enormous effort to raze Antonia and subsequently build a ramp on that side thanks to improved access, and even a road to bring forces up into that area more easily, that no specific mention is made of an attack from this platform. Ladders are only mentioned vaguely, being brought up to

the colonnades for climbing up. Thus, I suggest that ladders were used to descend the colonnade wall thanks to the ramp which may have levelled the top of the wall with the floor level of the razed Antonia. There are doubtless other theories one could propose, but my assumptions are meant to reconcile preceding details and hypotheses.

136. Josephus, 6.223–8.

137. Why this was not done at the start of the Temple assault is inexplicable. Did the Romans think that the Jews had built a large new wall behind it?

138. Josephus, 6.232.

139. Josephus, 6.241. As before, Josephus was presenting Flavian propaganda that Titus cared for the splendour and significance of the Temple.

140. Oddly there is no reference to the whereabouts of John ben Levi and Simon ben Giora. They were clearly insignificant at this point in Josephus' narrative.

141. Josephus, 6.244–9.

142. Josephus, 6.259.

143. Josephus, 261–6, describes Titus' attempt to save the building. I have assumed his motivation was because of the valuable contents and not because of any reverence for its sacred nature.

144. Time calculations are all approximations. First Temple construction is traditionally dated to the reign of King Solomon, 970–931 BC. Babylonian destruction was around 586 BC. King Cyrus' reign was 559–530. The Second Temple was completed in 515 BC.

145. Ammianus Marcellinus, *Res Gestae*, 23.1

146. Josephus, 6.271–85.

147. Josephus, 6.316–22.

148. Josephus, 6.199–218.

149. Josephus, 6.353.

150. Josephus, 6.323–54.

151. Josephus, 6.374–7.

152. Josephus, 6.381–6. Larger numbers being set free are asserted but may have been an exaggeration. Perhaps the massive numbers simply required a proportion to be set free.

153. Josephus, 6.387–91.

154. Josephus, 6.400–2. Only 'warlords' are mentioned as the leaders.

155. Josephus, 5.392 indicates that the rebels put up little or no resistance against the siege engines on 7 September and the Romans captured Herod's Palace on the same day and erected victory standards on the abandoned Herodian Towers. Pillaging commenced and on 8 September Jerusalem burned, 5.407. Tradition dates the fall of Jerusalem to 7 September but I disagree because the erection of the standards surely marks its fall.

156. Masada still remained, but generally the revolt was over.

157. Josephus, 6.404–6

158. Josephus, 6.409–19.

159. Josephus, 6.429–34.

160. Josephus, 7.1–4, 7.376–80. Eleazar ben Jairus was a later eyewitness to the razing.

161. Grossly estimated based on the Romans focusing on the Second Temple (including its massive Herodian stonework), city walls, fortifications, and significant public buildings, as well as the wealthier districts with substantial stone construction. Poorer districts, made of simpler structures (mud-brick, wood, plaster, and rubble), likely burned down or collapsed rather than being systematically dismantled or moved by Roman engineers. I assume around 420,000 m^3 in volume equating to around one million tonnes of stone materials dismantled or moved in the Roman destruction.

162. Josephus, 7.5.

163. Assuming a modest portion of meat was 230 g/8 oz, over 10,000kg of meat would be needed, with a likely yield of 196 kg per ox.

Chapter 7: *Caesar's Eastern Tour*

1. Josephus, 7.17–20.

2. Jones, 'Titus in the East AD 70–71'. Jones makes a compelling case that Titus was given specific instructions to remain in the East.

3. Levick, *Vespasian*, 'A New Emperor and his Opponents'. Brunt, P. A., 'Tacitus on the Batavian Revolt'. Julius Civilis, a Batavian chieftain, led the uprising.

4. Julius Caesar and Mark Antony, for example.

5. Josephus, 7.20.

6. Josephus, 7.23 is silent about the almost certain presence of Agrippa and Berenice.

7. Josephus, 7.31.

8. Josephus, 7.25–36.

9. Josephus, 7.37–8.

10. Josephus, 7.104. I assume this was the reason for Titus' inaction.

11. Millar, F., *The Roman Near East 31 BC–AD 337*, 'The Bridgehead and Dependent Kingdoms'. Knox M'Elderry, R., 'The Legions of the Euphrates Frontier.'

12. Bowman, Garnsey & Rathbone, 'The Flavians: Vespasian'. In Syria, III *Gallica*, VI *Ferrata*, X *Fretensis*, and XII *Fulminata*.

13. Luttwak, E. N., *The Grand Strategy of the Roman Empire – from the First Century AD to the Third*, 'From the Flavians to the Severi.'

14. Luttwak, 'From the Flavians to the Severi'.

15. In 20 AD, the Emperor Augustus sent the young Tiberius with an army to place their candidate, Tigranes, on the Armenian throne as a Roman vassal. Terms were agreed without conflict with Parthia.

16. Goldsworthy, A., *In the Name of Rome: The Men Who Won the Roman Empire*, 'Imperial Legate: Corbulo and Armenia.'

17. In 66, Nero crowned the Parthian prince Tiridates I as king of Armenia in Rome.

18. Bosworth, A. B., 'Vespasian's Reorganization of the North-East Frontier'. Bosworth provides a detailed evaluation of Suetonius' reference (*Vespasian* 8) to 'frequent barbarian raids'.

19. Vervaet, F. J., 'Domitius Corbulo and the Rise of the Flavian Dynasty.'

20. Mitford, T. B., 'The Inscriptions of Satala (Armenia Minor)'. Talbert, R., *Barrington Atlas of the Greek and Roman World*.

21. Millar, *The Roman Near East 31 BC–AD 337*, 'Imperialism and Expansion'. Bosworth, 'Vespasian's Reorganization of the North-East Frontier'. Millar describes evidence for auxiliary locations and Bosworth the importance of the *limes* to the security of the Anatolian plateau.

22. Knox M'Elderry, R., 'The Legions of the Euphrates Frontier'.

23. Syme, 'The New Emperor', *Tacitus*. Bosworth, 'Vespasian's Reorganization of the North-East Frontier'. Syme suggests Traianus as a possible candidate for the new consular Cappadocia province and the architect of Vespasian's plans, while Bosworth questions the time available to Traianus to implement the Cappadocia–Galatia complex. On balance, I assume Traianus' role remains a distinct possibility and he could have had three full years to do so, 71–73, before arriving to take over in Syria at the end of 73 or early 74, where he could continue implementation from Antioch.

24. Syme, 'The New Emperor', *Tacitus*.

25. Bosworth, 'Vespasian's Reorganization of the North-East Frontier'. See Bosworth for rationale for the annexation of Lesser Armenia, the date and the consequences.

26. Its not certain when XVI *Flavia* arrived in the east but I assume it was before the annexation of Lesser Armenia in 72 to provide the necessary military oversight.

27. Bosworth, 'Vespasian's Reorganization of the North-East Frontier'.

28. Josephus, 7.219–29. Knox M'Elderry, R., 'The Legions of the Euphrates Frontier.'

29. Millar, 'Imperialism and Expansion'.

30. Bosworth, 'Vespasian's Reorganization of the North-East Frontier'. Bosworth provides an extensive analysis of the evidence for this underappreciated extension of Roman influence.

31. Suetonius, *Histories*, 6.3. Tacitus, *Histories*, 4.51

32. Tacitus, *Histories*, 4.51

33. Josephus, 356. Jones, 'Titus in the East AD 70–71'.

34. Josephus, 6.357.

35. Josephus, 7.105–6. For the date, I assume a three-week stay in Berytus starting mid-November, sixteen days' march to Antioch, five days in Antioch and then thirteen days' march to Zeugma.

36. Accounting for attrition and detachments possibly still heading back from the west.

37. Josephus, 7.105–6.

38. Kouremenos, A., 'Trajan: Rome's Last Emperor'. I am grateful for Kouremenos' review that highlights the interplay between 'king' and 'emperor' in the East, citing Athenaeus VIII. 361.3, who refers to Hadrian as μουσικώτατος βασιλεύς.

39. Josephus, 7.112–15, describes Titus lamenting the destruction of the city. I assume it was rather a visit to confirm the postwar role of X *Fretensis* in Judea.
40. A fine example is preserved in Pompeii.
41. Suetonius, *Titus*, 5. The fact that Suetonius mentions this as 'especially' important verifies the spread of rumours back in Rome.
42. Suetonius, *Titus*, 5.
43. Jones, 'Role Under Vespasian'.

Chapter 8: *Augusti Filius in Rome*

1. Josephus, 7.120–1. I assume he landed at Ostia and crowds conveniently lined up in Rome after word of his arrival.
2. Josephus 7.121. Jones, 'Role under Vespasian'. Josephus dates these events to June 71, soon after Titus' return, so preparations must have started several months beforehand, not least to have troops from the legions in Rome. Jones agrees.
3. Josephus, 7.121–2. Father and both sons are mentioned. In the case of Domitian, it is unclear if Josephus is referring to his superfluous participation in quelling the Batavian uprising. Domitian is described as being on horseback during the event but not in a triumphal chariot like Vespasian and Titus, suggesting his inclusion was political rather than militarily deserved. Josephus was therefore probably exaggerating Domitian's award of a triumph.
4. Josephus, 7.123. Makin, E., 'The Triumphal Route, with Particular Reference to the Flavian Triumph'. Beard, M., *The Roman Triumph*. Josephus specifically states that the soldiers assembled close by the Temple of Isis.
5. Likely given that whole legions could not be spared.
6. Carandini, A. & Carafa, P., eds, *The Atlas of Ancient Rome*, 1 Text and Images, Region IX Circus Flaminius. I postulate that the *porticus triumphi* was not necessarily a single entity, especially given the enormous number of soldiers potentially involved in the triumph.
7. Josephus, 7.123. Beard, *The Roman Triumph*. Josephus' specific reference to Vespasian and Titus spending the night in the temple is an important fact that he was unlikely to mistake. Beard makes a strong case not to assume that all triumphs used the same venues nor identical routes.
8. Josephus, 7.124–5.
9. Carandini & Carafa, *The Atlas of Ancient Rome*, 2 Tables and Indexes, Tab 223.
10. Josephus, 7.124–9.
11. Beard, *The Roman Triumph*. Makin, 'The Triumphal Route'. Beard and Makin provide detailed reviews of the triumphal routes.
12. William Smith, *Triumphus. A Dictionary of Greek and Roman Antiquities*. The *toga picta* was worn over the *tunica palmata*.
13. Östenberg, I., 'Circum metas fertur: An alternative reading of the triumphal route'. Östenberg reviews various arguments for its location and points out that the gate used changed over time.

14. Josephus, 7.132–52. The only references to the sequence are ships after the floats, the Jewish Laws after the Temple spoils, and then Vespasian. I have made certain assumptions based on other triumphs and logical sequencing.
15. Josephus, 7.132.
16. Josephus, 7.522. Referred to as Lake Gennesaret.
17. Beard, *The Roman Triumph*, includes a thorough review of the historical evidence for Tertullian's quote in his *Apologeticus* and the complexities and possible diversities in Roman triumphs. There is no evidence to prove that it was a permanent fixture.
18. Östenberg, 'Circum metas fertur'.
19. Passing the Temple of Divus Augustus was probably a reverent moment for the victors and participants that is not described in modern studies, probably because the temple has not been excavated.
20. Beard, *The Roman Triumph*. Beard discusses the evidence for and against a detour around the Velabrum and concludes that the route passed this region rather than going through it.
21. Smith, *Triumphus*.
22. Beard, *The Roman Triumph*. Östenberg, 'Circum metas fertur'. Östenberg makes a convincing case for completing a circuit around the *spina* and not a straight pass through.
23. Östenberg, 'Circum metas fertur'. It cannot be ruled out that the Flavians took this route with the symbolism suggested by Östenberg of returning the land to the people of Rome.
24. Makin, 'The Triumphal Route, with Particular Reference to the Flavian Triumph'. JRS. 11:25–36.
25. Josephus, 7.153–4.
26. Suetonius, *Vespasian*, 12.
27. Josephus, 7.156–7.
28. Jones, 'Role Under Vespasian'. Jones explains Titus' titles and powers but not his status as an official co-ruler. I note that although Marcus Aurelius and Lucius were considered co-emperors, Marcus held more *auctoritas*; he had been consul once more than Lucius and he alone was *Pontifex Maximus*.
29. Talbert, *The Senate of Imperial Rome*, 'Emperor in the Senate'.
30. Jones, 'Role Under Vespasian'. 1 July was the probable date that the title was conferred.
31. Jones, 'Role Under Vespasian'. Unconventionally, Titus did not receive a salutation for his accession.
32. Talbert, 'The Senate'.
33. Jones, 'Role Under Vespasian', provides a thorough review of Titus' *ordinarius* appointments during Vespasian's reign.
34. Levick, 'Elites'.
35. Jones, 'Role Under Vespasian'.

36. Jones, 'Role Under Vespasian'. Jones cites a calculation that around 150 of these two type of appointment may have been awarded.
37. Suetonius, *Titus*, 6.
38. De La Bédoyère, G., *Praetorian*, 'Introduction'.
39. De La Bédoyère, *Praetorian*, 'To the Victor, the spoils'. De La Bédoyère suggests that the Flavian Praetorian cohorts were probably 1,000 strong and there could have been between nine and nineteen cohorts based on epigraphic evidence.
40. Suetonius, *Vitellius*, 10.
41. Dio Cassius, Histories, 52.24.2, describes the value of having two prefects. However, one was in sole charge when Augustus died. Tiberius used one prefect, Sejanus.
42. Father, Marcus Arrecinus Clemens.
43. Jones, 'Role Under Vespasian'. Jones points out that Titus' sole command of the Guard is an assumption. I also assume that his long tenure as commander from 71–79 was single-handed.
44. Suetonius, *Titus*, 6.
45. This is conjecture based on there being only one named individual in the ancient sources (Suetonius, *Titus*, 6) for the entire period of nine years he was commander.
46. Bowman, Garnsey & Rathbone, 'The High Empire AD 70–192: Vespasian'
47. Jones, 'Role under Vespasian'. Jones reviews extensively the role of Mucianus after Vespasian's accession and detects a decline in his influence after 72, becoming disrespectful and bitter, but not treasonous.
48. It is not attested, but I assume Domitilla II, Titus' sister, was born in 53, married around fifteen years of age in 68 and had her daughter, Domitilla III, in 69. This would fit with the understanding that Domitilla II died before her father became emperor but had a child.
49. Bowman, Garnsey & Rathbone, 'The High Empire AD 70–192: Vespasian'. Levick, B., Vespasian, 'Elites'.
50. Townend, G., 'Some Flavian Connections'.
51. Bowman, Garnsey & Rathbone, 'The High Empire AD 70–192: Vespasian'. Vespasian had a high regard for Marcellus.
52. Tacitus, *Dialogue*, 8. Jones, 'Role Under Vespasian'. Townend, G., 'Some Flavian Connections'.
53. Ibid.
54. Levick, B., Vespasian, 'Elites'.
55. Townend, 'Some Flavian Connections'.
56. Levick, *Vespasian*, 'Conclusions'.
57. Suetonius, *Vespasian*, 23
58. Brunt, P. A., 'Lex de Imperio Vespasiani'.
59. Suetonius, *Vespasian*, 1.
60. Bowman, Garnsey & Rathbone, 'The High Empire AD 70–192: Vespasian'.
61. It is not clear exactly what Helvidius did wrong but he was evidently too outspoken.
62. Dio Cassius, *Histories*, 65.12.

63. Bowman, Garnsey & Rathbone, 'The High Empire AD 70–192: Vespasian'. Dio Cassius, *Histories*, 65.12. Suetonius, *Vespasian*, 15.

64. Knox M'Elderry, R., 'Some Conjectures on the Reign of Vespasian'.

65. Jones, 'Reign of Titus'.

66. The inauguration year is debated and may have been later in 81.

67. Gallia, A., 'Nero's Divine Stepfather and the Flavian Regime'.

68. Suetonius, *Vespasian*, 9. Claridge, A., *Rome, An Oxford Archaeological Guide*, 'Imperial forums'.

69. Moormann, E., 'Some Observations on the *Templum Pacis*: A Summa of Flavian Politics'. Detailed description of the purpose, location and construction. A list of the artworks is included.

70. Overman, J. A., 'The First Revolt and Flavian Politics'.

71. Suetonius, *Vespasian*, 8.

72. Lindsay, H., 'Vespasian and the City of Rome: The Centrality of the Capitolium'.

73. Suetonius, *Vespasian*, 16. New and heavier taxes are discussed alongside 'avarice' and 'greed'. This appears unjust, as presumably the dire financial situation required Vespasian to appear greedy in acquiring funds.

74. Suetonius, *Vespasian*, 16.

75. Dio Cassius, *Histories*, 65.14

76. Levick, *Vespasian*, 'Financial Survival'. Levick provides an extensive review of financial matters under Vespasian.

77. Suetonius, *Domitian*, 17. If Phyllis was aged approximately 15 at the time of Domitian's birth in 51, then she would have been 28 years old when Julia was born in 64.

78. Baumgartel, K. L., Sneeringer, L., Cohen, S. M., 'From royal wet nurses to Facebook: The evolution of breastmilk sharing.'

79. Suetonius, *Domitian*, 22. The date is unclear but is generally thought to be in the early 70s.

80. Fraser, T. E., 'Domitia Longina: An underestimated Augusta (c. 52–126/8)'.

81. Suetonius, *Domitian*, 3.

82. Jones, 'Reign of Titus'.

83. Barrett, 'Vespasian's Wife'.

84. Suetonius, *Domitian*, 12.

85. Dio Cassius, 65.14. Caenis' death.

86. Levick, 'Conclusions'.

87. Suetonius, *Titus*, 7.

88. Jones, 'Role under Vespasian'. Jones outlines the possibility that Mucianus' death removed the barrier but thinks it was far more likely that Vespasian had vetoed her visit for fears of welcoming 'a second Cleopatra to Rome'.

89. Suetonius, *Titus*, 7. Dio Cassius, *Histories*, 65.15

90. Dio Cassius, *Histories*, 65.15

91. Jones, 'Judaea'. Jones astutely mentions this problem as arising early on in their relationship.

92. Suetonius, *Titus*, 7. Anagnostou-Laoutides & Charles, 'Titus and Berenice: the Elegiac Aura of an Historical Affair'. Keaveney, A. & Madden, J., 'Berenice at Rome'. Suetonius states that the couple did not want to part company. Anagnostou-Laoutides & Charles argue that she was dismissed immediately after Titus' accession in 79. Keaveney & Madden suggest that Suetonius was correct in assigning Titus' dismissal of Berenice to right after his accession. I postulate that Vespasian would have intervened and she was sent away in 79 before Titus became emperor. As emperor, the most powerful man in the world, why would he have sent her away?

93. Dio Cassius, *Histories*, 65.16. Suetonius, *Titus*, 6. Dio stated clearly that Vespasian was the target.

94. Dio Cassius, 66.17, for his gout.

95. Jones, 'Role under Vespasian'. Jones makes a convincing case that there were unlikely associates.

96. The identity of the troops is not known, but to have countered the Praetorians and urban cohorts in Rome, only legions would have been capable.

97. There are no attested trips outside Italy between 71 and 79, although one cannot exclude undocumented trips.

98. Suetonius, *Titus*, 3.

Chapter 9: *Accession and Reign*

1. Suetonius, *Titus*, 11. The same country house Titus would later die in.

2. Suetonius, *Vespasian*, 24. Dio Cassius, *Histories*, 66.17. Dio gives a sequence in which Vespasian's doctors chided him for continuing to work, to which he responded that he must remain on his feet and, convinced he was going to die, joked about becoming a god, mixed in with portents for his death. Suetonius describes more specific symptoms and the final bout of diarrhoea when he tried to rise to his feet and muttered that emperors should stay on their feet after which he collapsed and died. I assume that his joke about becoming a god was earlier on when he was still relatively alert and then mumbled about emperors on their feet as he made a final stand from his deathbed.

3. I dismiss the usual rumours associated with an emperor's death, such as the supposed belief by the Emperor Hadrian (Dio Cassius, *Histories*, 66.17.1) that Titus poisoned his father.

4. Pliny the Elder, *The Natural Histories,* 1 Dedications. Josephus, 3.235–8. Suetonius, *Titus*, 6. Pliny for Titus praising his father, Josephus for Titus' role as Vespasian's protector during his reign.

5. Jones, 'Reign of Titus'.

6. Dio Cassius, *Histories*, 53.16.

7. Jones, 'Reign of Titus'. Jones's hypothesis is adopted here.

8. Assumes around 150,000 legionaries, 125,000 auxiliaries, 20,000 *vigiles*, urban cohorts and Praetorians, and 35,000 navy.

9. Heller, J. L., 'Burial Customs of the Romans.'

10. Smith, W., 'Spectacle in the Roman Imperial Funeral Procession'. Smith provides a detailed overview of the documented funerals of Augustus, Pertinax and Septimius Severus.

11. Jones, 'Reign of Titus'. Jones examines the rationale for the delayed ceremony but earlier decision for Vespasian's deification, and I assume Titus would have been keen to use the funeral pyre per tradition to release the eagle. Moreover, an inscription shows Titus as *divi filius* between 1 July and the end of 79, supporting the notion that the decision was made then.

12. Bowman, Garnsey & Rathbone, 'The High Empire AD 70–192: Titus'.

13. Suetonius, *Titus*, 9.

14. RIC II 948 (Vespasian); RSC 65.

15. Sear, D. R., *Roman Coins I and Their Their Values*, Titus as Augustus (issues after he became emperor, AD 79–81).

16. Sear, *Roman Coins I*, 2489, TR P VIIII IMP XIIII COS VI PP.

17. Sear, *Roman Coins I*, 2490, TR P VIIII IMP XIIII COS VI PP & 2491, TR P VIIII IMP XIIII COS VI PP.

18. Sear, *Roman Coins I*, 2462.

19. Vitale, M., '*Iudaea Recepta*, eine neue legende auf goldmunzen Vespasians'.

20. Suetonius, *Titus*, 9.

21. Suetonius, *Titus*, 9.

22. Sear, *Roman Coins I*, 2538.

23. Tacitus, *Histories*, 4.52

24. Jones, 'Reign of Titus'. Jones provides a detailed assessment of the ancient sources and I agree with his conclusions that many of the salacious stories are dubious at best.

25. Suetonius, *Titus*, 3.

26. Suetonius, *Titus*, 6.

27. Suetonius, *Titus*, 7.

28. The full inscription reads: 'He lived 52 years. To the spirits of the departed Tiberius Claudius Secundus. Here he has everything with him, "bathing, wine and sex ruin our bodies, but only bathing, wine and sex make life worth living". Merope, freedwoman of Caesar made this for her dear companion, herself and their family and their descendants.'

29. Dio Cassius, *Histories*, 66.18. Berenice is clearly referred to as being in Rome 'again'.

30. Suetonius, *Titus*, 6.

31. Suetonius, *Titus*, 7.

32. Suetonius, *Titus*, 7. This reference to the dinners appears to mark the point in Suetonius' narrative when he begins writing about Titus as emperor because just a few sentences before he describes Titus' 'riotous living' as *Caesar*.

33. Suetonius, *Titus*, 8. Dio Cassius, *Histories*, 66.19.

34. Suetonius, *Titus*, 8.

35. Dio Cassius, *Histories*, 66.19.

36. Dio Cassius, *Histories*, 66.19.

37. Suetonius, *Titus*, 9.

38. Bowman, Garnsey & Rathbone, 'The High Empire AD 70–192: Titus'.

39. Ibid.

40. Jones, 'Reign of Titus'.

41. Jones, 'Reign of Titus'. Jones distinguishes between Vespasian and possible appointments made by Titus.

42. Jones, 'Reign of Titus'. Jones warns against definite conclusions as few positions are attested but a pattern is nevertheless detectable.

43. Evans, J. K., 'The Role of *Suffragium* in Imperial Political Decision-Making: A Flavian Example'. Evans provides a definitive evaluation of Tiberius Julius' role.

44. Vespasian posted the legion to Theveste (Tebessa, Algeria) in 75.

45. Evans, 'The Role of *Suffragium*'. Evans astutely highlights the later dilemma for Domitian, who sent Tiberius Julius into retirement. The innovative trial of related governors in charge of Numidia and Egypt would not be repeated.

46. Jones, 'Reign of Titus'.

47. Jones, 'Reign of Titus'.

48. Jones, 'Reign of Titus'.

49. Fraser, T. E., 'Domitia Longina'.

50. McDermott, W. C., '*Fabricius Veiento*'.

51. Jones, 'Reign of Titus'.

52. Tacitus, *Dialogue*, 8. Jones, 'Role Under Vespasian'. Townend, G., 'Some Flavian Connections'.

53. Ward Perkins, J. B., 'The Career of Sex. Julius Frontinus.'

54. Champlin, E., 'Pegasus.'

55. Torelli, M., 'The *Cursus Honorum* of M. Hirrius Fronto Neratius Pansa'.

56. Gallivan, P., 'Who Was Acilius?'

57. Bruun, C., 'Some Comments on the Status of Imperial Freedmen: the Case of Ti. Claudius Aug lib. Classicus'.

58. Carandini & Carafa, *The Atlas of Ancient Rome*, 1 Text and Images, Region III Isis et Serapis. Connolly, P., *Colosseum, Rome's Arena of Death*, 'Vespasian's Vision'.

59. www.statista.com, data from 2018.

60. Suetonius, *Titus*, 7.

61. Carandini & Carafa, *The Atlas of Ancient Rome*, 2 Tables & Indexes, Tab. 117.

62. Suetonius, *Titus*, 8.

63. Jones, 'Reign of Titus'. Jones reviews a number of works. For water system, see UNESCO Tentative Lists: Titus Tunnel.

64. Dio Cassius, *Histories*, 66.19, refers to his frugal nature and avoidance of unnecessary expenses.

65. Although many modern texts refer to 100 days of spectacles neither Suetonius nor Dio Cassius specifically cite this number.
66. Dio Cassius, *Histories*, 66.25.
67. Carter, M. J., 'Gladiatorial Combat: The Rules of Engagement'.
68. Dio Cassius, *Histories*, 66.25. Suetonius, *Titus*, 7.
69. Suetonius, *Titus*, 7. Dio Cassius, *Histories*, 66.25.
70. Polybius, *Histories*, 31.28.6, gives 750,000 HS as the cost of a generous gladiatorial show in the Republican period.
71. Examples include Tiberius', Caligula's and Claudius' enormous *donativa* to the Praetorian Guards: 1,000, 2,000 and 15,000 respectively. Claudius' *congiarium* in 45 AD was 300 HS per person on the corn dole. Vespasian gave a low amount to each legionary of 100 HS at the start of his reign because of the dire financial crisis resulting from civil war. Nerva is thought to have issued 150,000 on the corn dole – 300 HS each, for each legionary 400 HS, plus 1,000 HS each for the Praetorians. I assume for Titus' grand total: 150,000 citizens x 300 HS = 45m HS; 150,000 legionaries x 400HS = 60m HS rounded up to 75m HS to account for officers and Rome's urban cohorts and 2,000 HS x 9,000 Praetorians = 18m HS. The empire's annual budget is generally considered to be around 830m HS.
72. Suetonius, *Titus*, 7. Dio Cassius, 66.24
73. Suetonius, *Titus*, 7. I assume this alludes to emperors like Caligula, who allegedly brought charges against individuals for financial gain (Suetonius, *Caligula*, 41).
74. Jones, 'Reign of Titus'.
75. Jones, 'Reign of Titus'. Jones discusses the division of diplomas into three categories: (I) issued to serving soldiers only, (II) to both serving soldiers and veterans, and (III) to veterans only. He observes that Types I and II were already in use under Claudius, while the first known example of Type II belongs to Titus' reign.
76. Jones, 'Reign of Titus'. Jones reviews the bills in the *Digest* assembled by a team of lawyers commissioned by Justinian in AD 533 to collect everything of value from earlier Roman law.
77. Jones, 'Reign of Titus'. Jones provides detailed analyses of provincial activities.
78. A Parthian prince of the Arsacid line would sit on the Armenian throne, but his nomination needed Rome's approval.
79. Pappano, A. E., 'The False Neros'.
80. Carandini & Carafa, *The Atlas of Ancient Rome*, Region III Isis et Serapis., includes evidence about the Laocoön.
81. Dio Cassius, 65.10.
82. Cominesi, A. R., 'Flavian Architecture on the Palatine: Continuity or Break'. Provides a convincing argument for the Flavian distancing from Nero's residences.
83. Vinson, M. P., 'Domitia Longina, Julia Titi, and the Literary Tradition'. Kohn, T. D., 'The Enigma of Julia Augusta Titi'. Vinson believes that the later accusations of adultery between Domitian and Julia are untenable and based on the hostile nature of sources about Domitian. Kohn concludes that the rumours, although popular,

were highly questionable in accuracy. Suetonius, *Titus*, 22, referring to the adultery even while Titus was alive, appears very hard to accept, given Titus' substantial efforts to rebrand his image, award his daughter the virtuous title of *Augusta* and the generally hostile narrative by Suetonius against Domitian.

84. D'Ambra, E., 'Mode and Model in the Flavian Female Portrait'.
85. An inscription found in Herculaneum means the title was granted before the town's destruction in 79, and coins of 79–81 support the notion that it was therefore given very soon after Titus became emperor.
86. Sear, D., *Roman Coins and their Value*, 'Flavian Dynasty: Julia'.
87. Suetonius, *Domitian*, 3: '[Domitia] had presented Domitian with a daughter during his second consulship (74) and in the following year, with a son.'

Chapter 10: *Consecutive Disasters*

1. Dio Cassius, 66.24. Suetonius, *Titus*, 4.8. Properties without heirs belonged to the treasury, so Titus was essentially redirecting funds.
2. A spring visit would have allowed progress to be judged and fits with the likelihood that the fire in Rome happened in the spring or summer when drier conditions aided the scale of the conflagration.
3. Canter, H. V., 'Conflagrations in Ancient Rome'.
4. The origin is not known, but previous fires had originated in the Campus Martius and its unlikely it started in the Capitoline because in that case the fire would have had to spread downwards. Alternatively, it may have started in the Quirinal area and swept south-west.
5. Sear, *Roman Coins I*, 'Titus'.
6. Dio Cassius, *Histories*, 66.24. I assume additionally that the Velabrum was probably impacted along with the majority of residential buildings in the affected areas.
7. This assumes the urban area of Rome was 13.7 km². This works out as a far higher concentration of firefighters than in modern cities; present-day London has approximately 6,000 firefighters for more than 1,500 km².
8. Rainbird, J. S., 'The Fire Stations of Imperial Rome'. Rainbird provides a detailed assessment of the role of the *vigiles* and their facilities.
9. Tacitus, *Annales* 15.43; and Suetonius, *Nero*, 16.
10. There is no physical evidence for this deployment but its very probable.
11. Suetonius, *Titus*, 8.
12. Suetonius, *Titus*, 8. Dio Cassius, *Histories*, 66.23.
13. Lo Cascio, E., 'The Size of the Roman Population: Beloch and the Meaning of the Augustan Census Figures', Storey, G. R., 'The Population of Ancient Rome', Oates, W. J., 'The Population of Rome.' Lo Cascio, 600,000; Storey, 500,000; Oates, 1,250,000. I favour a mid-point towards the lower end of the range given the argument of population density.
14. Jerome, *Chronicle*, AD 78.

15. Cunha, B. A., 'The cause of the plague of Athens: plague, typhoid, typhus, smallpox, or measles?' Cunha finds the strongest association to symptoms related to either measles virus or orthopoxvirus.

16. The ancient sources make no reference to its continuation into the following year or into the reign of Domitian, which they surely would have done if an epidemic of this scale lasted so long.

17. Oates, 'The Population of Rome', for the proportion of children.

18. Farnsworth Gray, H., 'Sewerage in Ancient and Mediaeval Times.'

19. Dio Cassius, *Histories*, 66.23, links Vesuvius ash to the later 'terrible pestilence'. However, such air pollution would cause chronic respiratory diseases, not an acute, epidemic-like disease. I postulate it was the influx of people into Rome that added to conditions suitable for an outbreak.

20. As far as other pathogens are concerned, we can dismiss the possibility of hepatitis B virus as it typically results in asymptomatic infections and chronic disease. We can also eliminate influenza A virus H1N1 and H3N2 strains as they did not exist at the time. Malaria can be ruled out because it was endemic and well-known during that period, and the epidemic in Rome was described as being caused by a disease rarely seen before. Additionally, B19 parvovirus can be crossed off as infections are usually mild in otherwise healthy children and adults. I also dismiss tuberculosis on the basis that, in the eighteenth century in Western Europe, TB had become an epidemic with a mortality rate of around 900 deaths per 100,000 inhabitants per year – more elevated among young people. If ancestral strains were circulating in the first century, they would not have caused the apparent death toll in Rome in 80.

21. Suetonius, *Titus*, 8.

22. Atkinson, J. E., 'Turning Crises into Drama: The Management of Epidemics in Classical Antiquity'.

Chapter 11: *Death and Legacy*

1. Suetonius, *Titus*, 10.

2. Suetonius, *Titus*, 10. Dio Cassius, *Histories*, 66.26. Dio corroborates the point on carrying guilt but records Titus' last words as: 'I have made but one mistake.'

3. It has been speculated that this refers to an affair with his brother's wife but this can be dismissed as typical gossip for the period.

4. Dio Cassius, *Histories*, 66.26, only mentions Domitian but it is reasonable to assume that others were summoned because of the seriousness of Titus' decline.

5. Dio Cassius, *Histories*, 66.26.

6. Jones, 'Reign of Titus', provides the correct date for his death, which Suetonius gets wrong (*Titus*, 11).

7. Retief, F. & Cilliers, L., 'Malaria in Graeco-Roman Times'.

8. The ancient sources interpret this in a more sinister way, whereas it was more plausibly a practical means of preparing for the inevitable.

9. Suetonius, *Titus*, 11.

10. Jones, B. W., *The Emperor Domitian*, 'Early Career'.

11. Dio Cassius, *Histories*, 67.2.

12. Jones, 'Reign of Titus'.

13. Sear, *Roman Coins*, 2885.

14. Sear, *Roman Coins*, 2886.

15. Bowman, Garnsey & Rathbone, 'The High Empire AD 70–192: Domitian'.

16. Vinson, 'Domitia Longina, Julia Titi, and the Literary Tradition.'

17. Overman, 'The First Revolt and Flavian Politics', provides a compelling argument for the change in positioning of the Jewish War, as well as the observation regarding the absence of the *Judaicus* title.

18. Gittin 56b.

19. Suetonius, *Titus*, 7. Dio Cassius, *Histories*, 2.2, corroborates Suetonius' verdict: 'He spent his youth in the delights of self-indulgence, but he showed more restraint in his own reign than in that of his father.'

20. Suetonius, *Titus*, 1.

21. Dio Cassius, *Histories*, 66.18.

22. https://www.yu.edu/library/2022/08/03/tishah-bav-at-the-arch-of-titus-in-1926

BIBLIOGRAPHY

Ancient Authors and Prosopography

Dio Cassius, *Histories*, Books 61–70, trans. E. Cary, Loeb Classical Library, Harvard UP, 2000.

Jerome, *Chronicles*, trans. M. D. Donalson, Mellen UP, 1996.

Josephus, *The Jewish War*, trans. M. Hammond, Oxford World Classics, 2017

Josephus, *The Life of Flavius Josephus*, trans. W. Whiston, Project Gutenberg eBook.

Ammianus Marcellinus, *Res Gestae*, trans. J. C. Rolfe, Loeb Classical Library, Harvard UP, 1939–50.

Pliny the Elder, *Natural Histories*, trans. John Bostock, Taylor & Francis 1885, Perseus Catalogue.

Pliny the Younger, *Letters*, trans. B. Radice, Penguin Classics, 1969.

Polybius, *The Histories*, trans. W. R. Paton, Loeb Classical Library, Harvard UP, 1922–27.

Prosopographia Imperii Romani (PIR2), https://pir.bbaw.de.

Quintilian, *Institutio Oratoria*, trans. H. E. Butler, Loeb Classical Library, Harvard UP, 1920–22.

G. Suetonius Tranquillus, *The Twelve Caesars*, trans. M. Grant and R. Graves, Penguin, 1979.

Strabo, *Geography*, ed. H. L. Jones., Loeb Classical Library, Harvard UP, 1923.

Tacitus, *Annals*, trans. A. J. Church & W. Jackson Brodribb, Perseus 4.0 Digital Library.

Cornelius Tacitus, *A Dialogue on Oratory*, ed. A. J. Church & W. Jackson Brodribb, Perseus 4.0 Digital Library.

Talmud, The William Davidson (Talmud Bavli) Edition.

Virgil, *Bucolics, Aeneid, and Georgics of Virgil*, J. B. Greenough, Ginn & Co, 1900.

Modern Works

Abdy, R., *Legion, Life in the Roman Army*, The British Museum, 2024.

——, 'The Last Coin in Pompeii: A Re-Evaluation of the Coin Hoard from the House of the Golden Bracelet', *Numismatic Chronicle*, 173: 79–83, 2013.

Anagnostou-Laoutides, E. & M. B. Charles, 'Titus and Berenice: The Elegiac Aura of an Historical Affair', *Arethusa*, 48(1): 17–46, 2015.

Arbiv, K., 'Evidence of the Roman Attack on the Third Wall of Jerusalem at the End of the Second Temple Period', *Atiqot*, 111:103–18, 2023.

Atkinson, J. E., 'Turning Crises into Drama: The Management of Epidemics in Classical Antiquity', *Acta Classica*, 44: 35–52, 2001.

Aviam, M., 'Yodfat (Jotapata): The Life and Death of a Jewish Galilean Town', The David A. Kipper Ancient Israel Lecture Series, Oriental Institute, University of Chicago, 2018

Aylward, W. (ed.), 'Excavations at Zeugma. Conducted by Oxford Archaeology', Packard Humanities Institute, 2013.

Baldwin Bowsky, M., 'A. Larcius Lepidus Sulpicianus and a Newly Identified Proconsul of Crete and Cyrenaica', *Historia: Zeitschrift für Alte Geschichte*, 36(4): 502–8, 1987.

Barbieri, R., et al., 'Yersinia Pestis: the Natural History of Plague', Clin Microbiol Rev., 34(1):e00044–19, 2020.

Barrett, A., 'Vespasian's Wife', *Latomus* 64(2): 385–96, 2005.

Baumgartel, K. L., Sneeringer, L., Cohen, S. M., 'From Royal Wet Nurses to Facebook: the Evolution of Breastmilk Sharing', *Breastfeed Rev.*, 24(3): 25–32, 2016.

Beard, M., *The Roman Triumph*, Harvard UP, 2007.

Ben-Ami, D. & Y. Tchekhanovets, 'The Lower City of Jerusalem on the Eve of its Destruction, 70 C.E.: A View From Hanyon Givati', *Bulletin of the American Schools of Oriental Research*, 364: 61–85, 2011.

Birley, A. R., 'The Life and Death of Cornelius Tacitus', *Historia: Zeitschrift für Alte Geschichte*, 49(2): 230–47, 2000.

Bosworth, A. B., 'Vespasian's Reorganization of the North-East Frontier', *Antichthon*, 10:63–78, 1976.

Bowman, A. K., Garnsey, P., Rathbone, D. (eds), *The Cambridge Ancient History*, Vol. XI, *The High Empire* AD 70–192, Cambridge UP, 2nd edn., 2000.

Bradley, K. R., 'The Chronology of Nero's Visit to Greece A.D. 66/67', *Latomus*, 37:1, 1978.

——, 'Nero's Retinue in Greece, A.D. 66/67', *Illinois Classical Studies*, 4: 152–7, 1979.

Brunt, P. A., 'The Revolt of Vindex and the Fall of Nero,' *Latomus*, 18(3): 531–59, 1959.

——, 'Tacitus on the Batavian Revolt,' *Latomus*, 19(3):494–517, 1960)

——, 'Lex de Imperio Vespasiani', *Journal of Roman Studies*, 67: 95–116, 1977.

——, 'Nobilitas and Novitas', *Journal of Roman Studies*, 72: 1–17, 1982.

Bruun, C., 'Some Comments on the Status of Imperial Freedmen, the Case of Ti. Claudius Aug lib. Classicus', *Zeitschrift für Papyrologie und Epigraphik*, 82:271–85, 1990.

Bunson, M., *Encyclopedia of the Roman Empire*, Facts on File, 2002.

Burn, A. R., 'The Battle of the Medway, AD 43', *History*, 38(133), 105–15, 1953.

Caldwell, T., 'The Career of Licinius Mucianus', MA thesis, Univ. of Melbourne, 2015.

Campbell, D. B., 'Did Emperor Caligula plan to invade Britain? Caligula's capers on the North Sea Coast', *Ancient Warfare*, Vol. VI, 6: 49–53.

Canter, H. V., 'Conflagrations in Ancient Rome' *The Classical Journal*, 27(4): 270–88, 1932.

Capasso, L., 'Herculaneum Victims of the Volcanic Eruptions of Vesuvius in 79 AD', *Lancet*, 356:1344–6, 2000.

Carandini, A. & P. Carafa (eds), *The Atlas of Ancient Rome*, Princeton UP (2 vols, English translation), 2017.

Carlos, G., Gross, J, Jamil, S., Dela Cruz, C., Damby, D., Tam, E., 'Volcanic Eruptions and Threats to Respiratory Health', *Am J Respir Crit Care Med*, Vol. 197:21–2, 2018.

Carter, M. J., 'Gladiatorial Combat: The Rules of Engagement', *Classical Journal*, 102(2): 97–114, 2006.

Champlin, E., 'Pegasus', *Zeitschrift für Papyrologie und Epigraphik*, 32:269–78, 1978.

Cioni, R., Longo, A., Macedonio, G., Santacroce, R., Sbrana, A., Sulpizio, R., Andronico, D., 'Assessing pyroclastic fall hazard through field data and numerical simulations: Example from Vesuvius', *Chemistry and Physics of Minerals and Rocks/Volcanology*, 108, B2, 2003.

Cioni, R., Gurioli, L., Lanza, R., Zanella, E., 'Temperatures of the A.D. 79 pyroclastic density current deposits (Vesuvius, Italy)', *J. Geophys. Res.*, 109, B02207, 2004.

Claridge, A., *Rome, An Oxford Archaeological Guide*, Oxford UP, 1998.

Coarelli, F., Stephen, K., & Patterson, H., 'Investigations at Falacrinae, the Birthplace of Vespasian', *Papers of the British School at Rome*, 76: 47–73, 2008.

Cominesi, A. R., 'Flavian Architecture on the Palatine: Continuity or Break', in Heerink, M. & Meijer, E. (eds), *Flavian Responses to Nero's Rome*, Amsterdam UP, 2022.

Connolly, P., *Colosseum, Rome's Arena of Death*, BBC Books, 2003.

Cordes, L., 'Iuvenis Infandi Ingeni Scelerum Capaxque: Flavian Responses to Nero's Youth', in Heerink & Meijer (eds), *Flavian Responses to Nero's Rome*, Amsterdam UP, 2022.

Crook, J. A., 'Titus and Berenice', *American Journal of Philology*, 72(2): 162–75, 1951.

Cunha, B. A., 'The cause of the plague of Athens: plague, typhoid, typhus, smallpox, or measles?', *Infect Dis Clin North Am.*, 18(1): 29–43, 2004.

D'Ambra, E., 'Mode and Model in the Flavian Female Portrait', *American Journal of Archaeology*, 117(4): 511–25, 2013.

Dando-Collins, S., *Conquering Jerusalem*, Turner, 2021.

——, *Legions of Rome*, Thomas Dunne Books, 2010.

Davies, R. W., 'The Roman Military Diet', *Britannia*, 2:122–42, 1971.

De la Bédoyère, G., *Praetorian*, Yale UP, 2018.

Delile, H., Keenan-Jones, D., Blichert-Toft, J., Goiran J. P., Arnaud-Godet, F., Romano, P., Albarede, F., 'A lead isotope perspective on urban development in ancient Naples', *PNAS*, 113(22): 6148–53, 2016.

Dellino, P., et al., 'The Impact of pyroclastic density currents duration on humans: the case of the AD 79 eruption of Vesuvius', *Nature Scientific Reports*, 11:4959.

Doronzo, D. M., Di Vito, M. A., Arienzo, I., Bini, M., Calusi, B., Cerminara, M., Corradini, S., de Vita, S., Giaccio, B., Gurioli, L. Mannella, G., Ricciardi, G. P., Rucco, I., Sparice, D., Todesco, M., Trasatti, E., Zanchetta, G., 'The 79 CE Eruption of Vesuvius: A Lesson from the Past and the Need of a Multidisciplinary Approach for Developments in Vulcanology', *Earth Science Reviews*, 231: 104072, 2022.

Duncan-Jones, R., *Money and Government in the Roman Empire*, Cambridge UP, 1998.

Düx, A., et al., 'Measles virus and rinderpest virus divergence dated to the sixth century BCE', *Science*, 368:1367–70, 2020.

Elliot, S., *Great Battles of Early Imperial Rome*, Pen & Sword, 2023.

Elton, H., 'Zeugma's Military History in Light of the Rescue Excavations', Packard Humanities Institute, 2013.

Evans, J. K., 'The Role of *Suffragium* in Imperial Political Decision-Making: A Flavian Example', *Historia: Zeitschrift für Alte Geschichte*, 27(1): 102–28, 1978.

Farnsworth Gray, H., 'Sewerage in Ancient and Mediaeval Times', *Sewage Works Journal*, 12(5): 939–46, 1940.

Fields, N., *Britannia AD 43: The Claudian Invasion*, Osprey, 2020.

Foerster, G., 'The Early History of Caesarea', *Bulletin of the American Schools of Oriental Research. Supplementary Studies*, 19:9–22, 1975.

Forsyth, P. Y., 'In the Wake of Etna, 44 B.C.', *Classical Antiquity*, 7(1): 49–57, 1998.

Foss, P. W., *Pliny and the Eruption of Vesuvius*, Taylor & Francis, 2022.

Fraser, T. E., 'Domitia Longina: An Underestimated Augusta (*c.* 52–126/8)', *Ancient Society*, 45:205–66, 2015.

Gallia, A., 'Nero's Divine Stepfather and the Flavian Regime', in Heerink & Meijer, *Flavian Responses to Nero's Rome*, Amsterdam UP, 2022.

Gallivan, P., 'Who Was Acilius?', *Historia: Zeitschrift für Alte Geschichte*, 27(40): 621–5, 1978.

Garcia y Garcia, L., *Pupils, Teachers and Schools in Pompeii*, Bardi, 2005.

Giacomelli, L., Perrotta, A. M., Scandone, R., & Scarpati, C., 'The eruption of Vesuvius of 79 AD and its impact on human environment in Pompeii', *Episodes*, 26(3): 235–8, 2003.

Gisela, R., 'The Pheidian Zeus at Olympia', *Hesperia: Journal of the American School of Classical Studies at Athens*, 35(2): 166–70, 1966.

Giuffuida, A., 'Sensational: skeleton buried in Vesuvius eruption found at Herculaneum', *Guardian*, 15 October 2021.

Goldsworthy, A. K., *The Roman Army at War, 100BC–AD200*, Clarendon Press, 1998.

——, *In the Name of Rome: The Men Who Won the Roman Empire*, Phoenix Press, 2003.

Gordon, R. J., 'Fort of Antonia or Temple Mount?', *Independent*, 2017.

Griffin, M., *Nero, the End of a Dynasty*, Routledge, 1987.

Hassall, M., 'Batavians and the Roman Conquest of Britain', *Britannia*, 1:131–6, 1970.

Heller, J. L., 'Burial Customs of the Romans', *Classical Weekly*, 25(24):193–7, 1932.

Hiesinger, U., 'The Portraits of Nero', *American Journal of Archaeology*, 79(2): 113–24, 1975.

Horsley, R., 'The Zealots: Their Origin, Relationships and Importance in the Jewish Revolt', *Novum Testamentum*, 28(2):159–92, 1986.

Howe, T., 'The Social Status of the Villas of Stabiae', in A. Marzano & G. Métraux (eds), *The Roman Villa in the Mediterranean Basin: Late Republic to Late Antiquity*, 97–119, Cambridge UP, 2018.

Isaac, B. H., & Roll, I., 'A Milestone of A.D. 69 from Judea: The Elder Trajan and Vespasian', *Journal of Roman Studies*, 66:15–19, 1976.

Jackson, N., *Trajan: Rome's Last Conqueror*, Greenhill Books, 2022.

John, T. J., et al., 'Epidemiology and prevention of measles in rural south India', *Indian J Med Res*, 72: 153–8, 1980.

Jones, B. W., *The Emperor Domitian*, Routledge, 1992.

——, *The Emperor Titus*, Croom Helm/St. Martin's Press, 1984.

——, 'Agrippina and Vespasian', *Latomus* 43(3): 581–3, 1984.

——, 'Titus in the East AD 70–71', *Rheinisches Museum für Philologie*, 128(3/4): 346–52, 1985.

Jones, J. R., 'Mint magistrates in the early Roman Empire', *Bulletin of the Institute of Classical Studies*, 17: 70–8, 1970.

Kaye, S., 'The Roman invasion of Britain, 43 AD: riverine, wading and tidal studies as a means of limiting the possible locations of the invasion-ground and the two-day river battle', *Branda Arc Geophysics*, 2014.

Keaveney, A. & Madden, J., 'Berenice at Rome', *Museum Helveticum*, 60(1): 39–43, 2003.

Klebs, E., Rohden, P. von, & Dessau., H., *Prosopographia Imperii Romani (PRI) saeculi I, II, III*, Berolini, 1933.

de Kleijn, G., 'C. Licinius Mucianus, Leader in Time of Crisis', *Historia: Zeitschrift für Alte Geschichte*, 58(3): 311–24, 2009.

Kleijwegt, M., '"Iuvenes" and Roman Imperial Society', *Acta Classica,* 37: 79–10, 1994.

Knox M'Elderry, R., 'The Legions of the Euphrates Frontier', *Classical Quarterly*, 3(1):44–53, 1909.

——, 'Some Conjectures on the Reign of Vespasian', *Journal of Roman Studies*, 3:116–26, 1913.

Kohn, T. D., 'The Enigma of Julia Augusta Titi', *Historia* 71(4): 459–84, 2022.

Korfmann, M., 'The Sling as a Weapon', *Scientific American*, 229(4): 34–46, 1973.

Kouremenos, A., 'Trajan: Rome's Last Emperor', *Bryn Mawr Classical Review*, 2023.

La Monaca, V., 'Flavia Domitilla as "delicata": a new interpretation of Suetonius, Vesp. 3', *Ancient Society*, 43: 191–212, 2013.

Le Bohec, Y., & Wolff, C. (eds), *Les Légions de Rome sous le Haut-Empire*, Collection du
    Centre d'Études Romaines et Gallo-Romaines, Nouvelle série, no 20, 2002
Lepper, F., & Frere, S., *Trajan's Column*, Alan Sutton, 1988.
Levick, B., *Vespasian*, Routledge, 1999.
Lindsay, H., 'Vespasian and the City of Rome: The Centrality of the Capitolium', *Acta
    Classica*, 53:165–80, 2010.
Lo Cascio, E., 'The Size of the Roman Population: Beloch and the Meaning of the
    Augustan Census Figures', *Journal of Roman Studies*, 84: 23–40, 1994.
Luongo, G., Perrotta A., Scarpati, C., De Carolis, E., Patricelli, G., Ciarallo, A. M., 'Impact
    of the AD 79 explosive eruption on Pompeii, II. Causes of death of the inhabitants
    inferred by stratigraphic analysis and areal distribution of the human casualties', *J.
    Volcanology & Geothermal Res*, 126: 169–200, 2003.
Luttwak, E. N., *The Grand Strategy of the Roman Empire – from the First Century AD to the
    Third*, Johns Hopkins UP, 1979.

Macurdy, G. H. 'Julia Berenice', *American Journal of Philology*, 56(3): 256–53, 1935.
Makin, E., 'The Triumphal Route, with Particular Reference to the Flavian Triumph',
    Journal of Roman Studies, 11:25–36, 1921.
Manley, J., AD 43 *The Roman Invasion of Britain, A Reassessment*, Tempus, 1999.
Martin, E., *The Temples That Jerusalem Forgot*, Academy for Scriptural Knowledge, 1994
Mastrolorenzo, G., Petrone, P. P., Pagano, M., Incoronato, A., Baxter, P. J., Canzanella, A.,
    Fattore, L., 'Herculaneum Victims of Vesuvius in AD 79', *Nature*, 410(6830): 769–70,
    2001.
McAlindon, D., 'Entry to the Senate in the Early Empire', *Journal of Roman Studies*,
    47(1/2): 191–5, 1957.
McDermott, W. C., 'Fabricius Veiento', *American Journal of Philology*, 91(2): 129–48, 1970.
McNally, J. R., 'Toward a Definition of Rhetoric', *Philosophy & Rhetoric*, 3(2) 71–81, 1970.
McPake, R., 'A Note on the Cognomina of Legio XX', *Britannia* 12: 293–5, 1981.
Millar, F., *The Roman Near East, 31 BC–AD 337*, Harvard UP, 2001.
Mitford, T. B., 'The Inscriptions of Satala (Armenia Minor)', *Zeitschrift für Papyrologie und
    Epigraphik*, 115:137–67, 1997.
Moormann, E., 'Some Observations on the Templum Pacis: A Summa of Flavian
    Politics', in Heerink & Meijer, *Flavian Responses to Nero's Rome*, Amsterdam UP, 2022.
Morford, M., 'The Training of Three Roman Emperors', *Phoenix* 22(1): 57–72, 1968.
Mouratidis, J., 'Nero: The Artist, the Athlete and His Downfall', *Journal of Sport History*,
    12(1): 5–20, 1985.
Mühlemann, B., et al., 'Diverse variola virus (smallpox) strains were widespread in
    northern Europe in the Viking Age', *Science*, 369, eaaw8977, 2020.
Murphy-O'Connor, J., 'Where was the Antonia Fort?', *Revue Biblique* 111(1): 78–89, 2004.

Newhall, C. G. & Self, S., 'The Volcanic Explosivity Index (VEI): An Estimate of
    Explosive Magnitude for Historical Volcanism', *History of Geophysics*, 2(1).
Nicols, J., *Vespasian and the Partes Flavianae,* Franz Steiner Verlag, 1978.

Oates, W. J., 'The Population of Rome', *Classical Philology,* 29(2): 101–6, 1934.
Östenberg, I., 'Circum metas fertur: An alternative reading of the triumphal route',
    Historia: Zeitschrift für Alte Geschichte, 59(3): 303–20, 2010.
Overman, J. A., 'The First Revolt and Flavian Politics', in Berlin, A. M., & Overman, J. A.
    (eds), *The First Jewish Revolt, Archaeology, History and Ideology,* Routledge, 2002.

Pappano, A. E., 'The False Neros', *Classical Journal,* 32(7): 385–92, 1937.
Petrone, P., Pucci, P., Niola, M., Baxter, P., Fontanarosa, C., Giordano, G., Graziano,
    V., Sirano, F., Amoresano, A., 'Heat-Induced Brain Vitrification from the Vesuvius
    Eruption in C.E. 79', *N Engl J Med,* 382: 383–4, 2020.
Petrone, P., Pucci, P., Vergara, A., Amoresano, A., Birolo, L., Pane, F., et al., 'A hypothesis
    of sudden body fluid vaporization in the 79 AD victims of Vesuvius', *PLoS ONE,* 13(9):
    e0203210, 2018.
Power, T., 'Suetonius' Tacitus', *Journal of Roman Studies,* 104: 205–25, 2014.

Rainbird, J. S., 'The Fire Stations of Imperial Rome', *Papers of the British School at Rome,*
    54: 147–69, 1986.
Retief, F. & Cilliers, L., 'Malaria in Graeco-Roman Times', *Acta Classica,* 47: 127–37,
    2004.
Rogers, R. S., 'Heirs and Rivals to Nero', *Transactions and Proceedings of the American
    Philological Association,* 86: 190–212, 1955.

Sams, M., Antonia: 'The Fort Jerusalem Forgot', *Popular Archaeology,* Dec, 2015.
Scandone, R., Giacomelli, L., Rosi., M., 'Death, Survival and Damage during the 79 AD
    Eruption of Vesuvius which destroyed Pompeii and Herculaneum', *J. Res. Didactics in
    Geog.,* 2(8): 5–30, 2019.
Scorrano, G., Viva, S., Pinotti, T., Fabbri, P. F., Rickards, O., & Macciardi, F.,
    'Bioarchaeological and palaeogenomic portrait of two Pompeians that died during the
    eruption of Vesuvius in 79 AD', *Nature Scientific Reports,* 12: 6468.
Sear, D. R., *Roman Coins and Their Values,* Vol. 1, Spink reprint, 2017.
Sheppard, S. I., *The Jewish Revolt AD 66–74,* Osprey, 2013.
Sigurdsson, H., Carey, S., Cornell, W., & Pescatore, T., 'The Eruption of Vesuvius in A.D.
    79', *National Geographic Research,* 1(3): 332–87, 1985.
Sigurdsson, H., Cashdollar, S., & Sparks, S. R. J., 'The Eruption of Vesuvius in A.D. 79:
    Reconstruction from Historical and Volcanological Evidence', *American Journal of
    Archaeology,* 86(1): 39–51, 1982.
Smith, W., *A dictionary of Greek and Roman antiquities,* Harper, 1878.

Smith, W., 'Spectacle in the Roman Imperial Funeral Procession', *Theses, Dissertations, and Student Creative Activity, School of Art, Art History and Design*, Univ. of Nebraska, 2023.

Spyrou, M. A., et al., 'Analysis of 3800-year-old Yersinia pestis genomes suggests Bronze Age origin for bubonic plague', *Nat Commun.*, 9:2234, 2018.

Starr, C. G., 'Coastal Defense in the Roman World', *American Journal of Philology*, 64(1): 56–70, 1943.

Stewart, Z., 'Sejanus, Gaetulicus, and Seneca', *American Journal of Philology*, 74(1): 70–85, 1953.

Storey, G. R., 'The "Skyscrapers" of the Ancient Roman World', *Latomus* 62(1): 3–26, 2003.

——, 'The population of ancient Rome', *Antiquity*, 71: 966–78, 1997.

Syme, R., *Tacitus*, Vol. I, Oxford UP, 1958.

——, 'Partisans of Galba', *Historia: Zeitschrift für Alte Geschichte*, 31(4): 460–83, 1982.

Syon, D., Yavor, Z., Getzov, N., 'Gamla 1997–2000', Israel Antiquities Authority, 2005.

Tal, I., & Price, J., 'Seven Onomastic Problems in Josephus' Bellum Judaicum', *Jewish Quarterly Review*, 84(2/3):189–208, 1993.

Talbert, R., *The Senate of Imperial Rome*, Princeton UP, 1984.

——, *Barrington Atlas of the Greek and Roman World*, Princeton, 2000.

Thomas, C., 'Claudius and the Roman Army Reforms', *Historia: Zeitschrift für Alte Geschichte*, 53(4), 424–52, 2004.

Thornton, S., 'Water Works', *National Geographic Society*, October, 2023.

Torelli, M., 'The *Cursus Honorum* of M. Hirrius Fronto Neratius Pansa', *Journal of Roman Studies*, 58:170–5, 1968.

Townend, G., 'Some Flavian Connections', *Journal of Roman Studies*, 51: 54–62, 1961.

Turner, B., 'War losses and worldview: Reviewing the Roman funerary altar at Adamclisi'. *American Journal of Philology*, 134(2): 277–304, 2013.

Udoh, F., 'Taxation of Judea under the Governors', in *To Caesar What Is Caesar's: Tribute, Taxes, and Imperial Administration in Early Roman Palestine*, 207–43, Brown Judaic Studies, 2020.

Vervaet, F. J., 'Domitius Corbulo and the Rise of the Flavian Dynasty.' *Historia: Zeitschrift für Alte Geschichte*, 52(4): 436–64, 2003.

Vinson, M. P., 'Domitia Longina, Julia Titi, and the Literary Tradition', *Historia: Zeitschrift für Alte Geschichte*, 38(4): 431–50, 1989.

Vitale, M., '*Iudaea Recepta*, eine neue legende auf goldmunzen Vespasians', *Ancient Society*, 44:243–55, 2014.

Ward Perkins, J. B., 'The Career of Sex. Julius Frontinus', *Classical Quarterly*, 31(2): 102–5, 1937.

Wardle, D, 'Suetonius on Vespasian's rise to power under the Julio-Claudians', *Acta Classica*, 53: 101–15, 2010.

Waters, K. H., 'The Character of Domitian', *Phoenix*, 18(1): 49–77, 1964.

Wolfson, L. J., et al., 'Estimates of measles case fatality ratios: a comprehensive review of community-based studies', *Int J Epidemiol.*, 38(1):192–205, 2009.

Wunderman, R., ed., 'Global Volcanism Program, 1999. Report on Vesuvius (Italy)', *Bulletin of the Global Volcanism Network*, 24:10. Smithsonian Institution.

Yannicopoulos, A., 'The Pedagogue in Antiquity', *British Journal of Educational Studies* 33(2): 173–9, 1985.

Zeichmann, C. B., *The Roman Army and the New Testament*, Lexington Books, 2018.

GLOSSARY

Definitions are provided in the context of the imperial period covered in this biography. The singular in Latin precedes the plural.

aedileship: an administrative post to oversee the maintenance of public buildings and the regulation of public festivals that lost significant power during the early imperial period.

adlection: promotion of a non-member into the senate, or a member promoted in rank, by the emperor.

ala/alae: 'wing', regiment of cavalry.

aureus/aurei: standard Roman gold coin, worth twenty-five silver *denarii*.

aquilifer: Roman military standard bearer for the legion's eagle (*aquila*) standard.

auxiliary soldiers: generally non-citizen troops, often specialised in function, recruited into the Roman army.

ballista/ballistae: torsion-powered artillery catapult designed to throw rocks or arrow bolts.

Batavians: specialized Germanic Roman auxiliary troops.

bellum judaicum: Jewish War.

centurion: legionary officer responsible for leading a century of men, actually composed nominally of eighty legionaries.

collegium: a society or association.

cohort: main tactical unit of a Roman legion, 480 soldiers at full strength formed of six centuries.

comes/comites: a companion.

consilium (*principis*): the emperor's personal advisory council.

consul ordinarius: the 'regular' consul was the highest executive officer in the senate elected on 1 January each year. Two *consules ordinarii* were appointed concurrently. The *consul ordinarius* was significantly more prestigious than the *consul suffectus*.

consul suffectus: the 'replacement' consul appointed during the year when one of the *consules ordinarii* vacated their office.

curator aquarum: 'water curator', senatorial position responsible for Rome's aqueducts.

curia: the senate's meeting place.

cursus honorum: the 'course of honours' was the structured senatorial political career path.

decurion: officer in command of a *turma* (squadron) of cavalry, which typically consisted of about 10–30 cavalrymen.

delator/delatores: an 'informer' associated particularly with accusations of treason.

equestrians: the second tier of the upper class of Roman society often referred to as knights. The imperial administration increasingly looked to this class for senior positions.

Flavian: the imperial period referring to the reigns of Vespasian, Titus and Domitian.

grammaticus: a teacher who provided secondary education, focusing on advanced literacy, language and cultural education.

governor: official responsible for the administration of a Roman province: proconsul governors oversaw provinces under the control of the senate; propraetor governors lesser senatorial provinces; *legatus Augusti pro praetore* governed the imperial provinces; prefects were equestrian governors of strategically important provinces (e.g. Egypt); and procurators administered minor regions (e.g. Judea).

imperator: 'general' or 'commander', a title that transitioned from being a temporary military honorific for victorious generals to a permanent title for the emperor, symbolising his supreme command over the Roman military.

imperium: supreme authority to command, govern and enforce laws, particularly in military and provincial matters. This power became concentrated in the hands of the emperor, whose *imperium maius*, greater authority, placed him above all other officials, ensuring centralised control of the Roman state.

latus clavus: the broad purple stripe on the tunic that symbolised the senatorial class.

legatus legionis: 'legate of a legion', was the commander of a Roman legion whose appointment was a direct mandate of the emperor.

legatus Augusti pro praetore: governor of an imperial province, directly appointed by the emperor.

legionaries:. Roman citizens enlisted as paid professional heavy infantry soldiers.

lex: an official law passed by the senate.

maiestas: the crime of treason against the sovereign dignity of the emperor.

military tribune: senior officer in a Roman legion. A senatorial tribune (*tribunus laticlavius*), one per legion, was generally endorsed by the emperor and the commission served as part of his early political career. An equestrian tribune (*tribunus angusticlavius*), five per legion, were recruited from the equestrian class.

novus homo: a 'new man', an individual who was the first in his family to hold a significant political office.

ornamenta triumphalia: a prestigious military award that effectively replaced a triumph through the streets of Rome that was reserved for the emperors.

pater patriae: 'father of his country', an honorary title bestowed on the emperor, symbolising his role as the protector and father figure of the Roman state and its people.

patrician: a member of the Roman aristocracy, typically descended from ancient noble families. Patricians were generally the wealthiest, most politically influential and socially privileged class. By the early imperial period, many patrician families had been annihilated due to significant violence during times of civil conflict and political instability.

pedagogue: an individual responsible for the care, education and supervision of young children, especially the children of wealthy families.

plebeian: a member of the lower class in ancient Rome.

pontifex maximus: 'greatest bridge builder', the head of Roman state religion, a post usually held by the emperor.

praefectus castrorum: 'Camp Prefect', third most senior officer in a legion responsible for logistics and training. Duties could include commanding detachments on campaign.

praefectus urbi: 'prefect of the city (Rome)', a high-ranking official, typically selected by the emperor, responsible for maintaining law, order and administration within Rome. Importantly, the commander of Rome's urban paramilitary guards, *cohortes urbanae*.

praetorian guard: the elite unit of soldiers tasked with protecting the emperor in Rome, or while travelling or on the battlefield.

praetorship: senior senatorial position held for one year. Typically, praetors were judges. Completion qualified the propraetor to govern lesser senatorial provinces, command a legion or more rarely to directly seek the consulship.

primus pilus: 'first spear', the most senior centurion of a legion who commanded the first century of the first cohort that was composed of the most experienced legionaries.

Principate: the phase of rule under an emperor and not a republic, characterised by a system that preserved the outward appearance of republican institutions while concentrating real power in the hands of the emperor.

princeps: first or foremost, the title was adopted by Augustus to express his imperial position as 'first amongst equals'.

procurator castrensis: part of the emperor's administration who oversaw the running of the imperial residence.

quadriga: a four-horse chariot.

quaestorship: the first step in a senatorial career, signifying formal entry into the senate, with responsibilities primarily focused on financial matters.

rationibus: chief financial secretary to the emperor.

rhetor: a teacher in the art of rhetoric.

senate: the political institution that functioned as an advisory body to the emperor, composed of aristocratic members who held limited legislative and administrative authority under the imperial system.

sestertius/sestertii (abbreviated to HS): the principal base-metal coin of the imperial period, minted in brass; this was the standard financial unit.

testudo: 'tortoise', a military tactical formation when soldiers raised their shields above and along the side of their tightly closed formation to provide protection against missile fire while advancing.

toga virilis: 'toga of manhood', was a garment worn in ancient Rome symbolising a young Roman male's transition to adulthood typically around fifteen years of age.

tribune: high ranking officers: in a legion one *tribunus laticlavius*, a noble acting as second-in-command, while the other five were *tribuni angusticlavii*, equestrian officers handling administration and discipline; in auxiliary units the tribune was the commanding officer.

tribunicia potestas: 'tribunician power', referred to the legal powers and privileges associated with the Republican office of the tribune of the plebs (see *plebeian*), which were assumed by the emperor as part of his authority. This power became a cornerstone of the imperial system, enabling the emperor to exercise supreme authority while maintaining the appearance of adhering to Republican traditions.

vigiles: Rome's night watchmen and firefighters, acting primarily as a fire brigade force.

vigintivirate: 'the board of twenty', were twenty junior officials involved in financial, judicial or administrative roles. Not part of the official *cursus honorum*, it was typically a stepping stone before entry into the senate and candidates were normally selected by the emperor.